Barry R Boughen was born into a 1950s world of some austerity and strictness but he revelled absolutely in the freedom and simplicity those days offered. His love of wildlife and of life in general has brought him great joy as has his insatiable need and ability to think. Putting down his thoughts in print has brought great satisfaction and pride.

To Lucy, my Granddaughter

Barry R. Boughen

WONDERMENT

A BOOK OF LIFE, THOUGHT, LOVE, PHILOSOPHY AND REALITY (BUT MOSTLY REALITY)

AUSTIN MACAULEY
PUBLISHERS LTD.

A CIP catalogue record for this title is available from the British Library.

ISBN 978 1 78455 876 5 (Paperback)
ISBN 978 1 78455 877 2 (Hardback)
ISBN 978 1 78455 87 89 (E-Book)

www.austinmacauley.com

First Published (2016)
Austin Macauley Publishers Ltd.
25 Canada Square
Canary Wharf
London
E14 5LB

Contents

Preface

I dedicate this book to my granddaughter Lucy. A beautiful and intelligent 8 year old who is already one of the greatest loves of my life. I have seven grandchildren. All are wonderful and one or two of them are already thinking along the same lines as me. I love them all dearly but Lucy is just that little bit extra special to me because she is so much like me. Whether this is a good or bad thing for her is for others to comment upon. Some would say "poor child". Unusually for a child, she talks totally openly to me and tells me exactly what is on her mind. She conveys her thoughts more like an adult and her deepest thoughts are no secret. She is also just starting to question everything which is wonderful. Even as a small child she gives and gives but also hurts when that giving is not appreciated or acknowledged. We talk about the world or nature or dinosaurs or even teeth which all fascinate me though I must admit I am not quite so fascinated about her favourites, the boy band One Direction.

My concern for her is that she has not yet been taught by others too much of the Wonderment and reality of the world around her such as why day turns to night or how the seasons or tides work. Or why polar bears never eat penguins but already she is having her vulnerable little mind filled by them with things such as "God" and "dead people in the sky looking down on her". Of course, until now she has not questioned why or how. She has just taken it all in like an innocent little dry sponge eager for water. It is good to see things gradually changing.

Isn't it odd that if I was to tell Lucy that, in reality, God did not exist and dead people are just that, 'dead', and are not in the sky and do not have working eyes any more to, 'look down upon her from that sky', people would tell me I was wrong in doing so and yet they teach her this other nonsense without the slightest notion of thought or evidence.

I shall, when Lucy is a little older, tell her what and how I think but I shall not do it in any forceful way. I will tell her she must listen to what I say but she must also listen to what others say as well. The biggest thing I can teach her is to always listen carefully to both sides of any argument and then think long and hard about both of them before making her own decisions. By doing this she will truly be following her own mind, will be leading her own life and will be free.

I hope she will learn to live her life in a real world but if, after thinking hard, she says I am totally wrong and decides she wants to become a nun and devote her life to God and the church then so be it. She will have my blessing and I will still love her as dearly as I do today.

At the time of writing I have just finished reading Richard Dawkins' brilliant book 'The God Delusion' and have been inspired to put my own thoughts onto paper, thoughts which have been manifesting in my mind for many years.

Richard Dawkins is a very clever man with an intellect far beyond my own but we do share thoughts upon the same lines. At least I have this in common with him.

The 'God Delusion' is a brilliant book as I say and in no way am I knocking it but I thought I would write mine in a simpler way that could possibly connect more with the general public and also perhaps with older children who are the gullible recipients of religious brainwashing from church and church goers, from schools and even from their own ill-informed relatives.

I would like to teach them to think for themselves and enjoy the world for what is it. We live in a fantastic world full of fantastic things. If we think for ourselves and marvel at the Wonderment around us our lives can be fulfilled to an extent never reachable by just accepting from others that any god created it all and that is the simple, and to my mind, all too boring fact.

Children, and the rest of us, must also learn not only to think but to question and look for evidence for everything. (More on all this as the pages turn).

In its context, obviously, this book does do its best to dispel the myth of religion but it is not written as any kind of personal attack on the believers of anything. I am trying to dispel religion but I am also trying to dispel the belief in any superstition and am doing my utmost to highlight the pathetic love humans have for war and hurting each other. All I am really trying to do is teach everyone to live together and open their eyes and minds to what is around them and what is real. We teach Roman and Greek mythology in our schools and universities because they are topics of the past, topics that were once believed in. We know now these gods did not exist but we perfectly accept their place in history. So we teach it as the past. Why is it people still believe in a religious god when all these other gods have been discounted? Is it because of dogma? An affliction suffered by many and not only in a religious sense.

My father was not a religious man but was dogmatic in every way. If he was right he was right one hundred per cent which was fair enough when he was right but he was also one hundred per cent right even when he was blatantly wrong. This was frustrating and often upsetting for those around him but for him it was worse. Because of the dogma in his mind it was always closed and therefore he never learned. This was quite ironic really when one of his life mottos was 'never to be afraid to learn'. His life was dogged by dogma you could say. So many people suffer his same fate.

In this book my mind has delved deep into the culture of today's world and also deep into the minds of its population. I have set out views and some of those views are strong and powerful but I have done my best throughout the entire book to back up my thoughts, theories and opinions with logic, answers, proof and reasoning.

In writing I am certainly not going out of my way to evoke any kind of religious hatred. I am not that way inclined at all.

There is enough religious hatred around already without me joining in. What is surprising is the fact that religious hatred more often than not comes from religious people. It is either aimed at those of a different persuasion to theirs or towards atheists. Although atheists do not understand the beliefs of religionists and do try to enlighten them as to a different way they do not usually throw hatred towards them for their beliefs. They neither hate them or anyone else. It does seem that those who teach 'love thy neighbour' and 'turn the other cheek' are generally those who demonstrate the most anger themselves.

I talk about religionists and atheists but I do not really consider myself as being either. Being an atheist places you into a certain group, a non-believer as opposed to being a believer in religion, as if you have to be on one side or the other. I do not think there are real sides to be on. I write this book to try and enlighten people and to get them to think and wonder for themselves and see religion (as with other mythologies) and God as just quaint things of the yesterday. Things that people wanted and very often felt they needed in their lives in the past. It gave them all something to pray to for better things. The trouble was, and still is, that they were and still are also used as levers with which to threaten and persecute those around them.

People are persecuted for their religious beliefs, punished for wanting to be of another religion and even children are taught to be fearful of God and hell. Are they still told of the devil, fire, burning skin and red hot pokers for all eternity?

I am a non-believer in fire breathing dragons or green ogres or even a man called Humpy Dumpty who was made out of an egg but no one calls me an atheist for this. I am not an atheist in this case because these things, no matter how entertaining they are, could never have possibly existed. No one could say the bible isn't entertaining too with God making the earth in less than a week, Adam and Eve being the ancestors of us all and Noah and his family with their ark, carrying millions of animals. I am not an atheist in the religious sense for the same reason as

I am not an atheist in the Humpty Dumpty sense. I am not an atheist. I am me.

Yesterday I visited the church in East Bergholt Suffolk while on a day out with friends. One friend was particularly keen on seeing the bell cage there. After driving up what seemed like every street in the village we found the church and its bell cage, an outdoor set of bells set at ground level. This and the church itself were fascinating. I know I am totally against religion but it has to be said that without it there would never have been these wonderful buildings.

The reason I mention this is not to just extol the virtues of churches but to illustrate a point. While we were looking inside the church a man came in with his two lovely young daughters, the oldest of whom asked him a question. She was about eight or nine years old and she asked,

"Dad, do you believe in God?"

When her father answered that he supposed he did she answered, "Do I?"

This lovely and innocent young girl did not have the maturity to fully know her own mind but already she had not just accepted that God existed and that was that. Already she was using her brain to think and what a good sign for her future life that was.

Ricky Gervais

"If there is a god then why did he make me an atheist?"

We live on a small planet and that planet is filled to bursting with humans. Great problems lie ahead as we run short of all that is necessary for survival. In this book I travel from where we came from to where we are today and then from where we are today to what we must do in the future. If we wish to survive in any way even remotely close to the way we live today massive decisions and changes have to be made but will we make them?

Who, as leaders of the earth will ever stand up and say "Look, enough is enough".

We have lived almost hedonistic lifestyles and have pleased ourselves and our desires in every way for far too long. We have plundered the earth wantonly without any thought for the future. We will soon have to think and decisions will soon have to be made. Or will they?

Hopefully a few of you who read this book will not only learn something new from it but will also learn to see life in slightly a different, more interesting, passionate and illuminating way.

If though, my book serves only to make you think even more deeply of your religion, superstitions and beliefs and you completely shun both me and my views then that's fine too. At least it has made you think more about something. Not everyone's mind can be turned or eyes can be opened. Not everyone will listen at all but we are what we are. Neither being an atheist, a religionist or just being you makes you automatically a bad person.

Through my views and feelings I live a wonderful life. It is truly full, passionate and meaningful. I am not bound by beliefs or superstitions. I am not bound by what I do or when I do it or what I eat or drink or wear. I am the only person (apart from my wife) who tells me what to do and of course I do it all without causing harm or distress to anyone. I always try to give a little more than I take.

You could possibly see me as an intellectual and see my thoughts as the way to go in future. You may see me just as a person with a lot to say. You may see me as an interfering nuisance or you may see me simply as some kind of crackpot. Whatever you think is totally up to you but I do thank you for reading this book and analysing my thoughts. Your thoughts are your thoughts and luckily we live where we can openly think and say what we wish. We live in countries which rejoice in freedom of speech. Many do not have this luxury.

A few paragraphs earlier I talked about dogma and said this is an affliction suffered by many people. You would be perfectly within your rights and reasoning to say I must be totally dogmatic in my thoughts as well. Otherwise I would not be writing this book, but no. I do have my thoughts, ideas, beliefs and disbeliefs but show me a convincing argument for religion or superstition and I shall be religious or superstitious. Show me a hairy green goblin and I shall embrace him and believe in him. Look at a peach. It is quite a hairy little fruit and you may not think it edible at all let alone beautiful to eat. You may be asked to try one and if your mind is closed you may decline but if you do try one you realise a peach is truly one of the loveliest fruits you can eat. You have listened, found the evidence and have enjoyed. I have listened to many pro religion arguments in the past but have never heard one so far with any evidence that has been able to even slightly sway me. Please do try though. Sway me and I'm with you. Until that time I will have to just be me with my own thoughts and ideals.

"You are whatever you think you are in your own mind but to others you can only be what they think of you in theirs."

(That's profound isn't it? I just made it up.)

Prof Richard Dawkins is a hero of mine and I hold him in great respect. I have always been envious of his chance to air his views. I do apologise to him if some of the contents of this book seem very similar to his. They have to be really because our books are loosely based on the same subject. My thoughts are my own thoughts, but where they are not and I do quote him I shall mention his name. I do not wish to be sued for plagiarism.

Thank you Richard for your inspiration

Another person I would like to mention is another hero of mine, Prof Brian Cox. This man enthrals me with his infectious Wonderment of what is around him. He is a relatively young man but with so much knowledge. I have learned greatly from him. He is the kind of man that you could not possibly dislike. I am envious of him too. I'm sure if everyone had just a little of his passion we would all be enlightened and lose our need for any superstition.

I must also give a mention to a lovely young lady who I admire and have also learned much from. Her name is Professor Alice Roberts and I have followed her career from being a young lady archaeologist on Time Team through to her later television programmes such as 'Origins of us' 'Coast' and 'Ice age giants'. Her fervour for her subject is as plain to see as Brian Cox's and I have always thought they would have made a good couple but that's just the romantic me being silly. Most people are just one thing in their career but I see Alice listed as being an anatomist, osteoarchaeologist, anthropologist, paleopathologist, television presenter and author. That makes for some CV.

And on to perhaps one of the world's greatest and most respected men, the great Sir David Attenborough. He is another man you could not possibly dislike. I have followed his work ever since I was a child and have probably learned more from him than from any other individual. It was this man who inspired me to love wildlife and to travel much of the world in search of it. My greatest wildlife thrill ever was to sit in the middle of the mass migration of wildebeest and zebra on the plains of Tanzania. Now that did fill me with Wonderment and it was thanks largely to Sir David's passion that I was there.

My thanks go to all these people and to everyone else who has led me to where I am today.

Most of this book comes from my own mind and my own thoughts but there are parts of it that I have had to research and learn. I have learned from many sources but the source I have learned from most is the wonderful website Wikipedia. I thank them too for their free, varied and very well laid out information.

A special thank you must also go to my step-daughter Tori and her partner Matt for listening to me and my thoughts and also for reading the book as it progressed and putting me right.

Their comments, encouragement and knowledge have helped me greatly. Last but not least I must give a mention to Annierose for enlightening me on the illegal drugs scene which she knows much more about than I do. Not that she has ever indulged of course. She just knows because she is young.

Life.

"What if the Hokey Cokey really is what it is all about?"

Winnie McGoogan (Mrs Browns Boys)

1
The Wonder of Nothing and the Beginning

Before the beginning of the universe there was nothing. This is something that both scientists and religionists can agree on but after that they have to go their own totally separate ways.

Let us think awhile.

Nothing! What is nothing? We do not know. How can something suddenly come from nothing? How could there be totally nothing, nothing existing in nothing? The human brain is a wonderful thing, a vast and powerful biological computer but even with it we cannot get our heads around the concept of nothing. If your pockets are empty at least you still have pockets. If a balloon bursts you may no longer have a balloon but you do still have all the air that was compressed inside it. If you were sitting on a chair totally depressed that you have nothing in your life you do still have the chair. (Now that is getting silly) It may be silly but isn't it better to have silly thoughts rather than have no thoughts at all? To reach intelligent thoughts and conclusions we all have to think and then discount many silly thoughts along the way.

Carrying on in the slightly silly vein of things even if we were to write down nothing (0) it may mean nothing but you still have the outline of the zero and the paper it was written on. You still also have the pencil.

One definition I have come across on the Interweb is this. Nothing: 'Something that has no existence'. Fair enough I suppose but how can 'Something' have no existence? If it doesn't exist then how can it be called 'Something'? A better definition would be Nothing: 'No thing' or 'Not anything'. 'Not anything' rests quite comfortably on the mind.

According to science the universe started with a big bang. Or was it a big bang? Is this possibly the wrong name? 'Big Bang' infers what it says, a big 'bang!!' But was there a big bang? Was there a noise at all? There is no air in space and noise cannot travel without it to travel in. Or was there air? We have air on our earth and if everything on our earth came from the big bang then that air must have been present in some form at the moment of the big bang. We could argue in which form this did exist but of course, at this stage there was no life existing and therefore nothing to hear the bang so does it really matter if it 'banged' or not?

With the big bang theory, within a billionth of a second every single building block of the universe was present. It was still hugely compressed and hugely hot but it was there in all its glory. All 100 or so elements that make up everything in the universe had to have been there in some form. This compressed and hot mass would go on expanding and expanding for the next 13.7 billion years until we reach where we are today.

Where is the evidence for this you may ask? And ask you should for the whole purpose of this book is to get you to ask and question everything. If someone tells you the door on number 10 Downing Street is painted black or polar bears are white don't just accept they are and certainly don't scream "Oh no they are not!" because you think you know better. Take in what the people say to you, think hard about it and then investigate before making your own decision. Look for evidence. These days with the help of the Interweb all we have to do is tap something in and press search. The internet is a wonder in itself.

The evidence of a huge (noisy or not) explosion from the big bang is all around us. We study the stars and galaxies and see that they are still, even after billions of years, moving away from each other into an expanding universe. I nearly said an 'ever expanding' universe because it is thought that could well be the case as galaxies do seem to be accelerating away from each other.

Far more about the stars and galaxies later.

Now, onto the religionist view of things.

As we have said, again it all started with nothing but then God made the heaven and the earth and the earth was without form, and void; and darkness was upon the face of the deep and God said, "Let there be light." God later went on to make man in his own image.

Hang on a minute I, and you, should say! Isn't there a fundamental problem here? 'First there was nothing and then God made the earth.' He later made man in his 'own image.' If man was made in his own image this must mean God was a man (or woman of course). So if this man (excuse me if I don't say 'or woman' every time) made the earth from nothing where did God himself come from? He is said to have made Adam and Eve but then who made God? With the big bang theory life eventually comes to fruition after billions of years. With religion there was life (God) even when there was nothing. As we know we cannot have something (God) when there is only 'nothing'. If we have God we have something. We cannot have both.

The only evidence for God creating the earth and all upon it comes from the bible. As they say "It is written". Let's see what else the bible has to say about creation.

In the beginning God created the heaven. And the earth was without form, and void; and darkness was upon the face of the deep. And the spirit of God moved upon the face of the water. And God said, Let there be light; and there was light. And God saw the light, that it was good; and God divided the light from the darkness. And God called the light day, and the darkness he called night. And the evening and the morning were the first day.

And God said, let there be a firmament in the midst of the waters; and let it divide the waters from the waters. And God made the firmament, and divided the waters which were under the firmament from the waters which were above the firmament; and it was so. And God called the firmament heaven. And the evening and the morning were the second day.

And God said, let the waters under the heaven be gathered together unto one place, and let the dry land appear; and it was so.

And God called the dry land Earth; and the gathering together of the waters called the seas; and God saw that it was good.

And God said, let the Earth bring forth grass, the herb yielding seed; and the fruit tree yielding fruit after his kind, whose seed is in itself, upon the earth; and it was so.

And the earth brought forth grass, and herb yielding seed after his kind, and the tree yielding fruit, whose seed was in itself, after his kind; and God saw that it was good. And the evening and the morning were the third day.

And God said, Let there be lights in the firmament of the heaven to divide the day from the night; and let them be for signs, and for seasons, and for days, and years: and let them be for lights in the firmament of the heaven to give light upon the earth and it was so. And God made two great lights; the greater light to rule the day, and the lesser light to rule the night: he made the stars also. And God set them in the firmament of the heaven to give light upon the earth, and to rule over the day and over the night, and to divide the light from the darkness: and God saw that it was good. And the evening and the morning were the fourth day.

And God said, Let the waters bring forth abundantly the moving creature that hath life, and fowl that may fly above the earth in the open firmament of heaven. And God created great whales, and every living creature that moveth, which the waters brought forth abundantly, after their kind, and every winged fowl after his kind: And God saw that it was good. And God blessed them, saying Be fruitful and multiply, and fill the waters

*in the seas, and let fowl multiply in the earth. And the evening
and the morning were the fifth day.*

*And God said, Let earth bring forth the living creature after
his kind, cattle and creeping thing, and beast of the earth after
his kind: and it was so. And God made the beast of the earth
after his kind, and the cattle after their kind, and everything that
creepeth upon the earth after his kind: and God saw that it was
good. And God said, Let us make man in our image, after our
likeness: And let them have dominion over the fish of the sea,
and over the fowl of the air, and over the cattle, and over the
earth, and over every creeping thing that creepeth upon the
earth. So God created man in his own image, in the image of
God created he him; male and female created he them.*

*And God blessed them, and God said unto them, Be fruitful
and multiply, and replenish the earth, and subdue it: And have
dominion over the fish of the sea, and over the fowl of the air,
and every living thing that moveth upon the earth. And God said,
Behold, I have given you every herb bearing seed, which is upon
all the face of the earth, and every tree, in which is the fruit of
the tree yielding seed; to you it shall be for meat. And to every
beast of the earth, and to every fowl of the air, and to everything
that creepeth upon the earth, wherein there is life, I have given
every green herb for meat: and it was so. And God saw
everything he had made, and, behold, it was very good. And the
evening and the morning were the sixth day.*

*Thus the heavens and the earth were finished, and all host
of them. And on the seventh day God ended his work which he
had made; and he rested on the seventh day from all his work
which he had made. And God blessed the seventh day, and
sanctified it: because that in it he had rested from all his work
which God created and made.*

Right, what does all this mean? It obviously means God
created the earth and all upon it in six days. He had been a busy
chap but let's look at it step by step.

God, who himself was around when there was nothing, created the earth from nothing. So far little more ridiculous than a scientist's view of the big bang coming from nothing.

Day One.

'The earth was without form or void'. Again scientists would say the same thing. The earth did form from a mass of gas and dust which was at first without form. The only difference here is the fact that we now know the earth was formed a good 9 billion years after the big bang.

Another problem here is that the bible says, 'Darkness was upon the face of the deep and the spirit of God moved upon the face of the water'. If the earth was without form how was there water and where was it held? Where was the deep? How could the deep have formed if there was no form for it to form into?

And God said, "Let there be light and there was light." What light was this? It states in the bible text that God made the sun and stars on the fourth day. At this point we are still on day one.

Day Two.

And God said, "Let there be a firmament in the midst of the waters; And let it divide the waters from the waters." There were now waters below and waters above the firmament. And God called the firmament heaven.

So he used the firmament to divide the waters from the waters. I had to think about that one but of course what is meant is the firmament divided land water from rain water. The trouble is he called the firmament heaven and there were waters above heaven. So heaven is just the space between the earth and the clouds. I was always told and assumed that the bible's heaven was the infinite space above our heads. What happens when it is foggy? Do heaven and earth suddenly become mixed? We could be on a hilltop above the clouds and have to look down to heaven instead of up. Anyway, we are on a sphere. Which way is up? From what I can gather, the firmament at the time the bible was written was thought to be a dome above a flat earth and this dome housed the sun and stars.

Day Three.

And God said, "Let the water under heaven be gathered unto one place and let the dry land appear."

Fair enough. At least it gives some order to things. He called the water seas and grew grass, herbs and trees upon the land. Quite reasonable some might say but what a day. As we are discounting evolution at this stage we have to assume all the myriad of grasses, herbs, flowers and trees that we see today were made by God in just a few hours. They must have been because according to religion they have not evolved since.

Day Four.

And God said, "Let there be lights in the firmament of the heaven to divide the day from the night."

This is odd as we said in day one. It seems God has just made the sun and stars so where did the light come from in day one? Let's just assume it was magic, or God's torch. He had to see what he was doing I suppose.

On day three God was supposed to have made all the earth's plant species and then he made the sun the day after. Perhaps he didn't realise that plants need sunlight in order to thrive. Still, he may have done it the wrong way round but according to the bible he did it and to many that is all that matters.

So the lights in the firmament or heaven were set there to provide light for the earth and the earth was the first thing to be made. We know for a fact and not from any far-fetched scientific theory that the earth could not possibly have come into existence before the sun as we rely totally on the sun for light, warmth and stability. We are held in the sun's orbit and travel around it once every 365.25 days. The earth could not have possibly existed before the sun. Not even for just a few miraculous days.

Also, thinking about things, if the sun and the stars were put in the sky just for the convenience of the earth that would make the earth by far the most significant object in the universe. Nothing could be more wrong. To us our earth is totally significant but in the great universe our planet is just a tiny speck of dust floating around a rather insignificant star which is only one of hundreds of thousands of millions of stars in our galaxy and that galaxy is only one of hundreds of thousands of millions of galaxies. More on this in the chapter 'The Wonder Of The Universe.'

Day Five.

We looked at day three and wondered at the marvel of God creating all known plant species in one day but day five really is something. It was on day five that God made all living things of the land, sea and air. It is not agreed completely by scientists and scholars just how many different species there are but the number does run into millions, probably around 8 million. A vast group of the world's most brilliant scientists could not, all together, even come anywhere near listing them all in one day let alone making them. Science has come a long way in recent years and we have cloned animals but the brightest people on earth could not actually make one from nothing. The only thing that could possibly make a giraffe is mummy and daddy giraffe through evolution.

I heard a gentleman on the radio some years ago saying evolution cannot possibly exist because, as he argued, "If you threw all the ingredients for a sponge onto the floor they would not turn into one without intervention." He was right of course but I'm afraid it isn't all quite that simple. The argument can be answered simply though. All those ingredients would simply rot down to their chemical constituents and become part of the earth again. That is where animals came from and where we end up returning.

Also, day five sees God make all the other animals but not us human beings, Homo sapiens. Are we really so special as to have a whole new day devoted to just us? And why just Homo sapiens? Why not mention Homo Erectus, Homo Floresiensis, Neanderthals Etc. Etc.? Again, are we so special?

Day Six.

And God said, "Let us make man in our own image, and after our likeness."

God is said to have made the earth and man all by himself but this statement says in 'our' image and after 'our' likeness. What does 'our' denote? Does it denote that God was not alone? There is no mention of a helping hand, an apprentice perhaps?

As I have said it bothers me why God made all the other animals on day five but waited for another day before he made us, human beings or Homo sapiens. I know religionists tend to separate us and other animals into two distinct groups, us and them, but this is wrong.

As with the thought of the earth being the centre of the universe, the thought of us being superior to other animals is arrogant to say the least. We are animals. We are not descended from primates, we are Primates. We are no different from other animals apart from the fact we have a big enough brain to ruin the planet we live on and rely upon as home.

God told us to go forth and replenish the earth. Replenish it? 'Populate' the earth I could understand but to replenish it denotes that it had to have been populated once and that population has ceased. This is just an unfortunate wording perhaps.

God also gave us dominion over all plants and other creatures. They were ours. They belonged to us. We could I presume do with them as we wished. Other animals are not there just for us. They are also there for themselves. We do eat other animals and they do eat each other. That's the nature of things but most were here long before we were and it is highly likely some will still be here long after we have gone. The ones we have not made extinct in the meantime that is.

So God rested on the seventh day, the Sabbath. He made the heaven and the earth and everything on it in just six days. I know religionists love to believe this but in a real world I'm sorry but it just isn't true is it?

I remember Richard Dawkins putting forward a point on television as he was walking up an incline to the top of a sheer drop at the end of it. Let me explain:

Scientists say the earth is approximately 4.5 billion years old and life has been evolving for 3.5 billion of those years. The bible says the earth and life were created in just six days. Richard Dawkins says the long gentle incline he was on represented evolution and each step he took represented a step in that evolution. The slope had to be of a minute gradient and some vast length to show how long evolution has taken whereas the sheer drop at the end of it represented God's six days.

His argument is that it has to be far more likely that life evolved with minute steps along that gradient rather than suddenly bursting into a myriad of forms on the top of the sheer ridge in no real time at all.

Some religious people are now saying we should not take these six days literally and that a 'God day' could have lasted a billion years. This would make for a great lay in on Sundays. Others say no. A day is a day because it is written.

There is a massive discrepancy between science's 4.5 billion years and religion's six days and there is also a massive discrepancy between some religionists who say there are twenty-four hours in a day and others who say a billion years. Maybe the argument for evolution is so great that some people have had to adapt their thinking of the bible to fall in line with it, to keep it creditable.

Again there will be many who totally disagree with me when I say a god could not possibly have made the world at all, let alone in just six days but that's fine. I am expressing my own views and not everyone will share them. I would invite them to think deeply about it though.

Many do now say the bible is not meant to be taken literally but if you do not take it literally what have you got left, only a few quaint stories. The bible in its various forms has always been the very cornerstone and foundation of many of the world's religious thoughts. Without it being true and accurate surely there can be no religion and if the first words themselves are proven not to be true how can anyone possibly believe anything else that comes after?

As an illustration of this I would like to convey a little story regarding my brother. He and his partner split up at almost the exact time that my dear late wife died of cancer. So there we were, two middle-aged men, suddenly placed in a world where we were on our own. I hated it and missed my wife tremendously. In a practical sense I had no problems but emotionally I was useless. We have a local paper which lists single people who want to meet others. You know, men seeking women, women seeking men, women seeking women and men seeking sheep and all that (I jest but we do live in the country). Anyway, my brother answered an ad from a lady who said she was 'in her late 30s'. It turned out she was so far into her late 30s she was actually 42.

My reference to this lady is the same as for the bible. The very first thing she told my brother was not true. How could he sincerely believe anything else she ever uttered? Thankfully this relationship did not work out and he is settled again, as am I, with a good, honest woman.

Another thing I have thought of is this. Genesis keeps telling us that God said this and God said that. Even if God did exist and say these things how do we know what he actually said? As with the big bang there was no one there to listen and certainly no one there to write down what he said and include later in the bible. These were the days of prehistory, i.e. before the invention of writing so no transcript was ever formed. It is said that God later gave us Jesus and we see written all manner of

34

things that he was supposed to have said. Jesus was said to have lived only two thousand or so years ago but no one even knows what he actually said let alone what God said god knows how long ago. There were no tape recorders, computers, press cuttings or anything.

One religionist admitted the fact but said the bible was a record of what God and Jesus probably 'would have said'. Well, that's not good enough is it? How can that be a true historic account?

I heard a religious person argue once that the human eye is such a complex organ that it could never have possibly come about by evolution.

In part this person was correct. The human eye, or the eye of every other animal as well, is complex and it is remarkable that it came about through evolution. Her argument was that as she could not understand the evolution of the eye then it must have been made by God. How easy. Again it negates the need for thought. In that case how did God make it? You can't say things are so complex they could not have possibly come about by evolution and then, in the same breath, say God made everything from nothing. A statement of that magnitude is preposterous.

Thinking simply, what is more likely, the eye forming over billions of years in miniscule increments or God making it and every other body part in one day with no instructions? I hate the phrase 'that's a no-brainer' but in this instance I have just used it.

I remember sitting one day talking to lady who was a regular churchgoer. It seemed that word of my thoughts and opinions had travelled before me and she constantly goaded me into arguing about religion. I was in no mood for confrontation but eventually I did talk to her about my beliefs, or non-beliefs perhaps. I kept completely calm and just explained why I thought there was no such thing as God or any other creator as I sipped my coffee and ate digestive biscuits.

She didn't keep quite as calm though and suddenly and sarcastically (Her sarcasm was mixed with a good amount of venom) she said, "I know the kind of person you are. You are the kind of person who only ever believes in things that are real."

I was quite gobsmacked. I nearly typed 'godsmacked' then. I only believe in things that are real? Am I thick? I cannot work that one out. What else is there to believe in apart from reality? As children we do believe in many things such as the Tooth Fairy or Father Christmas or we have imaginary friends (My Lucy used to stand at the front door and talk to ET.) but we do grow up and realise these things are not real. I did not ask this lady to explain because she was genuinely enraged so I thought it best to ignore her and carried on with my coffee and biscuits for fear of her turning into the Incredible Hulk's great-grandmother. Obviously if a person can only argue in this ridiculous sense and rage then there is no point in arguing. She was a lady beyond reason or reasoning with. However, my silence did little to assuage her anger. If anything it only heightened it. Luckily within seconds another colleague walked in to the room and I could change the subject. Needless to say I was never classed as one of this lady's circle of closest friends but I did manage somehow to live without it.

Another work colleague sometime later asked me about my religious beliefs and when I said I had none she said I was, "A bad man who would suffer in hell."

"Well," I said. "With all that fire there at least it will be warm." She was, at best, displeased.

If there was a god and this god was all-powerful, all-seeing and all-forgiving then why should we be frightened of him? Why should we have this "fear of God" drummed into us? Even if everything religionists say were true and God is so great would he be vain enough to want us to kneel and pray to him all the time and sing songs to serenade him on a Sunday? Why do people pray? They pray to God but for what? Mostly for their own self benefit. So aren't religionists being more than a little self-centred in their prayers when they should be the unselfish ones?

If God did create the world why did he do it? What was the need? Was it a new hobby? Did he just think one morning, "Oh, I know what I will do, I will create a world." What was the point of this world? Surely up to then God had been living quite contentedly in nothing and had no worries. Why did he suddenly work so hard for those six days only to bring forth a population which soon drove him to despair with so much fighting, arguing and murdering each other that he had to eventually commit mass murder himself to get rid of them?

Also if God had lived a life where he had absolutely nothing to do and then he decided to start this new hobby out of boredom why did he feel he had to hurry and do it all in six days? They say he is still alive today. Surely there was no hurry at all.

In my writing you will notice a, probably somewhat perverse and wry sense of humour. This is not done as a deliberate attack on anyone or anything. It is just my relaxed way of living and expression. I mean no harm by it but just enjoy life in a light-hearted, free and easy manner. Life can be fun if you enjoy it in a bright but realistic way.

In this chapter we have looked at God's creation of the world and in the next couple of chapters we shall look at a couple of other very nice and also naively entertaining bible stories, ones which have captivated many a child and adult for many a past century. Look at them as reality and you close your mind to real reality but look at them as lovely old pieces of entertaining scripture as I do and you will love them.

2

The Wonder of Adam and Eve

"God made man from dust"

This statement is partially true as we do come from the earth. We are made of chemicals from the earth and when we die we return to the earth as those same chemicals. Ashes to ashes, dust to dust.

More like ashes to ashes, compost to chemicals I would say but then no. Let's leave this one because the bible has had a good go at describing the procedure.

"God breathed the breath of life into the man's nostrils and the man became a living soul."

The fact that God breathed breath into the man again confirms that God was a living, breathing human being. He had lungs to breathe with, he had a mouth to speak and he had a brain to think but what did 'he' breathe before he invented the universe and lived in nothing? We find out in this chapter that he had legs and could walk as well, yet another human trait. Any body needs sustenance, warmth and oxygen. How did God live when there were none of these when he lived in nothing?

So God is getting all the credit in the bible for making every animal and eventually man and woman.

He is ranked so highly for doing so but there had to be something higher than God to make him and then who made them, and them and them? We could labour on but instead let's get on with the story.

The Garden of Eden.

And the Lord God planted a garden to the east of Eden and there he put the man he had formed. The garden was full of every tree that is pleasant to the sight and good for food.

In the midst of the garden was planted the tree of life and also the tree of knowledge of good and evil.

Lord God put the man in the garden to dress it and to keep it.

And the Lord God commanded the man saying of every tree in the garden thou mayest freely eat: But of the tree of knowledge of good and evil, thou shalt not eat of it for in the day that thou eatest thereof thou shalt surely die.

And the Lord God said, it is not good that the man should be alone; I will make an help for him.

And out of the ground the Lord formed every beast of the field and every fowl of the air; and brought them unto Adam to see what he would call them: and whatsoever Adam called every living creature, that was the name thereof.

Adam did this without an help so the Lord caused a deep sleep to fall upon Adam, and he slept, and he took one of Adam's ribs, and closed up the flesh instead thereof; and the rib, which the Lord God had taken from the man, made he a woman, and brought her unto the man.

And Adam said, This is now bone of my bones, and flesh of my flesh; She shall be called woman because she was taken out of man. Thereof shall a man leave his father and his mother, and shall cleave unto his wife: and they shall be one flesh. And they were both naked, the man and his wife, and they were not ashamed.

Before we go on with the story let's just pause awhile and consider the above.

If we forget the fact for a while that neither man nor other animals could ever have been made by a god or any other great being we can look at this part as being quite innocuous. God has made man (Adam) and he has provided him with a nice place to live. It seems Eden was set somewhere in Africa so the temperature was warm and God had filled Adam's garden with all manner of fruits, herbs and meats for him to enjoy. All Adam had to do was look after his land as would any gardener or smallholder today.

And God told Adam he could eat the fruit of whatever tree he liked but he was not to eat from the tree of knowledge of good and evil because if he did he would die the day he ate it.

Again fair enough, God had set the rules and they were simple enough. It seems Adam had plenty of other trees to eat from so he had no need to eat from the tree of knowledge of good and evil did he? But guess what. Like a naughty child, he would. He would be led astray by a woman. Haven't we all been? (That was a joke in a non-misogynistic way.) Trouble here is this woman was not alone. She had a companion, a sidekick. A talking snake of all things and Adam would be beguiled by them both.

Adam was shown all beasts around him and was told to name them. I take it these were only the ones in the Garden of Eden otherwise there would be millions of them. He must have called them Elephant, Zebra, Impala, Rhinoceros, Baboon and Ostrich. I bet as he looked at a big cat with a mane and called him Lion the lion was looking right back at Adam and thinking he could call him 'Lunch'.

God sent Adam into a deep sleep and took a rib from him and from the rib he formed a woman. Then he closed Adam's wound.

Sorry, but how unlikely is this? I can see the beauty of man and woman being so close they seem of the same flesh but a woman is more than just a rib bone. A woman has to be made of the same ingredients as a man but then Adam was just made from dust. Perhaps a bone is preferable.

God was a knowledgeable kind of chap but was he a trained surgeon? He has just operated on Adam and taken a rib from him when neither anaesthetic nor medical instruments were invented. Clever but still, that's nothing I suppose when you think he made a complete woman out of that one bone and he had already made the whole world and all upon it in just six days.

A man shall *'cleave unto his wife'*.

The word cleave is a little disturbing because it generally means to split. This brings to mind some kind of violence from Adam towards his wife but in the biblical sense the word 'cleave' seems to have had the exact opposite meaning. Instead of meaning to split it actually meant to join. So to cleave unto his wife meant they would be joined together.

'And they were naked, the man and his wife and they were not ashamed.'

Perhaps if they were in a crowded supermarket and they were naked they ought to be ashamed but here they were husband and wife, of one flesh, alone in the garden. Why should they be ashamed?

My wife and I may look a bit haggard with no clothes on these days but we are never ashamed and nor should anyone else be. My wife and I are of one flesh. The problem is most of that flesh is not really where it is supposed to be any more.

Less of the stupidity and back to the story.

The Fall.

Now the serpent was more subtil than any other beast of the field which the Lord God had made. And he said unto the woman, Yea, hath God said, Ye shall not eat of every tree in the garden? And the woman said unto the serpent, we may eat of the fruit of the trees of the garden: But of the fruit of the tree which is in the midst of the garden, God hath said, Ye shall not eat of it. Neither shall you touch it, lest ye die. And the serpent said unto the woman, Ye shall not surely die; For God doth know that in the day ye eat thereof, then your eyes shall be opened, and ye shall be as gods knowing good and evil. And when the woman saw that the tree was good for food, and that it was pleasant to the eye, and a tree to be desired to make one wise, she took of the fruit thereof, and did eat, and gave also unto her husband with her; And he did eat. And the eyes of them both were opened and they knew that they both were naked; And sewed fig leaves together, and made aprons.

Before we talk about this part of the story I feel I ought to explain the meaning of the word subtil.

It is not a word commonly used today and in fact my computer underlines it in red every time I type it. Even that is confused.

Subtil means Sly, Artful, Cunning or Crafty.

As I said, this snake is talking! (He talked with a forked tongue perhaps) And it is talking quite articulately it seems. It is also quite clever because it knows the secret of the tree of knowledge and beguiles the woman into eating the fruit of it. It seems that in the beginning snakes were more intellectual than humans.

The woman saw that the tree was good for food. How did she see this? Just because a thing looks good to eat it doesn't mean it is good to eat. I picked a mushroom once years ago because it looked good to eat. It did look good and it tasted even better than it actually looked. The trouble was what I thought was a field mushroom was in fact a yellow staining mushroom. I was not well for a few hours but it did open my eyes. I will not be eating one again.

When it says here that Adam and the woman (Eve, but she has not been named yet) had their eyes opened I do suppose it means in the same wisdom sense as I have just mentioned. After all, the woman did see that the tree was good for food before she ate the fruit. She must have had sight then.

In many depictions of Adam and Eve eating the forbidden fruit it depicts the fruit as an apple. This would be silly because if it were true then religionists all over the world would refrain from eating them and poor old Granny Smith would be out of business. The bible does not actually say which fruit the forbidden one was. Talking of depictions, every depiction I see of Adam and Eve portrays them as white people. Surely if they were African they would have been black. Isn't this a little bit racist? Mind you, it is lucky for us that they all spoke English.

So Adam and Eve's eyes were opened to knowledge and to good and evil. With knowledge there was so much to wonder about. Even with the bible's account of creation there were masses of stars in the sky at night and in the day the sun was shining. They were surrounded by animals of all kinds both on the land and in the air and trees around them brought forth fruit of every kind. They had eaten the forbidden fruit so they were now as gods knowing good and evil and as gods they had the power to do anything. There was so much now to think about and do. The world was theirs and they had dominion over it. They may have had the power and freedom to do and think anything but what did they think of first? The only thing they could think of it seems was the fact their naughty bits were showing so they conjured up a couple of needles and threads and made aprons out of leaves. So they have only just realised they were naked and yet, in the previous section it says, *"And they were naked, the man and his wife, and they were not ashamed."*

A lovely story so far but trouble was brewing just around the corner.

I say a lovely story but, do you know, having read it through again in order to write this book I realise, so far, it is a truly charming story. Few these days would fight their corner by swearing it is absolutely true but, accepting this, it is charming.

I once saw Richard Dawkins talking to one of the heads of the Jewish church and even he had to admit Adam and Eve's tale was only a story. It is just a bit of a novelette really which was written by someone with a naïve but imaginative brain. Dickens and Shakespeare would have been proud of them.

Let's move on again because their story is about to take a sinister and menacing turn.

And they heard the voice of the Lord God walking in the garden in the cool of the day: And Adam and his wife hid themselves from the presence of the Lord God amongst the trees of the garden. And the Lord called unto Adam, and said unto him, Where art thou? And he said, I heard thy voice in the garden, and I was afraid, because I was naked; and I hid myself. And he said, Who told thee that thou wast naked? Hast thou eaten of the tree, whereof I commanded thee that thou shouldest not eat? And the man said, The woman whom thou gavest to be with, she gave me of the tree, and I did eat. And the Lord God said unto the woman, What is this thou hast done? And the woman said, The serpent beguiled me, and I did eat. And the Lord God said unto the serpent, Because thou hast done this, thou art cursed above all cattle, and above every beast of the field; upon thy belly shalt thou go, and dust shalt thou eat all the days of thy life; and I will put an enmity between thee and the woman, and between thy seed and her seed; it shall bruise thy head, and thou shalt bruise his heel. Unto the woman he said, I will greatly multiply thy sorrow and thy conception; in sorrow thou shalt bring forth children; and thy desire shall be to thy husband, and he shall rule over thee.

And unto Adam he said, Because thou hast hearkened unto the voice of thy wife, and hast eaten of the tree, of which I commanded thee, saying, Thou shalt not eat if it; cursed is the ground for thy sake; in sorrow shalt thou eat of it all the days of thy life; thorns also and thistles shall it bring forth to thee; and thou shalt eat the herb of the field; in the seat of thy face shalt thou eat bread, till thou return unto the ground; for out it wast thou taken: for dust thou art, and unto dust shalt thou return. And Adam called his wife's name Eve; because she was the mother of all living, Unto Adam and also to his wife did the Lord God make coats of skin, and he clothed them.

And the Lord God said, Behold, the man is become as one of us, to know good and evil; and now, lest he put forward his hand, and take also of the tree of life, and eat, and live forever:

therefore the Lord God sent him forth from the Garden of Eden, to till the ground from whence it was taken. So he drove out the man; and he placed at the east of the Garden of Eden Cherubims, and a flaming sword which turned every way, to keep the way of the tree of life.

We will analyse this a little:

The Lord God called to Adam and asked where he was. Adam said he had hidden himself because he was naked. Hadn't he and his wife already sewn fig leaves together to form aprons to cover themselves so they were not naked?

God quickly realised they had been naughty and had eaten from the forbidden tree. Adam was truly a human wasn't he? When he was accused he automatically blamed someone else. He blamed his wife. In my house this has changed. My wife automatically blames me. The clever thing is no matter what it is she wants to blame me for she can find a perfectly valid reason why even if it had nothing to do with me at all or even if I was nowhere near when it happened. In this bible case the woman just threw all responsibility onto the poor old talking snake.

The Lord turned to the snake and cursed him to go upon his belly. Of course he would go upon his belly. He was a snake wasn't he? Would he have been a snake if he had legs? More like a newt or lizard perhaps. Mind you, snakes do have evidence within their skeletons that they did evolve from walking creatures. Could God have done this? God also commanded that the snake would eat dust for the rest of his life. Of course, there can be no truth in this statement as we all know no creature could possibly live on dust. Or could they? Adam was formed of dust so were other animals formed of the same material? We do all have the same biological make-up. So when the snake crawled upon his belly to catch and eat another animal was he in essence just eating dust?

God also put an enmity between the snake and the woman meaning that the warm relationship they seemed to have had was now turned to a hostile one. Humans, even these days, do

45

have enmity between themselves and snakes. Is this an ingrained feeling because of the bible story? Snakes are a wonderful product of evolution, marvellous animals that have adapted in many forms to populate the earth. We should wonder at them and certainly not have enmity towards them.

If it could ever possibly have happened, God's command to make them crawl upon their bellies actually gave a great advantage to the snake. Just imagine the advantage of stalking and catching your prey when you are lying flat on the ground. The slightest of plants or stones can be used as cover. I should think the snake was delighted with his curse.

'It shall bruise thy head, and thou shalt bruise his heel'.

This statement did make me wonder but I have found the following explanation on the internet. It reads:

When you read there in Genesis where the Lord said to Eve- He gives a prophecy to Eve, who is the symbol of the church, saying that her Seed, meaning her Descendant, who would be the Messiah, would bruise the head of the serpent but the serpent would bruise his heel. The only way to kill a serpent is, you don't bang it on the tail, you have to smash it on the head and the word 'bruise' there means to smash the head of the serpent.

When a person is bitten on the heel, it means it impedes their progress and the devil has successfully hindered the progress of the church but it has not been a mortal wound. It has not stopped its motion. So it's telling about the war, the enmity, between the children of the devil and the children of the woman, or the church, of Christ, and it's an allegory of that battle between good and evil. Incidentally, if you go to Revelation 12, and read about the dragon pursuing the church, that is a bigger picture of that prophecy.

So to bruise its head means you kill a snake by smashing it on the head. I know there is still enmity between humans and snakes but do we need the bible to promote the killing of them, especially by smashing them on the head.

If we think about this just a little more deeply though isn't religion saying here that the snake represents evil and therefore the snake should be smashed. Not talked to and reasoned with but smashed. Hasn't this been true of the path of religion throughout the ages? I look at common everyday hymns that are sung in church:

> Onwards Christian soldiers
> Fight the good fight with all thy might
> Nor shall my sword sleep in my hand

These are calling to religionists to fight for their beliefs, and fight they do.

We see this today in religious extremism throughout the world. "Let's not sit down and talk matters over like educated adults. No, that would be far too boring. Let's invade each other's countries or pop out and blow each other to pieces. That would be much more fun."

As I have said before snakes are wonderful creatures. How wrong it is to see the poor things used as such a symbol of hate.

To be bitten on the heel seems to mean the devil has successfully managed to hinder the progress of the church. The devil is already playing a big part in the scheme of things but, like God, where did he come from? God made everything out of nothing so did God also make the devil? That was a bit of a slip-up wasn't it? God made everything so easily. He had the power to do anything he desired so why did he not just get rid of the devil? Think about it though. Did he keep the devil so he had someone to blame all the bad things on? Now, that's clever.

The writer of the above also says it is telling about the war, the enmity, between the children of the devil and the children of the woman, or the church of Christ. But we are still in the Garden of Eden with just God, Adam, Eve and the talking snake. Where are the children of either the woman or the devil and where is the church of God? Surely a 'church' takes more than three people and a serpent.

We could go on to talk about Revelation 12 and the dragon pursuing the church but I do not wish to go into the whole bible or dragons.

God told the woman he would greatly multiply her sorrow and conception. He said that in sorrow she would bring forth children and her desire would be towards her husband and he would rule over her.

So did this mean she was to live a miserable life and conception was to be sorrowful as well? He said he would multiply both her sorrow and conception. What is it to multiply a conception? Does it mean she (and other women after her) would have many children? Correct me if I am wrong but I do feel what is being said here is that she would be sorrowful in conception. Isn't it true in many cases and religions that women are not supposed to enjoy the act of making love and conception? I have known women who sincerely believed sex was purely for the procreation of children and is certainly not something to be enjoyed. Also, isn't this the reason why some religions still carry out the totally barbaric and ridiculous practise of female genital mutilation, to take the pleasure of love making away from women? Do we mutilate females just because of superstition? I do feel particularly strongly against this so I shall cover it fully in another chapter.

And what of *'In sorrow thou shalt bring forth children'*.

I have never had a baby of course but I have witnessed birth both in animals and humans. I don't think children are brought forth in sorrow but it does look bloody painful. Is it especially painful in humans because our pelvises have evolved slightly different because we walk upright or are our children born earlier and almost prematurely to compensate for this? Most wild animals give birth to young who walk after a few minutes but ours take around a year. I do not know just how painful it is for a woman or perhaps a wildebeest. I use wildebeest as an example because I sat once on the back of a truck and watched one giving birth. Our schedule was such that we couldn't stay long enough for the whole birth but from what I did see the mother wildebeest did seem in much pain. Unlike human mothers she also had the worry of her baby being eaten by predators as soon as it was born. This is why their babies have to get up and run pretty quickly.

I wonder here if God actually made childbirth painful there and then whilst reprimanding Eve or does the bible blame Eve in the time of its writing because through experience they knew then that childbirth was painful. "Let's teach women that their pain in childbirth is because of Eve disobeying God. That will frighten them and make them fear God and do as they are commanded. For if God can punish Eve in this way he could punish all women in whatever way he chose."

'Her desire would be towards her husband and he would rule over her'. What?

Again, I know this is the case is many religions and societies but why? By saying 'her desire would be towards her husband', is condemning Eve, and every other woman since to see her husband's desires as paramount. Her husband's desires are far above her own and she must do as he commands because he rules over her. I don't think so, although this rash statement, in an ancient book of stories, is still used by many today as an excuse to treat women as little more than dross to be ordered and pushed around at her man's will. It is only in the last two or three decades in this country that attitudes have changed. Women here do now have equal rights. Her place is not chained to the sink anymore and she has a right to voice her feelings and opinions. After all why shouldn't she? It wasn't long ago that men were laughed at because they did some cooking or knew where the vacuum cleaner was kept. I have been told I was wrong to tell a wife I loved her because it was soppy and not at all manly. Why? (I say 'a' wife because I have had a few.)

A woman's place is not to react to each and every one of her husband's desires and do as he commands. He doesn't rule over her. Every woman is a man's equal and unless this is truly believed and understood there can be no true relationship between them.

The Lord then turned to Adam and said, *"Cursed is the ground for thy sake; in sorrow shall thou eat of it all the days of thy life. Thorns and thistles shall it bring forth to thee."*

Once again, as with Eve and childbirth, humans at the time of the writing of the bible already knew how hard life was. They knew that tilling the ground for food was back-breaking work. How easy it was to retrospectively blame this on Adam's misdemeanour.

So Adam's only punishment was to work hard to produce a living for his family (don't we all) when poor old Eve was made to be his slave and suffer greatly in childbirth. Once again the man has come out on top. Adam was also to have thorns and thistles in his garden. He ought to see mine.

I have called the woman Eve all along because I thought it a bit rude just to call her woman but in the bible this is when Adam actually names her. Funny really when right from the very beginning he found names for all the animals. Perhaps calling her woman for so long symbolised his and God's disrespect for the female of the species. Adam called his wife Eve because she was the 'Mother of all living'. We shall examine this in a little while.

The Lord then drove Adam and Eve out of the Garden of Eden. He put in place Cherubims (winged angels) and a flaming sword which turned every way to stop them returning. Cherubims and a flaming sword eh? Whatever will they think of next?

Cain and Abel. The story says:

And Adam knew his wife Eve; and she conceived, and bare Cain, and said, I have gotten a man from the Lord. And she again bare his brother Abel. And Abel was a keeper of sheep, but Cain was a tiller of the ground. And in process of time it came to pass, that Cain brought of the fruit of the ground an offering unto the Lord. And Abel, he also brought of the firstlings of his flock and the fat thereof. And the Lord had respect unto Abel and to his offering; but unto Cain and to his offspring he had no respect. And Cain was very wroth, and countenance fell. And the Lord said unto Cain. Why art thou wroth? And why is thy countenance fallen? If thou doest well, shalt thou not be accepted? And if thou doest not well, sin lieth at the door. And unto thee shall be his desire, and thou shalt rule over him. And Cain talked with Abel his brother, and it came to pass, when they were in the field, that Cain rose up against Abel his brother, and slew him.

What can we make of this?

'And Adam knew his wife'. Isn't that lovely? I've 'known' many women in my life but not in this way. (Well, perhaps one or two in this way.) To 'know' someone in the bible means to have sex, or make love. Anyway, Eve gave birth to a son, Cain. I bet all through her labour she cursed the day she ate that ruddy fruit bless her. She said she had gotten a man from the Lord. I thought it was her husband she knew. I jest. Eve then went on to give birth to Abel.

Abel became a shepherd and Cain became an arable farmer. They were successful it seems because they had enough spare produce to offer to the Lord. Cain gave him fruit and Abel gave him meat. The Lord had respect for Abel but not for Cain. This was a bit unfair wasn't it? Obviously the Lord liked meat more than veg but what else could poor old Cain offer? This is what he grew in his profession. He was an arable farmer. He couldn't give unto the Lord a big fat Hereford bull could he? The Lord gave him and his offspring no respect. This must mean any future offspring as we have not mentioned children in this generation as yet.

Cain was very annoyed and the Lord said to him if he did well he would be accepted. He had done his best. Cain was treated rather unfairly and had become angry so what did he do? He could have turned to his brother for comfort and solace but no. None of this business was Abel's fault but Cain murdered him anyway. Human beings don't change do they?

Continuing:

And the Lord said unto Cain, Where is Abel, thy brother? And he said, I know not. Am I my brother's keeper? And he said. What hast thou done? The voice of thy brother's blood crieth unto me from the ground. And now art thou cursed from the earth, which has opened her mouth to receive thy brother's blood from thy hand; when thou tillest the ground, it shall not henceforth yield unto thee her strength; a fugitive and a vagabond shalt thou be in the earth. And Cain said unto the Lord, my punishment is greater than I can bear. Behold, thou hast driven me out this day from the face of the earth; and from thy face shall I be hid; and I shall be a fugitive and a vagabond in the earth; and it shall come to pass, that every one that findeth me shall slay me. And the Lord said unto him, Therefore whosoever slayeth Cain, vengeance shall be taken on him sevenfold. And the Lord set a mark upon Cain, lest any finding him should kill him

The Lord asked Cain where his brother was and Cain said he didn't know. Surely this was an all seeing, all knowing god. If he saw everything then why did he need to ask? But it seems the Lord was just toying with Cain a little because he knew the voice of Abel's blood was crying unto him. The voice of his blood? We now have blood talking as well as a snake!

The Lord said Cain was cursed from the earth which had opened her mouth to receive Cain's brother's blood. Now the earth has a mouth. Will that be talking next?

Cain was banished from the land to live life as a fugitive and vagabond. He accepted this but was worried about being murdered by whoever he met. This could be a big worry these days perhaps but if Cain had thought a little, all he had to do was stay away from his mother and father. Think about it.

And Cain went out from the presence of the lord and dwelt in the land of Nod, on the east of Eden. And Cain knew his wife; and she conceived, and bare Enoch: and he builded a city, and called the name of the city, after the name of his son Enoch. And unto Enoch was born Irad; and Irad begat Mehujael: and Mehujael begat Methusael: and Methusael begat Lamech.

Wooah! Hold on! Hold back! Stop a minute! Put the handbrake on!

It says here that Cain knew his wife and she conceived and bare Enoch. I don't understand. Have you spotted a bit of a flaw here? I have and it is not just a 'bit of a flaw'. His mother Eve was the mother of all creation. She only gave birth to Cain and Abel so on earth we had God, Adam, Eve and Cain. (And the talking snake.) Where has Cain's wife suddenly sprung up from when there was only one woman on earth? Oh dear, did Cain marry and know his own mother and if so wasn't that just a shade unholy? Is this why the bible doesn't mention his wife's name? Are we promoting incest here? Cain's son was called Enoch and he had a son Irad. That's nice but who was Enoch's wife and the mother of his children? No! Please not his own Grandmother? That is pushing even my fervid imagination a little too far.

Cain builded a city and named it after his son Enoch, Enoch City. Sounds like a good football team to me but why did he builded a city? Including God there were only six people on the planet. A small hamlet would have been plenty big enough surely.

Going on:

And Lamech took unto him two wives: the name of one was Adah, and the name of the other Zillah. And Adah bare Jabal: he was the father of such as dwell in tents, and of such as have cattle. And his brother's name was Jubal: he was the father of all such as handle the harp and organ.

And Zillah, she also bare Tubal-cain, an instructor of every artificer in brass and iron; and the sister of Tubal-cain was Naamah, And Lamech said unto his wives,

"Adah and Zillah, Hear my voice; Ye wives of Lamech, harken unto my speech: For I have slain a man to my wounding, And a young man to my hurt. If Cain shall be avenged sevenfold, Truly Lamech seventy and sevenfold.

And Adam knew his wife again; and she bare a son, and called his name Seth: For God, said she, hath appointed me another seed instead of Abel, whom Cain slew. And to Seth, to him also there was born a son; and he called him Enos: then began men to call upon the name of the Lord.

Lamech took two wives, Adah and Zillah. Adah had a child called Jabal and Zilla had one called Tubal-cain who was an instructor in the Iron Age.

Lamech gathered his wives together and admitted to them he had murdered a man and a young man. Two murders? (Am I reading this correctly?) Anyway it seems murdering ran in the family.

Then, after all this Adam knew his wife again and she bore a son, Seth. This is all well and good and congratulations to them I say but look at the passage above. We now have a family tree of Cain, Enoch, Irad, Mehujael, Methusael, Lamech and Jabal. Poor, or lucky, (whichever way you look at it) old wife of Adam has just given birth when she is already a g-g-g-g-g-grandmother. Let's say Cain's wife was 25 years old when she gave birth to Enoch and we will take 25 years after that to represent a generation. This makes Eve somewhere in the region of 175 years old by the time Seth was born. Didn't she do well? Mind you we find in the next chapter that the people of these times certainly were said to have lived long lives.

It also says God had appointed her another seed instead of Abel. So was the long dead Abel the father of Seth?

And Seth then had a son and called him Enos. 'Then began men to call upon the name of the Lord.'

So presumably Enos became a vicar or priest.

So this is the story of Adam and Eve. As I have said, it is delightful as a story but in examination the story cannot possibly be true or indeed have any real meaning in a real world. Some of you will, no doubt, still believe every word of it and if you do that's fine with me. As with God's creation of the world and our next story, if they are not possibly true accounts of real history then what place have they in it apart from being things that people used to believe before they learned better? Why is so much importance and reliance put upon them? How can we pray vehemently to something which cannot be real? Adam and Eve is a wonderful story. Sweet and naively entertaining but even this is nowhere as entertaining or unrealistic as the next chapter The Wonder Of Noah.

3
The Wonder of Noah

Even I went to Sunday school once long ago. I was only about seven years old and, like my granddaughter Lucy, was not old enough or wise enough to know any different. It was what children did on a Sunday morning. The story of Noah's Ark sticks in my mind from those days. I remember the bright colours in the pictures of all the animals and, looking back, I think it was the animals in the pictures that enthralled me more than the story. God arranged for Noah to make an ark because of a great flood and the animals went in two by two. This was all I took in at the time but as I grew older I realised there was far more to the story.

In Adam and Eve I wrote parts of the story and then went into my thoughts before moving on but please forgive me if I indulge myself a little here and give you the complete story first. We shall analyse the story in detail at the end but I really do not want to spoil it by butting in. Again, as with other parts of the bible, the story is so profoundly naïve and should never be taken seriously but some of course do. I shall touch on an account I have read on the Interweb in which someone does try to justify his belief in the story's reality and how it could have happened. His understanding and explanations are priceless. Even television has aired programmes on the subject where they have searched for the ark's resting place.

Despite its ludicrous content it is a truly lovely story so let's enjoy it as I did in Sunday school.

Noah's Ark:

And God said unto Noah, The end of all flesh is coming before me; for the earth is filled with violence through them; and behold, I will destroy them with the earth. Make thee an ark of gopher wood; rooms shalt thou make in the ark, and shalt pitch it within and without with pitch. And this is the fashion which thou shalt make it of; The length of the ark shall be three hundred cubits, the breadth of it fifty cubits, and the height of it thirty cubits. A window shalt thou make to the ark, and in a cubit shalt thou finish it above; and the door of the ark shalt thou set in the side thereof; with lower, second, and third stories shalt thou make it. And behold I, even I, do bring a flood of waters upon the earth, to destroy all flesh, wherein is the breath of life, from under heaven; and everything that is in the earth shall die.

But with thee will I establish my covenant; and thou shalt come into the ark, thou, and thy sons, and thy wife, and thy sons' wives with thee. Any of every living thing of all flesh, two of every sort shalt thou bring into the ark, to keep them alive with thee; they shall be male and female. Of fowls after their kind, and of cattle after their kind, of every creeping thing of the earth after his kind, two of every sort shall come unto thee, to keep them alive. And take thou unto thee of all food that is eaten and thou shalt gather it to thee: and it shall be for food for thee, and for them. Thus did Noah; according to all that God commanded him, so did he.

And the lord said unto Noah, Come thou and all thy house into the ark; for thee have I seen righteous before me in this generation. Of every clean beast thou shalt take thee sevens, the male and his female: and of beast that are not clean by two, the male and his female. Of fowls also of the air by sevens, the male and the female; to keep seed alive upon the face of all the earth. For yet seven days, and I will cause it to rain upon the earth forty days and forty nights; and every living substance that I have made will I destroy from off the face of the earth. And Noah did according unto all that the Lord commanded him. And Noah was six hundred years old when the flood of waters was upon the earth.

And Noah went in, and his sons, and his wife, and his sons' wives with him, into the ark, because of the waters of the flood. Of clean beasts, and of beasts that are not clean, and of fowls, and of everything that creepeth upon the earth, there went in two and two unto Noah into the ark, the male and the female, as God had commanded Noah. And it came to pass after seven days, that the waters of the flood were upon the earth.

The Great Flood:

In the six hundredth year of Noah's life, in the second month, the seventeenth day of the month, the same day were all the fountains of the great deep broken up, and the windows of heaven were opened. And the rain was upon the earth forty days and forty nights. In the self same day entered Noah, and Shem, and Ham, and Japheth, the sons of Noah, and Noah's wife, and the three wives of his sons with them, into the ark; they, and every beast after his kind, and all the cattle after their kind, and every creeping thing that creepeth upon the earth after his kind, and every fowl after his kind, every bird of every sort. And they went in unto Noah into the ark, two and two of all flesh, wherein is the breath of life. And they that went in, went in male and female of all flesh: As God had commanded him: and the Lord shut him in. And the flood was forty days upon the earth; and the waters increased, and bare up the ark, and it was lift up above the earth. And the waters prevailed, and were Increased greatly upon the earth; and the ark went upon the face of the waters. And the waters prevailed exceedingly upon the earth; and all the high hills, that were under the whole heaven were covered. Fifteen cubits upward did the waters prevail; and the mountains were covered. And all flesh died that moved upon the earth, both of fowl, and of cattle, and of beast, and of every creeping thing that creepeth upon the earth, and every man; all in whose nostrils was the breath of life, of all that was in the dry land, died. And every living substance was destroyed which was upon the face of the ground, both man, and cattle, and the creeping things, and the fowl of the heaven; and they were destroyed from the earth: And Noah only remained alive, and they that were with him in the ark. And the waters prevailed upon the earth an hundred and fifty days.

And God remembered Noah, and every living thing, and all the cattle that was with him in the ark; and God made a wind to pass over the earth, and the waters asswaged; the fountains of the deep and the windows of heaven were stopped, and the rain from heaven was restrained; and the waters returned from off the earth continually: and after the end of the hundred and fifty days the waters were abated. And the ark rested in the seventh month, on the seventeenth day of the month, upon the mountains of Ararat. And the waters decreased continually until the tenth month, on the first day of the month, were the tops of the mountains seen.

And it came to pass at the end of forty days, that Noah opened the window of the ark which he had made: and he sent forth a raven, which went forth to and fro, until the waters were dried up from off the earth. Also he sent forth a dove from him, to see if the waters were abated from off the face of the ground; but the dove found no rest for the sole of her foot, and she returned unto him into the ark, for the waters were on the face of the whole earth; then he put forth his hand, and took her, and pulled her in unto the ark. And he stayed yet another seven days; and again he sent forth the dove out of the ark; and the dove came in to him in the evening; and, lo, in her mouth was an olive leaf plucked off; so Noah knew that the waters were abated from the face of the earth. And he stayed yet another seven days; and sent forth the dove; which returned not again unto him anymore.

And it came to pass in the six hundredth and first year, In the first month, the first day of the month, the waters were dried up from off the earth: and Noah removed the covering of the ark, and looked, and, behold, the face of the ground was dry. And in the second month, on the seven and twentieth day of the month, was the earth dried.

And God spoke unto Noah, saying, Go forth of the ark, thou and thy wife, and thy sons, and thy sons' wives with thee. Bring forth with thee every living thing that is with thee, of all flesh, both of fowl, and of cattle, and of every creeping thing that creepeth upon the earth, that they may breed abundantly in the earth, and be fruitful, and multiply upon the earth. And Noah went forth, and his sons, and his wife, and his sons' wives with him; every beast, every creeping thing, and every fowl and whatsoever creepeth upon the earth, after their kinds, went forth out of the ark.

And Noah builded an altar unto the lord; and took of every clean beast, and of every clean fowl, and offered burnt offerings on the altar. And the Lord smelled a sweet savour; and the Lord said in his heart, I will not again curse the ground any more for man's sake; for the imagination of man's heart is evil from his youth; neither will I again smite any more everything living, as I have done. While the earth remaineth, seedtime and harvest, and cold and heat, and summer and winter, and day and night shall not cease.

And God blessed Noah and his sons, and said unto them, Be fruitful and multiply, and replenish the earth. And the fear of you and the dread of you shall be upon every beast of the earth, and upon every fowl of the air, upon all that moveth upon the earth, and all the fishes of the sea; into your hand they are delivered. Every moving thing that liveth shall be meat for you; even as the green herb have I given you all things. But flesh with the life thereof, which is the blood thereof, shall ye not eat. And surely your blood of your lives will I require; at the hand of every beast will I require it, and at the hand of man; at the hand of every man's brother will I require the life of man' Whoso sheddeth man's blood, by man shall his blood be shed: for in the image of God made he man.

And you, be you fruitful, and multiply; bring forth abundantly in the earth, and multiply therein.

The Rainbow:

And God spake unto Noah, and to his sons with him, saying, And I, behold, I establish my covenant with you, and with your seed after you; and with every living creature that is with you, of the fowl, of the cattle, and of every beast of the earth with you; from all that go out of the ark, to every beast of the earth. And I will establish my covenant with you; neither shall all flesh be cut off any more by the waters of a flood; neither shall there be any more a flood to destroy the earth. And God said, This is the token of the covenant which I make between me and the earth. And it shall come to pass, when I bring a cloud over the earth, that the bow shall be seen in the cloud: and I will remember the covenant, which is between me and you and every living creature of all flesh; and the waters shall no more become a flood to destroy all flesh. And the bow shall be in the cloud; and I will look upon it, that I may remember the everlasting covenant between God and every living creature of all flesh that is upon the earth.

And God said unto Noah, This is the token of the covenant, which I have established between me and all flesh that is upon the earth.

And the sons of Noah, that went forth of the ark, were Shem, and Ham, and Japheth; and Ham is the father of Canaan. These are the three sons of Noah: and of them was the whole earth overspread.

And Noah began to be an husbandman, and he planted a vineyard: and he drank of the wine, and was drunken; and he was uncovered within his tent. And Ham the father of Canaan, saw the nakedness of his father, and told his two brethren without. And Shem and Japheth took a garment, and laid it upon both their shoulders, and went backward, and covered the nakedness of their father; and their faces were backward, and they saw not their father's nakedness. And Noah awoke from his wine, and knew what his younger son had done unto him. And he said,

Cursed be Canaan;

A servant of servants shall he be unto his brethren.
And he said,
Blessed be the Lord God of Shem;
And Canaan shall be his servant.
God shall enlarge Japheth,
And he shall dwell in the tents of Shem;
And Canaan shall be his servant.

And Noah lived after the flood three hundred and fifty years. And all the days of Noah were nine hundred and fifty years: and he died.

This is the story of Noah and his ark. In the time of the bible being written people tried desperately to tell how the world had come about and what happened after but they did not have the benefits of science that we have today. There are still many questions today that remain unanswered and we will never know it all but at least we do have a good, stable base to stand on. Writers and philosophers in bible writing times had no such knowledge to lean on and only had their own imaginations to turn to. They did their best but their imaginations did go a little wild bless them. We do thank them for their stories and the world would be a worse place without them but please do not take them seriously as do so many even now.

And so God had made the world and all who dwelt in it but things had not turned out quite the way he had expected. Right from the start with Adam and Eve eating the forbidden fruit and then Cain slaying his brother Abel, followed by Lamech also turning out to be a murderer, you can imagine God not being too pleased.

So people were causing havoc everywhere and God came up with a cunning plan to rid the earth of them. He would cause a great flood to come upon the earth and drown everyone and everything. But was every human in that time so vicious? Surely the whole world was not full of sinners. Just how many totally innocent, loving and lovely people did God murder? Was Noah such a wonderful man in himself? Was he really above all other human beings? Could this great God really have been the world's first mass murderer?

The trouble was he needed someone to repopulate the earth after the flood and the best candidate he could think of was a 480yr old boat builder and his family.

Can you imagine poor old Noah's shock? He was not exactly in the prime of his life and you would think he would be enjoying a good, long restful retirement, but no. Here he was suddenly burdened with the responsibility of building a ship big enough and strong enough to save the world.

God gave him very rudimentary guidelines but left the rest for Noah to think out for himself. It doesn't say in the story from my bible just how long it took Noah to build the ark but the common census of opinion seems to be 120yrs. God was pretty ratty with civilisation and you would have thought he would have specified a much quicker build time and introduced tough penalty clauses for late completion but Noah was an old gentleman and at that age I would have thought everything took time.

He did have his sons Shem, Ham and Japheth to help him (Isn't it odd how they all had sons in those days). The brain automatically sees 'sons' as young fit men but even they were old men by this time. Even if Noah had followed Adam's lead in fathering a child when he was about 175yrs old, his sons would themselves be around 305yrs old when they had to help with the ark but at least it was a good long contract for them to rely on. Not many boat-builders have this kind of security. So there was dad and his three sons beavering away on the massive boat and they would have had an age total of somewhere in the region of 1090yrs between them.

Noah and his wife and his sons and their wives were to repopulate the earth but by the time the ark was finished Noah was 600 and his sons were at least 425yrs old. Could any of them have reproduced at that age? Biologically impossible you must admit. Biologically impossible to even live anywhere near that long let alone reproduce.

With our feet on the ground and our minds open we all know that even with vast advances in medical techniques and treatments and drugs to combat almost anything over the last one hundred or so years we still do not get many humans living even for the amount of years it took Noah to build the ark. They certainly could never reproduce at that age.

While we are still talking about Noah and his family let's ask another question, one which typifies again the bible's attitude towards women. Noah and his sons are named but their wives are 'just their wives'. In bible terms they are not even worthy of being given names. The bible, certainly at this stage does seem to give no credence or respect to women at all. Such is the way in some religions and societies today. Noah and his sons may have built the ark but I bet their wives did their share of the cooking, cleaning, washing and mucking out.

I said wryly a few paragraphs ago that they all seem to have given birth to sons in those days. When I look at it closer I realise my wry humour was actually almost correct in fact. The names we have for biblical offspring so far are Cain, Abel, Irad, Mehujael, Methusael, Lamech, Jabal, Shem, Ham Naamah and Japeth. Every offspring, apart from Naamah, was male, or perhaps not. Were there other female offspring as well but the bible writers did not consider them worthy of a mention at all let alone naming them?

Also, we have no written evidence at all of the history of the ark. Not a word was written and handed down. No one knows when it was supposed to have happened and no one actually knows a single thing about it that is factual. All we have is a lovely simple story from the heads of bible writers. So if we do have nothing apart from the bible which was written way after the event how on earth do we know the names of even the men on board? No wonder we have no names for the lesser females.

Let's get on to the actual ark itself.

The ark was to be made of gopher wood. That's what it says in my bible but in other bible stories it says it was made of other woods. Whatever the wood was, let's look at its construction. The ark was not a small boat. God said it should be 300 cubits long, 50 cubits wide and 30 high. A cubit is roughly the length of a man's forearm and hand, in other words the measurement from his elbow to tip of his fingers. This works out at about 18 inches. So the ark measured 450ftx75ftx45ft. It is not a massive ship like the Titanic but, as I say, not a small boat either.

This ship was to stay afloat for months and was to house thousands of tons of animals and all their food and water so it was not to be thrown together. Was Noah a master ship builder? It doesn't actually mention what Noah did for a trade only that he was righteous. It is hoped he was a master boat-builder but perhaps he was a master greengrocer and that is why it took 120yrs to build it.

Right from the start there would have been design issues. Noah had to design a boat to house members of every single animal species in the world. How did he even know what all the animals to come were let alone what type of accommodation they needed? Also it would be no good putting the tigers in with the antelope would it?

I doubt if, in those days, Noah was a very well-travelled man. He would have had no idea what a tiger, moose or muntjac deer looked like let alone what sized cabin they needed. Cameras had not been invented so God couldn't even show him photographs. He also had a problem (a big problem) with diet. He never knew what the animals to come looked like so how did he know what they ate?

The ark was supposed to be afloat for a year so taking just one tiny species into consideration how did Noah collect and keep alive the flowers needed for each hummingbird, such a small bird but such a huge consideration. He would have had to collect the hundreds of species of nectar bearing flowers that the bird species relied on. To do this he would have had to have travelled the length of the continent of America. He would also then have had to keep them in a very specially heated and humidified greenhouse in order to feed all three hundred plus species. This is just highlighting one tiny species of bird so you can imagine what he was up against. This consideration would be the same for every single species in the world. In illustrations I have seen the ark as just three floors with pens. I'm afraid it would have to have been far more elaborate and sophisticated than that.

I am no shipbuilder myself but I do wonder if four men and their wives could possibly even launch such a vessel. I doubt if they would have had much help from neighbouring shipbuilders or anyone else. Can you imagine them building the ark with Noah knowing they would be left at the quayside to drown?

Also God told Noah to put 'a' window in the ark. A good idea but a few hundred would have been better. Just imagine all those animals packed closely together with all that effluent. I doubt if one window would have been enough to stop everything being overcome and dying from inhaling noxious gasses.

I said earlier that I have read an account on the Interweb which argues that the animals could easily be cared for. This gentleman suggests that several animals could be harnessed to slow moving rotary fans to keep the air flowing and clean. The same person suggests that waste from the animals would simply be left to drop through slatted floors. This is all well and good but what about the poor creatures on the floor below? Is this why some of the animals were classed as 'unclean'?

On to the animals of the ark:

Different accounts I have read give different numbers on animals which the ark would have housed. Some say the number was in the tens of thousands and some say even hundreds of thousands. Again let's open our eyes and minds. Let's think and be realistic. There would have to have been millions, millions of species and at least two of each. On our planet we do have millions of species of animals not just a few thousand. Religionists say far fewer actually travelled in the ark. The earth is home to approximately 8.7 million species including no less than 950,000 species of insect.

They are not suggesting the rest 'evolved' after the flood are they?

God did say that of clean beasts there would be seven and seven. That again multiplies the numbers. But what of 'clean' and 'unclean' animals? A clean mammal is supposed to be one that has a cloven hoof and chews the cud. Why that makes it 'clean' I do not know. Neither do I know which birds are classed as 'clean' and neither do other people it seems. I have just read a statement which says,

"It is hard for rabbinical authorities to distinguish clean from unclean birds, as the scripture (Lev. XI. 13-19) enumerates only the birds which shall not be eaten, without giving any of the marks which distinguish them from the clean birds. This is all the more important as the names of some of the birds mentioned in the scriptures are followed by the word lemino or leminehu – i.e. after its kind- and it is therefore necessary to recognise certain fixed distinguishing characteristics. The following rules are fixed by the Talmud, by which a clean bird may be distinguished. It must not be a bird of prey; it must have a front toe if that be the meaning of (then there is a word which I do not understand but it looks like musical symbols), but according to most explanations the hind toe is meant.

This explanation goes on and on and gets no more lucid. Why can't we just be sensible and call a bird a bird. He can't help it if his toe points forward or backwards can he? That's the way he was born. And would which way his toes pointed necessarily bother us if we were starving? We cut those bits off before we eat the bird anyway.

Let us leave and forget the 'clean' and 'unclean' issue for now and move on and let's just say the animals went in two by two. So in our ark there would just be two of everything and the unclean animals were the ones on the bottom deck covered in dung.

In the story it simply says that God told Noah and his family to go aboard the ark with all the animals. For some reason it neglects to mention how all the animals managed to get there. How did they get there? How could they have got there? They say the ark ended up on Mount Ararat which is in Turkey so let's assume it started off in that area. This means two polar bears had to travel down from the arctic, two jaguars had to pop over from South America, two Kangaroos had to hop across from Australia and two little field mice had to travel from England. Maybe the elephants packed all their belongings in their trunks. Sorry that was a terrible joke.

How did they all know where to go? How did they decide who should go? How did the polar bears reach Turkey without dying of heat stroke? What did they eat along the way? How did the raccoon, the buffalo, the puma, the elk, the moose and the rattle snake manage to cross the Atlantic Ocean from North America? How did ants and millipedes cross continents?

And what of the fish? "Well, they can swim", I hear you say. "They were left in the sea."

The sea is what all the water would be turned to. The rivers and lakes would be gone and freshwater fish cannot survive in salt water. Admittedly with all the rain that was to come the sea would be a little less salty but it still could not be home for thousands of freshwater fish species. And with it being less salty could it even have been home any more to sea fish? Perhaps all of the fish species would have to be housed in the ark. And how would the freshwater species get there before the arrival of the flood when the vast majority of them would have to cross a still salty ocean along the way? Fish would also have had to cross land and as we know there are very few that can do that.

Noah would have had to build giant aquariums, all at different temperatures for different species of different climates and he would have had to know which species ate which food.

How did he heat the aquariums? The only fuel he could have had was wood but was that a good idea with all that pitch without and within the ark?

He would also have had to have known not to drop a couple of pike in with the roach, rudd and bream.

There is another type of animal that is not mentioned in the bible and one which does not get much of a mention in real life either because of its size. We see mammals, fish, birds, insects and reptiles but we do not see microbes. Microbes are single cell organisms so tiny that millions can fit into the eye of a needle. They are the oldest form of life on earth. Microbe fossils date back to 3.5 billion years. That is billions of years before even dinosaurs roamed the earth. It is said there are more microbes living on a human hand than there are humans in the entire world. These tiny creatures, bacteria, archaea, fungi and protists are everywhere and we depend upon them. I have read that we could not possibly live without them but they could live very well without us. I think the rest of the planet feels the same. They are so important and fascinating that they really deserve their own book. Although there would be countless billions of them on Noah, his family and his cargo there are many more types that live in the ground and of course all of these would be wiped out by a worldwide flood. They too would have had to come on board, but how? How do you tell a microbe to make its way to a wooden ship being built by a nearly six hundred year old man and his ageing family? How would you convince them you are telling the truth? Also, in the ground are larger creatures such as worms, beetle larvae, leatherjackets etc. etc. etc. All of these would have to reach the ark and be housed.

When you think about it Noah had to have been a highly intelligent scientist. Perhaps the equivalent of Charles Darwin but I doubt if they would ever have met because only one of them was ever real.

According to the bible I am wrong and they did all reach the ark but then suddenly there was poor old Noah surrounded by millions of totally unfamiliar animals. How did he know where to house them and who to house with whom? I bet the tiger did soon pipe up and say he would be quite happy to share the penthouse suite with a few antelope. Did Noah have an inventory or did he have to ask them what type of animal they were? Perhaps, like the snake in Adam and Eve, they too could talk. Even if we were to say the ark was big enough to house two of all the animals in the world and they did all miraculously find their way to Noah, how was the boarding ever organised? And I bet there were a few disgruntled passengers when they found out they were going to have to live on the bottom deck and get caked in you know what.

Anyway, so the ark was filled and they all waited for the rain. God said it would rain for forty days and forty nights. I remember Mrs Brown of television's Mrs Brown's Boys saying to a couple of young Mormon lads.

*"Forty days and forty nights and they call that a disaster. In Ireland we call that the ******* summer".*

Here I admit to being wrong. Earlier I said would it be possible for so few people to launch such a large ship? They didn't have to did they? The flood waters would have risen and the ark would have been launched automatically. I am wrong again but there is nothing wrong with being wrong so long as it is admitted and we learn from our mistakes.

God shut Noah and all inside the ark. Please take a while here to imagine the sights, sounds and smells within the ark with its one window while they waited for the waters to come. There are eight people on board who have to care for millions of animals and these were wild animals that had never been accustomed to being shut in. I cannot see that the craft was exactly a tranquil haven of love and peace. I have recently watched the film Noah with Russell Crowe looking very young and fit for a six hundred year old man. The writers of the story realised the chaos that would ensue with all these animals on board so Russell Crowe went round with some smoke and made them all go to sleep. What a way out. Well done for the imagination. They slept for the whole journey and therefore did not have the need to eat, urinate or defecate. The film wasn't true to the bible story but that didn't matter when the bible story is so far-fetched anyway but having said this I did enjoy the film as an adult just as I enjoyed the original story as a child. The film did prove though God's idea that man and animals are different because although the smoke sent the elephants and all to sleep, the humans were not affected. Also, according to the film, the great flood happened sometime after about 1250BC. I thought it was supposed to have happened much earlier but Russell Crowe and Ray Winstone were using an awful lot of iron. I could pick at it all day but as I say it was entertaining and I did enjoy it.

The flood:

So it is now the seventeenth of February, or even the seventeenth of April if it all happened before around 713BC when the months of January and February were added to the calendar by the Romans, and Noah is six hundred years old and God is about to let loose the flood of all floods. Isn't it odd that the bible doesn't have names for the women on board the ark, cannot give any method of how the animals arrived at the ark and doesn't even begin to account for any of the actual facts regarding the story at all but it does know the exact date the flood began. It gives the exact date but not the actual year which is a bit of a cop-out isn't it?

'The fountains of the great deep were broken up and the windows of heaven were opened'

So this is how the flood is said to have occurred. The fountains of the great deep were broken up. What does this mean? It seems water is coming from the water. It is suggested that all this water was stored in vast fissures under the seas and it has been caused to rise up and flood the land. How could water under the sea rise up? It can't.

We do have high tides and tsunamis which can flood land but that is only in certain areas. If the land is flooded by a high tide somewhere there has to be a low tide somewhere else.

Let's analyse these 'fountains of the deep'.

If these vast areas of water said to be underneath the sea are sealed there then they cannot rise. If these areas are not sealed then they are all part of the sea anyway. Think of a model. We have a bowl filled to the brim with water with an upturned dish in it. The water under the dish is not part of the rest of the bowl as it is enclosed. If the dish was perforated then the water in the dish would be part of the rest of the bowl. Either way the water in the bowl could not possible flood over the rim of the bowl even if the dish was removed. Water, cannot possibly just well up to the surface and flood it because, as with everything else in the universe, it is held in place by gravity.

So this just leaves rain to flood the earth, forty days and forty nights worth. In this short time the water was to rise from the original sea level up to a height that would cover all the mountains. We all know that Everest is the highest point on earth and some will know it stands 8,848 metres or 29,029 feet above sea level. So in forty days, or 960 hours, rain had to fall to a depth of 29,000 plus feet. That is 30.24 feet every hour or 9.22 metres. The best ship in the world would not survive the downpour. To put the deluge in perspective, we have an average annual rainfall in Britain of a little under one meter. During the biblical downpour almost ten times that amount would be falling every hour. Can you imagine the chaos? I am trying but my mind cannot do it justice.

All the trees of the mountains and hillsides would be immediately uprooted and hillsides would be washed away. Floating debris would be scattered upon the seas in vast amounts and even if the ark could have possibly managed to survive the downpour would it have been completely scuppered by floating debris?

The deepest place in the world's oceans is the Mariana or Marianas Trench which at its deepest is 36,000 feet or 10,911 metres. When you look at the height of Everest you see that normal sea level is not far from half way between Everest's summit and Mariana's sea floor. Where did all the water come from? There was as much rain falling upon the earth as there was water already existing in the seas. It could not have been imported from another planet and could not possibly have been held in clouds. The pressure of the atmosphere alone would have destroyed everything beneath it.

And talking of pressure, the pressure upon us at sea level is 15psi. Everything at the old sea level after the flood would have been almost that of the Mariana Trench, i.e. 15,000psi, 1000 times normal pressure. I know it was supposed to be God's intention to kill off all human and animal life and it certainly would have worked but with the effects of salt water and this massive pressure every plant on earth would have been destroyed as well. The bible doesn't seem to have mentioned Noah's need to gather together all the plants of the world before the flood as well as all the animals. It is said there are approximately one million species of plants counting fungi. Poor old Noah would have had to gather them all and keep them in the manner they were accustomed to.

Their Time Afloat:

So Noah and his ark of millions have somehow miraculously survived the downpour and debris and they are now floating at almost the height of a Boeing 747 jumbo jet cruise flight. When we travel in a jumbo we have an artificial air pressure and temperature. Noah would not have had this luxury. He, his crew and all the animals (apart from the likes of bar headed geese that live at the height of Everest) would be suffering dreadfully from a shortness of breath and severe coldness. Few animals would actually be able to exist at this height for even a short amount of time let alone the best part of a year. The temperature outside a jumbo jet is something in the region of -60degrees. At least those animals on the bottom deck which were covered in dung did now have an advantage. They may have been caked and smelly but at least dung is warm. Even when it was dry this would have provided good insulation.

Feeding the Animals:

In the passage on the Interweb I have already quoted it says feeding all the animals would be easy. This religionist gentleman says only 16,000 animals were on the ark. This does fall slightly short of the actually 16 million there would have been. This man explains how easy it would be to feed the animals, including all the dinosaurs. Dinosaurs? Whooa! What is this poor chap thinking? It states that he has come to his conclusions after a twenty year study. We know Noah and dinosaurs never saw each other never mind share an ark together. They missed each other by 60 million years. It seems to me this poor deluded gentleman has wasted twenty years of his life doing this study but then again he will think I am wasting my time writing this book which he will, quite rightly in his own mind, class as dross.

He states that the herbivores would eat compressed hay and the carnivores would eat dried meat. He also states that the largest of all the animals weighs only a few hundred pounds. In his twenty years of study did he never see an elephant, a rhino or a hippo? I have seen many given weights for elephants and none of them say a few hundred pounds. The best I can see is anywhere between 8,800 and 15,400 pounds. I would say the average would be 4 to 5.5 tons. I have sat and watched as a massive bull elephant walked nonchalantly passed the truck we were sitting on. I can tell you for a fact he weighed more than just a few hundred pounds. He was huge, huge and beautiful!

Our man then goes on to say that animals which have very specialized diets today may not have had specialized diets in the days of the flood. Is he referring to evolution again by any chance?

So without wishing to go on and on about caring for the animals let's sum up by doing a simple calculation. We have 8 humans looking after 16 million animals. So each human, man or woman, named or not named, has to feed, bed and muck out 2 million animals each every day for a year. They also had to work as vets as it would be impossible for all the animals to be well for all of the time.

Even if all the food for all the animals could possibly have been gathered together it would have taken a vast fleet of ships to carry it all let alone the animals it was to be fed to. They would also have needed a huge fleet of ships just to carry the water needed. Noah would not have had enormous desalination plants on board. And let's be honest, it would have taken many thousands of people to even come anywhere near supplying all the animals' needs.

So could it all have happened? I shall leave you to make up your own minds.

The Waters Asswaged:

I know the spelling of 'asswaged' is not as we spell it today but this is the way it is spelled in the bible and it is quite quaint and what a lovely word.

After 150 days the waters assuaged and God remembered Noah. It was a good job he did. And on the 1st October the tops of the mountains were seen. So the waters were abating but where were they abating to? They could not have flowed down rivers to the sea because all the original river systems were thousands of meters below the sea and they couldn't flow into the sea could they? So the only way the waters could abate was through evaporation but even if the sun was shining, at 5.5 miles above the old sea level there would not have been much heat to cause evaporation to take place. Everything would have been frozen. Even if the weak sun at that height did manage to turn the water into water vapour, there would have been too much in the atmosphere to allow survival. As with all the other figures I have researched, the figures for the amount of water on earth do vary but it says on one web site (which looks reliable) that there are 360,000,000,000,000,000,000 gallons of water upon the earth. In the great flood the depth of water virtually doubled before heading back to the sky. At school I learned that 'A pint of water weighs a pound and a quarter'. So a gallon of water weighs ten pounds. This means we have to add another nought onto our gallon figure to find the weight of water in the flood. We do this and we then have to divide the figure by 2,240 (Pounds in a ton) to find the weight in tons, I.e. 1,607,142,857,142,857,000 tons.

I have read passages which explain where the water went and one is particularly brilliant. It says simply, "After the waters covered the mountains, God rebuked them and they fled." Now, why didn't I think of that? It is so obvious. I don't think any of this was at all possible but again, for the sake of the story, we shall say it happened.

Noah sent forth a dove and it eventually came back to him with an olive leaf in its beak. As we have said before the earth would have been ruined by the flood. Everything would have been completely crushed by the great pressure of the water above it and the torrents of water flowing down hills and mountains. There would have been nothing left apart from a vast devastation; a devastation that would have been so horrendous that the earth would have taken millions of years to recover from it. The whole of the earth would have been contaminated by salt as well so when Noah eventually set out to replant it nothing would have grown. In the story though God just told all to go forth and multiply and they did, all these very aged people.

Looking back upon the story, God has approached a 480yr old man and asked him and his sons and their wives to build an ark to carry them and at least two of all the animals in the world. The building of the ark was such a monumental task that it took them 120yrs to complete.

Once ready the ark had to be loaded with food and water to last everything a year and two of all species of animal somehow had to hear about the ark and then find their way to it. Many species do not even have a life cycle long enough to travel. What happened to them along the way?

When they all reached the ark Noah had to house them and bed them down before the sky opened up to let leash the torrent of all torrents. It rained for forty days and forty nights until the water covered Mount Everest, destroying everything beneath it.

Noah and his family beavered away feeding, bedding, nursing and mucking out all their charges until the waters asswaged. They then had to release all the animals into a devastated world where they all had to go forth and multiply.

All this was a giant undertaking for them all but why did God do it this way? In the beginning God created all the animals in a single day and followed this by creating man the following day. If the behaviour of man had become so terrible and God was so all powerful why did he devise this complicated and truly unworkable 121yr plan to right matters when all he had to do was make everyone disappear and create some more? There was no need for the ark or the floods and no need to destroy the earth and such a vast majority of animal and plant life upon it.

The Rainbow:

Before we end this chapter we shall take a quick look at the last section of the story regarding the rainbow.

God made a covenant with Noah that never again would he destroy the earth and life upon it. As we have just said above, he didn't have to. He was a brilliant man but the ark was not one of his better brainwaves. He decided he would put a rainbow in the sky to remind himself and Noah of the covenant. So do religionists today look at rainbows and immediately think of God and Noah. I don't know. I suppose some must.

After the flood ordeal was over Noah grew a vineyard, made wine and became drunken. Who could blame him after what he had been through and achieved? I enjoy a glass of wine sometimes after I have worked just a plain and ordinary day. I would say Noah had every right to take a good tipple.

The trouble was though one day he got rather tipsy and fell asleep naked in his tent and his son walked in and saw him there and this was desperately frowned upon. Why was accidently seeing his father naked such a crime and why, in the bible, is nakedness seen as such a big thing? Adam and Eve had eaten the forbidden fruit and were surrounded by Wonderment but all they could think of was their nakedness and now seeing a naked man was a crime.

Noah has saved the world and there is so much to do. We have just covered a remarkable story and you would think it would have a remarkable ending but it hasn't. The world has been put right and all the sinners have been murdered. Noah and his family have to clear up and repopulate the earth but the story does not end with any of this. It ends with a man seeing his father in the buff.

It was Noah's son Ham who stumbled upon his father's nakedness so why was it Ham's son Canaan who was punished? That's a bit unfair isn't it? Ham finding his father like this was a complete accident so why would even he be punished let lone his innocent son. Poor old Canaan was condemned to be a servant for no reason.

Biblical names such as Canaan, Shem, Irad, Lamech and Jabal are lovely and perhaps should be used more these days. I wonder though if Ham could ever be a Jewish name.

Philosophers and religionists both believe in something but a philosopher feels he has the duty to justify his beliefs.

4

The Wonder of the Universe and Numbers

We have talked at length about the bible and its entertaining stories but this book is not purely about proving them false and therefore being an inadequate way to describe how the earth came about. I could go on about burning bushes, people being turned into pillars of salt, walking on water, loaves and fishes and the parting of the waves but I really want to move on and talk about the real world and Wonderment. After all that is what the book is called.

The bible says God made the earth and it is both the centre of and most important thing in the universe. The sun is only there to provide light for us during the day and all the other stars we see in the sky are set there only to provide light for us during darkness. Religionists still believe this but let me attempt to describe what really happened and what is out there. Here I admit I am not Richard Dawkins or Brian Cox or Stephen Hawking. They are professors and I am just a man who thinks. My knowledge is nowhere near as great as theirs but hopefully I can entertain you as I try my best. I certainly do not know everything and even the three great gentlemen I have just mentioned would keenly admit neither do they, but just to think is the greatest thing we can do. Nobody knows everything and wouldn't it be boring if we did?

It is a generally accepted hypothesis that the big bang led to the beginning of the universe. As I have said before, this is based on the evidence we have before us such as the fact that if the universe is seen to be expanding then sometime in the distant past it must have been much smaller. This theory is then expanded (or contracted) with the universe being originally just a single dot or even nothing. As I have also said, we still cannot really understand the 'nothing' that was there before but one day a 'eureka' moment will occur in someone's mind and a perfectly simple and understandable answer will be found. This is how we learn.

My mind goes to a very early machine powered form of transport which I saw the late Fred Dibnah driving. It was massive and consisted of a horse carriage body mounted on a simple chassis and engine. Because travel had always been by horse and carriage it seemed the natural progression of things was to take away the horse and put an engine on a carriage (or vice versa) but then 'eureka', someone realised as they didn't need horses anymore they didn't need a carriage either. We then didn't have a 'horseless carriage' but a motor car.

Extending this little interlude further and still talking about cars, we have all known for years that the wing of an aeroplane gives lift and therefore allows it to take off. Again someone had a 'eureka' moment as they realised what was looking them squarely in the face all along. If an aeroplane wing provides lift then surely an upside down wing would provide a downward force. This is why today all formula 1 racing cars have adopted this theory and to their great advantage.

My favourite 'eureka' moment was a gentleman by the name of Percy Shaw who invented the 'cats eye' in the 1930s. This was a simple invention with no great technical knowhow required in their production but just look how his 'eureka' moment took off. Today there are many millions of 'cats eyes' on our roads and each is doing a great job and is saving lives. It is said that Mr Shaw had his idea when he saw a cat walking towards him in the road and he saw the reflection of the cat's eyes in his headlights. I suppose if he had seen the cat walking the other way he would have invented the pencil sharpener. Either way he was on to a winner.

The big bang theory does seem to hold for now but will something else be realised or will we just learn to understand it more? Was there just the one big bang or were there big bangs happening everywhere? Are there big bangs still happening today in parallel universes? Stars are born and stars die and explode, thus giving life to new stars and planets. Could this happen to big bangs? How many big bangs have there been and how many will there be in future? To look at this scientists use what they call the 'bubble theory'. Imagine a child blowing a string of bubbles. Each bubble has its own entity and identity and each goes its own way. The bubble theory sees these bubbles as universes. They coexist alongside one another without actually interfering with each other. No part of one bubble ever reaches any part of another but they are there. Whacky perhaps but as I have said before we do have to have whacky thoughts in order to get anywhere. Anyway though, thinking about it. Is it really so whacky? There is no evidence or theory to say it could not happen.

There used to be a wild theory of black holes, vast areas of extreme gravity that swallow up everything around them. People mocked but it turned out there is actually a black hole at the centre of every galaxy.

A theory my late father used to have was one in which we were all germs inside a body and we were all spreading out to invade that body. The universe is spreading as do germs and I can see the delight in his theory. It may seem rubbish but at least he was thinking. The trouble with this theory is that if we were germs inside another body then that body would have to be a germ inside another body and so on ad infinitum. Rather like inter stacking Russian dolls. It would be a bit like God really. God made the earth but someone must have made him and someone else must have made them and so on, and on and on and on.

We know so much about our universe but there is still much left to learn. We have the greatest minds on the planet working on it but we do not have all the answers yet. (Sorry religionists but this doesn't mean it had to be made by God). We also have the greatest minds on earth working on space travel and we have all, collectively, poured many billions of pounds or dollars or whatever into it for many years but still man has only travelled as far as the moon, a mere quarter of a million miles away. We will eventually go to Mars but even that is only our next door neighbour. Will we be able to travel beyond Mars before we destroy the very planet we are trying to fly from and which supports us?

Rather than think of 'nothing' some scientists say the big bang began with the explosion of a minute particle which contained all we see today. They say this particle was much smaller than an atom. I say no matter how small this particle was, it was there and therefore existed. Surely if it was there, like God, it needed something to exist in. My mind rests easier with the universe coming somehow from nothing but we do not yet understand 'nothing'. I feel we somehow have to grasp the reality of infinity and get our heads around it. We are clever beings but I think we are still in our infancy when it comes to understanding. Do we have to get away from our own laws of physics as we know them? Are these laws that we think by actually holding us back? Perhaps we need millions of silly thoughts until we happen upon one which maybe is, again, not quite so silly after all.

The beginning of the universe, like Eve's snake, is beguiling and intriguing but what intrigues and fascinates me most is the fact that you and I and everything else was there at the very beginning.

Although it all began over 13 billion years ago, we were there, you and I, and so was every frog, every tulip, every stick insect and every stick it ever sat on. We were there in one form or another on that day because everything came from the big bang and everything that came from it is still here today. Nothing has been added or taken away. All matter and energy (really matter is a form of energy) is as it always was and always will be.

Even the space of 'space' had to be there somehow. The space between your house and your neighbour's house, the space between your eyes and this book and even the space between our star, the sun, and our next nearest star Proxima Centauri which is 10,000 times further away than Neptune (Some 4.2 light years away) were all there at the big bang. If you hold out your hands and look at the space between them, that space has been there for 13.7 billion years.

We say that the energy in the universe has always been there and it has but energy can change form. It can morph from one form very simply into another. Let's talk about a wheelbarrow.

"He's gone crazy again", I can hear you say but no not quite yet.

A wheelbarrow will never move itself. Leave it in the garden and ten years later it will still be sitting there. It needs energy to move but a wheelbarrow cannot produce that energy. Where can it get its energy from? That is where you come in. You push the wheelbarrow because you have eaten food and have converted the energy within that food to physical energy. Your physical energy allows you to pick up the handles of the wheelbarrow and push it forward thus converting that energy again into the energy of movement. We have now converted the energy of potatoes, carrots and meat into movement. Your potatoes, carrots and meat have just moved a wheelbarrow. It is still the same amount of energy but has a totally different form.

The actual beginning of the universe:

In my younger days I concocted my own theory to age the universe. It was very simple as I shall show.

My theory was this.

If $Speed = \dfrac{Distance}{Time}$

Then $Time = \dfrac{Distance}{}$

Speed

(Multiply both sides by Time and divide both sides by Speed)

i.e. *Time* = $\dfrac{120\ miles}{60\ mph}$ = *2hours*

Therefore if we know the speed of the expanding universe and also the distance the universe has travelled since the big bang then we have our parameters for my theory and therefore would have the answer, its age. Simple eh? 'Eureka!!'

The trouble with my theory was that we do not have a constant speed for the expanding universe as it seems galaxies are actually accelerating away from each other and we do not know where the big bang actually took place exactly so we have no idea just how far it has actually travelled. My theory seemed logical to a fourteen year old but it didn't hold much water did it? I have since accepted scientists better theories.

We now know the universe (one universe or many) came from the big bang in whatever form it took. The universe just after the big bang (I mean the smallest of small fractions of a second after) was a gigantic mass of unorganised heat (energy). Then things started to change. I could talk in detail about baryon numbers and quarks and antiquarks or leptons or anti leptons but I doubt if many of you would understand. I certainly don't myself to any great extent. So let's try and keep things on a keel that most people like you and I will understand. I shall skip lightly through the early stages so as not to bore you. All I want to do is quickly describe the factors which led to the wonderful universe we can see today.

Let's start with the very early universe and this gigantic mass. That smallest of a small fraction of a second I have mentioned. Scientists would say roughly 10 to the minus 34 seconds or 0.0000000000000000000000000000000001 of a second. I said it was a small fraction didn't I?

In this time the universe is said to have doubled in size 90 times into a giant bubble. So am I wrong after all? In my mind the universe came from nothing so if it doubled in size 90 times, 900 times or even 900 million times it would still be nothing. So if scientists are correct it must have begun with something.

Anyway, let's look at what was in the universe at this time. This first fraction of a second saw a time of huge and rapid inflation and the universe was filled with a 'quark-gluon plasma' or 'quark soup'.

Moving on in time to a mere one billionth of a second after the big bang sub-atomic particles suddenly acquired mass and substance for the first time and amongst these substances were the Quarks.

'Quarks'

As I said we will not go into too much detail about various forms of matter but the quark does deserve a special mention as it is a fundamental constituent of matter. Quarks combine to form composite particles called hadrons. The most stable of which are protons and neutrons which are the components of atomic nuclei. This all happened before the universe was one minute old. Quarks are still in existence today but only within other particles. They can never be observed in their own right.

There are six types of quark (Up, Down, Charm, Strange, Bottom and Top) but let's not worry about all of these. As I have said the quark has led us to atomic nuclei so we can briefly move on to them.

Atomic Nuclei:

When the universe was approximately 10 seconds old the temperature fell to a point where atomic nuclei started to form.

Protons and neutrons began to form into atomic nuclei in the process of nuclear fusion.

After approximately 3 minutes a process took place which we call nucleosynthesis. Free neutrons combined with protons to form deuterium and this rapidly fused into helium. Nucleosynthesis only lasted for about 17 minutes before the temperature of the universe fell to a level where nuclear fusion could no longer take place spontaneously. We shall talk more about nuclear fusion later as the universe developed.

Atoms:

A nucleus is the centre of an atom. It is made up of protons and neutrons and is surrounded by the electron cloud (The space inside an atom). The size of the nucleus depends upon the type of atom it inhabits. The nucleus inside a light atom such as hydrogen is smaller than that inside a heavier atom such as uranium.

An atom is the smallest piece of ordinary matter and to put it very very simply, every atom is made from protons and neutrons surrounded by an electron cloud and everything in the universe is made from atoms and all this started 10 seconds after the big bang.

We have space in 'space' and much of every atom also consists of space. We humans and all rocks and everything else are made of atoms and so much of us and them is actually space and all that space was there at the big bang.

Atoms cluster together to form 'elements'.

Elements:

As the universe continued to cool and became less dense atoms formed into elements which are substances formed entirely from one kind of atom. The most common of all the elements is Hydrogen and this contains just one proton and one electron and from hydrogen all the other elements can be made. If two protons are fused together then one of them turns into a neutron and we then have a different element. The next in the chain you could say. This element is called Deuterium which is still a form of Hydrogen because it still, like Hydrogen, has only one proton in its nucleus and it is the number of protons that denote which element it is.

If you combine together two Deuterium nuclei you then have an element containing two protons and two neutrons and this is now called Helium.

As you add together more and more protons and neutrons you get different elements right through the whole 100 or so until you finally reach the heavier of the elements such as Osmium, Iridium, Platinum, Rhenium, Neptunium, Lead, Uranium and Gold.

This process of making the various elements is called Nuclear Fusion.

Nuclear Fusion:

From what I have just written, it seems simple to build elements. Just combine neutrons and protons. But simple as it sounds, it certainly isn't. If it was then we would all be doing it to make Platinum or Gold in our garden sheds.

There is only one place in the universe where this actually occurs and this place is inside stars. They are the only places in the universe which have the correct heat and density to do it. Our own Sun is a star and is 15million degrees C deep beneath its surface (6,000 degrees C at its surface) but even here in this vast heat all our Sun can do is turn Hydrogen into Helium. This takes a vast amount of energy and gives off a vast amount of light and heat, which is lucky for us because it is this light and heat that warms our planet and keeps us alive.

So our Sun only turns Hydrogen into Helium so where are all the other elements made? We shall look at this in detail in a while but first let's ask a question. Everything out there is made of elements so which of these elements are we human beings made from?

Answer. We are made from Oxygen 65%, Carbon 18.5%, Hydrogen 9.5%, Nitrogen 3.2%, Calcium 1.5%, Phosphorus 1.1%, Potassium 0.4%, Sulphur 0.3%, Sodium 0.2%, Chlorine 0.1% and Magnesium 0.1% together with other trace elements of 1%.

As we have said, our Sun does not make these elements so if we were not made by a god and we were not made by the sun, where exactly did all the elements come from to make us and our planet? Stars like our Sun are still in the prime of their lives but to make the heavier elements stars have to die. They may be there for billions of years and because of this the night sky seems to look the same night after night and year after year but in the end stars do die. The Sun is a little over 4.5 billion years old and is about halfway through its life cycle but in the end it will die as will our earth. Stars can only ever live as long as they have a store of Hydrogen to burn. Any fire is the same, the fuel runs out and the fire goes out. Stars don't just go out though, they go with an almighty bang.

Question:

The sun burns Hydrogen and on earth fire burns both it and Oxygen so if water is a mixture of Hydrogen and Oxygen, (H2O) then why does water put out a fire instead of fuelling it?

The death of a star:

Once a star runs out of fuel (Hydrogen) its death is certain. You would think at this stage with its fuel running out the star would cool dramatically but the opposite actually happens. It suddenly gets much hotter and with a great flash it starts to expand and eventually becomes hundreds of times its normal size. This sequence doesn't happen overnight but takes tens of thousands of years. Our Sun will eventually do this and it will become so large that it will actually engulf the earth within it. It will then be classed as a 'Red Giant'.

We do not see this every day of course because stars do last for billions of years but we do have one such red giant as a near neighbour. I say near neighbour because in the scale of the universe although this star is some 600 light years from us it is still relatively close. This dying star is called Beetlejuice (Or Betelgeuse) and it is so massive that the sun and all our planets right out to Jupiter could fit inside it.

While a star is burning Hydrogen the outward pressure of this burning counteracts the force of gravity which is trying to implode it. Burning and gravity will keep a star stable but as fuel runs out this effect is thrown out of balance and the core of the star has to succumb to gravity and will collapse. As it does its temperature will rise again until at approximately 100 million degrees, Helium nuclei fuse together forming into new elements, Carbon and Oxygen. The star then expands and contracts and in doing so other elements along the scale are produced. At the end of its life and with no more fuel to burn the star will fall in on itself totally but even in this great implosion normal stars will only produce about one third of the elements we have.

The other elements are produced in very rare events through the universe. The death of the very largest stars (10 times the magnitude of our Sun) because it is only these that can produce the massive temperatures needed to produce the heavier elements. They do this as they implode rapidly and then rebound with a force massive enough to collide with the outer layers and produce a temperature of 100 billion degrees. It is in these conditions and at these temperatures that the heaviest elements such as gold are formed. These explosions are called Supernovae and it is out of the death of such a star and it's resulting Supernovae that us, our Sun and all the other planets in our solar system were born. A star has died and given forth new life.

Isn't this true for all life whether that life is a star or even just a plant or you and I? A plant dies, we put it on a compost heap, it rots down to its chemical constituents and then we put it back on the garden to use those chemicals to feed the next generation of plants. We are the same. We die are buried and then we rot down to our constituent chemicals and new life will again form from us. So a rotting dead frog in your garden could well one day be part of a carrot or your late great grandmother could become part of a tree. Try not to worry the next time you are eating a carrot though that you might actually be chewing on a dead frog. As I say, it is only the chemicals that are left which are absorbed by the carrot. Farmers have always put manure on their fields but it doesn't mean we eat poo does it? At least I don't think so. I shall have to think about that one. All life has to end and then be recycled. After all, we only have what the earth has to offer. Without recycling on earth there would be nothing and the same applies throughout the universe.

We have talked about Beetlejuice and nebulae and also about high mass stars and Supernovae. The death of Beetlejuice and that of a high mass star are two separate happenings which I shall endeavour to explain before I move on.

Because of the mass of Beetlejuice being less than that of a high mass star, the death of it causes what we call a planetary nebula. In this case the outer envelope of the star is ejected while the core of the star becomes a 'White Dwarf' star. In the case of high mass stars the story is completely different. The resulting titanic explosion (called the supernova), leaves behind a neutron star or black hole. The exploded remains of the star form what is known as a 'Supernova Remnant' and it is from one of these that our solar system was born.

Everything in the universe is, always has been and always will be governed by the force of gravity. It holds your feet on the ground, it holds the earth in orbit around the sun and it holds the sun in its position in the galaxy. Even our galaxy is held in place by it. Gravity keeps us stable today but it also formed us in the first place.

Even the smallest particle exerts gravity and as our supernova cooled, gravity drew together particles within it. These particles became bigger and the bigger they got the more mass they achieved and therefore the more gravity they exerted. Eventually enough matter had formed together to begin the lives of new stars with planets orbiting them. The whole cycle had started again and our home planet was eventually formed. Let's look at our birth.

The sun gradually formed and this was surrounded by a mass of rock and gas which eventually formed into planets, satellites (Moons), and various smaller rocky items such as asteroids, comets and meteors. It is thought that as many as one hundred planets first evolved but gravity caused them to collide and form into fewer planets. In these blasts rocks were thrown out to either form parts of other planets or to become meteors or asteroids, millions of which inhabit the solar system today. Even our moon was once part of the earth and was blasted out during a massive collision.

The solar system as we see it today contains the Sun and the planets Mercury, Venus, Earth, Mars, Jupiter, Saturn, Uranus, Neptune and Pluto although Pluto is now classed as a dwarf planet. Below I have set out a quick chart of the planets.

Planet	Distance From Sun km	Equatorial Diameter km (Av)	Earth Day	Orbit (Days)
Mercury	57,910,000	4,880	58days 15hrs	87.96
Venus	108,200,000	12,103	243 days	224.68
Earth	149,600,000	12,756	24hr	365.25
Mars	227,940,000	6,794	24hr 39min	686,98

Jupiter	778,330,000	142,984	9hr 9min	4,332
Saturn	1,429,400,000	120,536	10hr 39min	10,832
Uranus	2,870,990,000	51,118	17hr 14min	30,799
Neptune	4,504,000,000	49,532	16hr 6min	60,190
Pluto	5,906,380,000	2,302	6hr 4min	90,520

If we look at the above chart we see that the size of our planets differs tremendously with Mars being just over half the size of Earth but Jupiter being some eleven times larger yet the earth turns on its own axis every 24hrs while Jupiter does it in a little over 9hrs. We lie just 149.6 million km (93 million miles) from the sun but Pluto is almost 6 billion km away.

A year on Venus is actually slightly shorter than its day and Neptune's orbit of the sun is so long and slow that in 2011 it completed its first full orbit of the Sun since its discovery in 1846.

We have not yet discovered life on other planets in our solar system or anywhere else but scientists are fascinated by the chance of life on one of Jupiter's 63 moons, Europa. Europa's surface seems to be a thick crust of ice which covers a global salty ocean which stays in a liquid state due to tidal heating caused by the interaction between Europa, Jupiter and other surrounding moons. It is incredible to think there could possibly be extra-terrestrial life this close to home. This life would not be human life of course but if it evolved in water, as did life on Earth originally, it could well resemble other aquatic life that we see here. With cost restraints in place I doubt if we shall ever see this life if it does exist but wouldn't it be mind-blowing if we could? I have seen Jupiter and a few of its moons through a telescope and I yearned then to see just what my imagination was thinking. I will not see it but will my descendants have the chance one day?

Jupiter is a fascinating planet with its gigantic size, its composition and its multitude of moons but we also rely upon it for our very existence. Although it lies a distant 600 million kilometres from us it is so vast that the gravity it exerts shields us from bombardment from various rocks flying around in space. They are generally pulled towards Jupiter rather than crash into us. It has failed in the past to divert every one of them and it will fail again in the future but 'we are certainly here because of Jupiter's size and power'. This is what has always been thought and believed by everyone including myself but could Jupiter actually catapult huge lumps of rock towards us? When we explore the solar system we use other planets to catapult us faster and further. Scientists are now theorising this as a possibility for Jupiter's forces as well.

I have also looked at Saturn through a small telescope. Even though it lies way over a billion kilometres from Earth its rings were plain to see. What I saw was just a tiny object with rings but the actual size of the rings is amazing. They stretch out thousands of kilometres from the planet and consist of mainly water ice particles with some rocks as well. The size of these particles ranges from the size of your fingernail to the size of a car. They were first observed by Galileo in1610.

I wonder, in those early days as this great man observed the skies, what Galileo thought to himself. Did he think God was a wonderfully imaginative inventor to make such entities or did he think there was no way that any mind could possibly even think of making them let alone actually achieve it all? If he thought the latter I doubt if in those days he would ever have done so without fear. What a heretic.

Galileo Galilei 1564-1642 made amazing advances in science and was called 'The father of modern observational astronomy'. We know so much more today through more modern advances in technology and experience but in the 15 and 16 hundreds Galileo's findings were incredible. To find something new now is very difficult and costly but imagine the world then. It knew very little apart from religion and for anyone as brilliant as Galileo there was so much to discover. As he studied his mind must have almost exploded with Wonderment.

I love the term 'The Goldilocks Zone'. This term has been coined to show just how perfect conditions on Earth are to support life. If we were closer to the Sun our planet would be too hot and if we were further away we would too cold but where we lie is just right. If we were closer to the sun our liquid water would disappear as vapour and if we were further from the sun it would only consist as ice and we need liquid water for survival. We also have Jupiter there to protect and watch over us (or throw rocks at us) and also the Earth's magnetic poles attract otherwise harmful rays from the Sun. We are lucky to be where we are and as we are but then again if we were not that lucky we would not be here at all and I would not be writing this.

If we think about it the universe is just the same. It in itself could show the 'Goldilocks' theory. It is so well balanced with the right amount of heat throughout and just the right force of gravity. Everything about our planet and the whole universe is 'just' right to support life and doesn't that make you think? Is it by chance that everything is 'just' right everywhere or did it have to be designed and made by something? (No, not in any biblical sense.) I can understand and accept that the earth has conditions perfect to sustain life while billions of other planets may not be so lucky but with the whole universe being 'just' perfect as well it is a wonder. What is it all about? Again, if something or 'someone' invented it all then who invented them? We are back to the 'God Dilemma' again. Let's hope someone has a huge 'eureka' moment soon because it baffles me just to think about it. We know there are billions of galaxies in our universe but are there billions of universes and are these universes all capable of supporting life? Did they just happen to be as they are or were they all 'designed'? Will we ever know and does it matter if we ever know? Of course it does.

We have talked about possible life on Europa but what about possible life on other planets in the universe. So many times you hear people talking about life on other planets and could any possibly exist. "Are we alone?" they say. "Is there anyone there?" (No, that is what spiritualists say isn't it?) Of course we are not alone. The universe just by its sheer size and by the massive figures involved has to support an absolute myriad of life. Again, we just have to open our minds and think. Let's look at another of my favourite things, figures.

Our planet is one of nine in our solar system that orbit the sun. (I am including Pluto here because I have always seen it as a planet. Isn't calling it a dwarf planet being a little sizeist if that is a word?) The Sun is one of between 100 and 400 billion stars in our galaxy, the Milky Way, (depending on which figures you believe), and our galaxy is one of at least 100 billion galaxies in the universe. This makes for a lovely sum.

Let's say that there are 250 billion stars in our galaxy (Midway between estimates of 100 and 400 billion) then we assume the number of planets orbiting each is an average of nine as we have. This means in our galaxy alone there could well be 2,250 billion planets.

Then we have to multiply this number by the number of galaxies in the universe. This gives the possible total number of planets as 225,000,000,000,000,000,000,000,000 or 225,000 billion billion.

Of course not all stars can support planets and not all planets can support life. The chance of life on a planet in our solar system is one in nine, or two in nine if life exists on Europa but let's not be that optimistic. Let's say the chance of life existing on any planet is not one in nine but is one in a million. (My wife said I was one in a million once but then she had been on the Vino.) Getting back to reality, if this is the case there would still be 225,000,000,000,000,000 or 225,000 million million planets supporting life.

Taking this another step further, and taking in the consideration there is a giant leap between basic life on a planet and human type life that has the ability and wish to explore, let's say the chance of a life form being like us is yet another 50 million to one. This still gives the number of planets supporting our type of life as 4,500,000,000 million or 4.5 billion.

We may live in our Goldilocks zone and be protected by our magnetic poles and Jupiter and have just the right atmosphere etc. but even with these things needed to support life figures alone say we must only be one of a vast amount of populated planets. Although how will we ever know? Will we ever see another life form from a different planet? Will we and other civilisations on other planets destroy ourselves before we ever have time to develop the technology needed to meet and greet each other?

Another thought.

What would be the point of a universe that had no intelligent life in it which could question why it exists?

Many people have seen UFOs and conspiracy theories have arisen everywhere saying we have been visited by aliens but never has there been proof. If you think about it there has always been proof of UFOs but this is simply because UFO means Unidentified Flying Object. It can mean anything that cannot, at the time, be identified. In the States some years ago there were sightings of a triangular shaped object seen in the sky. This was, at first, a UFO but then it was released that the sightings were not of an alien craft visiting us from deep space 9 but were in fact the new stealth bomber which was being developed by the USAF. The shape was so radical that it was easy to see why it was thought not to be of earthly origins.

To my mind there are vast amounts of planets out there which support intelligent life but they are all such a long way away that travelling to them, taking our laws of physics into account, would be all but impossible. Who knows though, we as travellers in space are still a very backward race. What if people from a different planet have come up with a far superior mode of transport and can possibly teleport themselves from one galaxy to another in just a second or two. Impossible for us maybe but who knows what others have invented. It may be a silly thought again but what if they see the universe in a totally different way to us? We see it as vast and foreboding and containing mind-blowing distances. Could their concept of it be much smaller and simpler? Some people would look at a trip to Australia from Britain as a long and foreboding journey but others may very possibly see it as nothing because that is what they do all the time. Then because they understand it better they would look at it in a totally different way.

So there could be aliens after all but if we did meet them what would we do? Would we all run and hide? Would we greet them warmly with open arms or would we kill them just to be on the safe side? Knowing human nature it would probably be the latter.

Intergalactic travel for us.

The distances involved in the Solar System are so vast that although light travels at 186,000 miles every second and we are just the third planet from the Sun it still takes over 8 minutes for the Sun's light to reach us so when we look at it, it is already 8 minutes older than what we are actually seeing. This does seem a long way and a long while but when we look at the bigger picture the distances in our Solar System pale into total insignificance as we stop talking about light reaching places in minutes and start talking about light taking millions of years.

Quarks are something that many people will not understand but most people will have heard about light years. Just in case this is something you haven't come across though I will explain.

I have already said light travels at a speed of 186,000 miles per second. So a light year is the distance it travels in a year, i.e. 186,000 (miles per second) x 60 (miles per minute) x 60 (miles per hour) x 24 (miles per day) x 365.25 (miles per year or 1 light year).

If I get my slate and chalk out I figure that to be:

186,000 miles per second
11,160,000 miles per minute
669,600,000 miles per hour
16,070,400,000 miles per day
5,869,713,600,000 miles per year

Taking these figures into account this means that Proxima Centauri our nearest star (apart from the Sun) lies a mere 24,652,797,120,000 miles away and even if we could travel to it at a constant 50,000 mph it would still take around 50,000 years to get there.

Our fastest mode of propulsion so far consists of men or cargo sitting on top of a giant firework but somehow, sometime and somewhere in the mind of someone who thinks there has to be yet another eureka moment to enable us to go faster. We do not just need to go faster. We need to go much much faster. After all, even if we could travel at the speed of light it would still take 4.2 years just to reach Proxima Centauri which is a near neighbour.

Scientists have found another planet which possibly inhabits a Goldilocks zone such as ours. This is a wonderful find but they say if we travelled to it at our current space travel speed it would take 350,000 years to get there.

I have tried to verify the above figures on the Interweb but it seems everyone uses the same miles per second figure but they come up with all sorts of figures at the end. My figures are from my head, my slate and chalk, and my aging calculator, and if they are not completely correct I do apologise. They are there not as any precise calculations but simply to illustrate the utter vastness of the universe around us. I'm sorry religionists but again if they do happen to be incorrect it does not mean the universe had to be made by God.

As I say I love figures and combining this with a love of the facts of the universe gives you all sorts of thoughts and Wonderment. Please do not close your minds off to it. You will be missing out on so much. Try and think of this. If the earth was represented on a piece of paper by just a single tiny dot, then Proxima Centauri would, on that scale, still have to be drawn five miles away. Boggling isn't it?

Also, as I have said, although light travels at a speed of 186,00 miles per second it takes 4.2 years to reach us from Proxima Centauri and that is the sun's nearest neighbour. Our galaxy's nearest neighbour, the Andromeda galaxy lies so far away its light actually takes 2.5 million years to reach us. I will not go into another sum but just think about it.

And another thought. Above I say "if it was possible to travel at 50,000mph". Have you ever thought just how fast we are already travelling through space? It seems to us we are sitting still but we know we must be turning on our own axis and are also orbiting the sun. We are in fact turning on our axis at approximately 1,000mph. This seems fast until we realise our planet is actually hurtling through space at over 67,000mph. Don't worry though, you are not about to spill your tea.

Before I abandon this chapter to move on I just want to talk about and explain another cosmic happening that fascinates me. This is called CMBR or Cosmic Microwave Background Radiation. This is electromagnetism that fills the universe. This radiation is left over from the very beginning of the universe. The Big Bang theory says that CMBR fills the whole of space and most radiation energy in space is CMBR.

I am not going to go into this in great detail but what fascinates me is the simple fact that when you turn on a radio and in between channels you hear a lot of hissing and fuzzing what you are in fact listening to is the Cosmic Microwave Background Radiation that was there at the very early time of the beginning of the universe. So next time you hear it try not to get annoyed because you cannot find your station. Just take a moment to think just what it is you are listening to. It will make it just a little less boring and frustrating.

In this chapter I have just touched upon the universe and its wonders. Hopefully it has taught you a little something. If you want to know more there are plenty of very good books on the subject, books by the likes of Stephen Hawking, a great man and thinker.

I have merely skimmed the surface of science but I hope it has given you a good insight into basic cosmology. I am not trying to teach you everything about the different subjects in this book. I am trying to give you a broad base upon which to form a platform, a platform from which you can think for yourself and fully enjoy the Wonderment of the Wonder of the Universe and Numbers.

5
The Wonder of Evolution

If I see a peacock fanning its tail or a peacock butterfly sipping nectar from a buddleia bush or I look at the beautifully formed compartments inside a wasps nest or marvel at a kestrel hovering ready to attack its prey I don't just stand there and think "Oh well, God made those and that is that." That is all too simple. Too simple, totally wrong and yes, again all too boring.

Anyone who closes their eyes and minds to the world around them either through religious dogma or through a lack of imagination and Wonderment, (I suppose in a way they could be one and the same thing.) is truly losing out on the wonder of everything around them. Whether they are peacocks or kestrels or wasps or any other animal, they were not made by any god. They have evolved over thousands of millions of years by minute increments rather than be made in one day just like that.

It is believed that birds were originally dinosaurs. God didn't just make a dinosaur and then a bird. These days we have fossils of animals which could be classed as the 'missing link' between dinosaurs and birds. We actually have feathered dinosaurs, one if which we have called 'Archaeopteryx'. This is a small dinosaur-bird or 'birdosaur' and on some of the fossils you can clearly see its dinosaur features but you can also see feathers. Feathers are thought to be modified scales which, with a little thought, seems quite logical. If you were to close a feather and harden it slightly you would have a kind of scale. Are all the birds we see today in our skies and hedgerows actually dinosaurs? Now that makes you wonder.

I find evolution quite simple to understand but if it troubles you at all I shall explain it in detail in a while but first of all let me illustrate it simply in a story, one as simple, and hopefully as enchanting, as those in the bible. It is a story I have thought of and have kept in my mind for some thirty years because I think it says a lot in its simplicity.

Once upon a time, long long ago there lived a family of moths who had a big big problem. These moths loved to feast on the sap of the silver birch tree. They found (unknowingly of course) that birch sap gave them all the protein and goodness they needed for life and birch trees were plentiful. They even learned they could lay their eggs on the inside of peeling birch bark so their hatchling caterpillars could feast on the succulent young spring leaves. If this wasn't enough to give them happiness it also happened that their pupating chrysalides looked just like birch leaves as well so they would mature unhindered by predators. So why was there a big problem you may ask?

Despite the moths having it all seemingly there was one thing which almost drove them to extinction. This was the fact that they had beautiful pure white wings which, when they were sipping birch sap, made them stand out like a sore thumb against the mottled birch bark, a beacon to all their hungry predators. The moths ate well and bred well but they were soon eaten. Things progressed because the more moths that were eaten the more predators were able to keep in tip-top condition and breed and so on. The moths soon became very scarce and looked doomed until a strange thing happened.

One group of moth eggs hatched and nothing new was seen in either the caterpillars or chrysalides but eventually as they turned into adults a mutation was noticed. Some of the new adults looked odd because their wings were not pure white, (If they were humans any deformity would probably have been laughed at). They had curious brown markings on them. They were nowhere near as beautiful as the other moths but because they didn't stand out so much on the trees they were more likely to be missed by predators. The moths that were still pure white still got eaten but those that were not managed to survive more and breed more. When they did breed they were very likely to pass on their genes to the next generation and these genes included the propensity for their young to have mottled wings. The more mottled their wings became the more they tended to survive and the more they survived the more mottled their wings became. This made them harder and harder to see and therefore the predators which relied upon them for food had less food to eat and then it was their numbers that decreased instead while the moths survived and thrived. The 'white winged birch moth' was no longer white winged but it had become a survivor.

This story may not be a real one. I use it just as a typical example but how brilliant it is to look at the Wonderment of our moths' story and marvel at its complexity and good and bad fortunes. How brilliant it is to look at all the other real moths around us and wonder about their stories and journeys through evolution. We should wonder at what they are, how they are what they are and where they came from and where they started. Imagine saying to one of our white winged birch moths, "God made you". He might well look back at you and say, "Oh no he didn't old mate. My ancestors struggled long and hard so that I could be here. They survived all sorts of predators and other trials and tribulations just so that I could be born and breathe. I am sitting on this tree in the sunshine because of them not because of some creator."

As I said in the chapter concerning Noah and his ark, there are literally millions of animal species on the planet. Whether that animal is an ant or an aardvark, a whelk or a whale, or a hare or a human, every one of them is filled with wonder. How can an ant, something so tiny, have the strength to lift so much? How can a blue whale manage to feed its massive body? How can a cheetah, such a relatively small animal, be the fastest animal on the planet? It is all because of tiny steps in evolution. Try hard to imagine it as we continue.

My moth story is a simple story of a simple act of evolution but it does not answer all the questions of where we and all other life came from. To grasp the story of evolution isn't easy but in this chapter I shall endeavour to explain. Because people cannot grasp it they do find it simpler to believe that a god did it all. To a thinking person it is far harder to understand how a god could have made us all on just one Friday and Saturday rather than think how we evolved over many years.

The first thing we have to realise is we are not just talking of a few years of evolution. The earth was formed 4.5 billion years ago and life started to form approximately a billion years later. This means that life has been forming and changing for 3.5 billion years. That's three and a half thousand million years. If we look back to the Battle of Hastings (1066) we think it happened a very long time ago but it only actually happened less than one thousand years ago. Life has not been evolving for just this tiny amount of time. It has been evolving for this time multiplied by 3.5 million. That is absolutely ample time for things to come about. All it needed was the correct circumstances and a start. Look at nature everywhere. Just give it a chance and it will flourish.

Going back to the gentleman at the beginning of the book who said if he dropped all the ingredients for a Victoria sponge onto the floor it would not evolve into one and therefore evolution could not possibly happen so (you guessed it), God had to have made everything. This gentleman certainly would not understand what I am going to try to explain even if I do it in as simple a way as possible. He would not understand and neither would he wish to. Intransigence I think they call it.

As I say, the earth formed a billion years before life began to evolve even in its simplest form. This was because of the fact the earth was so hot that nothing could survive. It was a massive ball of molten rock which was (as in the bible) without form. Eventually though it cooled enough for a rocky crust to form. The dominant force on the planet was volcanoes. The earth was covered in them and these helped keep the earth warm as the sun in these early days gave us only 75% of the heat it does today.

At this early stage if it had not been for volcanoes the earth would have been just a frozen globe.

As you can imagine though, with all this volcanic action, the atmosphere would not have been the same as we know it today. It was filled with hydrogen and oxygen but also contained carbon monoxide, carbon dioxide, hydrochloric acid, methane, ammonia, nitrogen and sulphur gases. It was an atmosphere we would not appreciate today. Another thing it did contain much of was water vapour. This condensed and eventually formed the oceans and once we had water it was possible for life to evolve.

As with the beginning of the universe no one is still quite sure exactly what happened but let me put it quite simply from my own mind before I do try to expand things properly. At the moment of the big bang everything was there. All the chemicals needed to build everything. We and every other animal are made from chemicals so why is it so mind-blowingly difficult to comprehend. If you have all the ingredients to make a sponge it will not make itself before it rots back to its constituent chemicals but if you have all the constituent chemical ingredients to make life then that life is alive, will not rot and will eventually evolve. I have recently read an article on the Interweb which says it shows 'ultimate proof' of God's existence and work. It says that because the earth is in a perfect Goldilocks zone and contains just the right chemicals in just the right temperature it had to be designed by God. I say yes everything is just right but it had to be for us to be here. If things were different we would not be here debating anything but it was all down to chance and numbers not some divine intervention. The chances of winning £100m on the Euro Lottery are so very slim that it is hardly worth the effort of buying a ticket but it has been won. Even the chances of winning the jackpot on the British Lotto are around 14 million to one. They say if you buy a ticket on a Monday you are more likely to die before Saturday than you are to win the jackpot. That's a cheery thought isn't it? I think the balls decide who wins lotteries and not any god. Why would a fair god award all this money to just one person while denying others who probably desperately need some of it? So even if the odds are high either for the lottery or the Goldilocks zone it does happen. As I have already said it is my educated guess that out there in our vast universe there are many millions or billions of such planets which inhabit their own Goldilocks zone and contain life just as our planet does and it all came about by natural forces.

At the moment of the big bang everything was there for the universe to form and it did. Isn't it the same for life on earth? Again everything needed was there for life to form and it did. As I say, give nature a chance and it will flourish.

So far I have just written what is in my own mind but let me try to explain what actually happened.

For life to have evolved the planet first needed to have amino acids which are the very building blocks of life. We talk about amino acids and because they are so fundamental to our story they sound perhaps prohibitively complex but amino acids are simply a mixture of chemicals. In their case they are a mixture of carbon, hydrogen, oxygen and nitrogen. So already we have the simple building blocks of life made from simple chemicals. (The four major chemicals that make us are Hydrogen, Carbon and Oxygen and Nitrogen.) Once chemicals have joined to form amino acids you may not suddenly have a myriad of life but remember we are only talking about the early history of life some 3.5 billion years ago.

These now formed amino acids (some scientists say these came from the earth's collisions with meteors) then formed together to make what have been named as peptides which are proteins that form the basis of cells. Peptides are just short chains of amino acids linked by peptide bonds. They are thought to have evolved around undersea volcanoes. Again this sounds complicated but all that is happening is chemicals are joining together. So we have already gone from talking about volcanoes to amino acids and then peptides forming the basis of cells. Cells then joined together (Or failed to separate) to form more complicated life. We are getting there.

Of course it is not all quite as simple as that. Prokaryotic cells such as bacteria formed in early times but it took another billion years for multicellular life to form. It is only in the last 570 million years that life has evolved to the types of creatures we are familiar with, starting with arthropods followed by fish which appeared 530 million years ago and mammals only 200 million years ago. Homo Sapiens (or us) only appeared on the earth 200,000 years ago, just a tiny fraction of life's time here. Again you can study it all in detail further if you wish and there are plenty of books to help but I would rather move on than bore you. I have looked at it all in quite a simple way but that is the way my mind sees it. It simply happened and happened simply. It started to happen 3.5 billion years ago and now we are here. It was never some miraculous two day event but a continuous and progressive drudge over thousands of millions of years. Let me try to put this into context with another simple analogy.

On its fourth birthday, a child says 1x2=2 and then on its fifth birthday it says 2x2=4. This goes on with a whole year in between each simple sum and the drudge seems endless. On its tenth birthday the child has only reached 12 in its sum and even if the child manages to live to the wonderful old age of 104yrs it has still only made the sum come to 200.

But now if we use this analogy for the amount of years that life has been forming and evolving we get the figure of 7,000,000,000 or seven billion.

The analogy may be simple but it illustrates clearly that by minute increments over a vast amount of time, life will evolve and flourish into the vast array we see today.

Eventually, as time progressed, more land appeared and the atmosphere changed. Cyanobacteria evolved and began sucking in carbon and giving out oxygen (taking the carbon out of carbon dioxide). They gained their energy through photosynthesis and oxygen was the by-product. Cyanobacteria is not a word we have all heard before but I'm sure we have all heard of its other name 'Blue-green algae' which blights our lakes and ponds during hot summer spells.

Because of the make-up and temperature of volcanoes, those under the sea (Hydrothermal vents) actually sucked oxygen out of the atmosphere whereas those above ground did not. As more land formed and more volcanoes were on the land less oxygen was taken out of the atmosphere and as we saw an increase in oxygen levels we also saw a greater diversity of life forming.

If we looked at life on earth in one big 3.5 billion year chunk it would be mind-boggling so scientists have broken it down into several eras or periods or epochs such as Archaean, Cambrian, Triassic, Jurassic and many others.

Scientific studies of genetic material indicates that a group of today's single celled organisms called Archaea, may well share many features with early life on earth. Archaea live today in hot springs and deep sea vents. Their similarity to early life has led the first period of life to be named the Archaean Period. Each geological period is separated by a major geological or palaeontological event such as mass extinctions etc.

As I have said, multicellular life forms began around a billion years after the first cellular life appeared. Complex multicellular life included animals, brown algae, red algae, green algae, plants and fungi. All this is interesting enough but we shall jump forward 2 billion years to the Cambrian period otherwise this book will go on to infinity and beyond.

The Cambrian period 545 - 495 million years ago, is a time of great evolution and prolific life on earth. Scientists have found boundless amounts of fossils from this period especially in the Burgess Shale in the Rocky Mountains of British Columbia. The shale is famous for its preservation of soft parts of fossils as well as for a very diverse group of animals called the arthropods. Among these are the Trilobites which themselves evolved into as many as 50,000 forms. Arthropods are animals such as trilobites and today's ants, shrimps, crabs, lobsters and wasps. They are all invertebrate animals which have an exoskeleton, a segmented body and jointed appendages.

Many arthropods have become extinct over time but even today there are as many as one million described species.

The arthropods' external skeleton gave them protection but it did also limit their size to some extent. There were never any the size of an elephant or buffalo but they did manage to evolve into creatures of up to three feet (almost a metre) in length.

Going back to chemicals evolving into animal life, trilobites evolved complex eyes and the lenses of some of them were actually formed from calcite which is a carbonate mineral. Again life is just using chemicals. Whereas we only have one lens per eye, some trilobites actually had as many as 5,000 lenses per eye. Trilobites are found in the Burgess Shale but they are also found in North Africa and other parts of the world so it is easy to see just what a successful creature this was. Although we have to put this into some perspective by realising that the earth was not the same then as it is today. Continents have formed and moved since then. The trilobites' closest living relatives today are horseshoe crabs.

Trilobites mostly lived in fairly shallow water and were benthic (bottom dwellers). They walked on the bottom and most likely fed on detritus but as simple plants began to flourish on land some trilobites and other arthropods were tempted out to feed upon them. They could not just do this though because they were water animals but in time evolution gave a hand and land animals came about and thrived.

Below is a timeline for the appearance of other species up to and beyond the one animal that fascinates everyone, the dinosaur which I shall again go into in more detail shortly. The dates are set in millions of years ago.

485 First vertebrates with true bones.

440 First Agnathan fish. (Jawless fish including lampreys)

420 Ray finned fish.

410 First fish to have teeth.

363 Insects roamed the land and would soon be able to fly. Sharks had also evolved.

340 Amphibians became diverse.

280 Earliest beetles.

251.4 The Permian-Triassic extinction event wipes out 90% of marine species.

245 Earliest Ichthyosaurs (Large marine reptiles) appeared.

225 Earliest dinosaurs, cycads and conifers evolve. Also the first mammals.

220 Forests dominate the land and herbivores grow to massive sizes to accommodate the amount of gut necessary to digest the giant amounts they needed to eat in order to gain enough from their nutrient poor diet.

170 Dinosaurs still evolving and diversifying along with salamanders and newts.

155 Archaeopteryx.

130 Flowering plants developed structures that attracted insects so as to spread pollen.

100 Earliest bees.

90 Extinction of the Ichthyosaurs and first appearance of snakes.

80 Ants.

68 The first appearance of Tyrannosaurus.

66 The cretaceous-paleogene event occurred which wiped out half of the entire animal species. This included ammonites, mosasaurs, pterosaurs and plesiosaurs.

66 Onwards. Mammals became the dominant species.

60 Earliest true primates appear.

55 Modern bird groups thrive.

52 The first bats appear.

50 Camels, rhinoceroses and tapir evolve.

40 Appearance of first butterflies and moths.

37 Sabre toothed cats.

25 Various species of deer appear.

20 Bears and giraffes are first seen.

15 Kangaroos.

10 Grasslands and savannahs appear giving food and life to a vast amount of animal species.

6.5 The first hominin, Sahelanthropus appeared.

6 Australopithecines diversify.

4.8 Mammoths

2 The first of the genus Homo appear.

1.7 The extinction of the Australopithecines.

1.2 The evolution of Homo Antecessor.

.6 The evolution of Homo Heidelbergensis.

.35 The evolution of Neanderthals.

.2 Modern humans first appear in Africa.

.03 The Neanderthals die out and the first domesticated dogs appear.

.01 The mammoths die out.

We do want to talk about the dinosaurs but please bear with me while I try to explain one or two of the above items.

The Permian-Triassic Extinction Event (251.4 million years ago):

In the earth's history this is the greatest and most severe extinction event. There are various theories as to what actually caused it, theories such as climate change, increased volcanism and impact events. Although we are not too sure of this we do know that it destroyed 90% of marine species and 70% of all terrestrial vertebrates. So much was lost that it took 10 million years for the earth to recover.

The Cretaceous-Paleogene Event or K-Pg Event:

Because it is called the Cretaceous-Paleogene Event it sounds quite highbrow but this is a happening we all know about. This is the event which killed off many of the non-avian dinosaurs. It wiped out as many as 75% of the earth's plant and animal species.

It is widely recognised now that this was caused by a giant asteroid plummeting to earth and impacting in the Gulf of Mexico. A crater there has been measured at 180km wide. Scientist have found a very thin layer of sediment called the K-Pg boundary which can be found throughout the world in rocks. This layer contains high levels of the element Iridium which is rare on earth but is abundant in asteroids. Not all scientists agree on this theory but it seems likely and logical to me.

This event was a terrible blow to life on earth but it did offer up an opportunity for life to adapt to new conditions and flourish again into many new forms such as horses, whales, primates, and birds.

We lost the dinosaurs as we knew them but if this event had not have happened we would probably not be here to talk about them anyway.

Sahelanthropus:

Sahelanthropus Tchadensis is an extinct hominin species. It may be a common ancestor of both humans and chimpanzees. The fossils were found in Chad in 2002.

Australopithecines:

These were bipedal (walked upright) and were dentally similar to humans but their brains were not much larger than those of apes. They had an average height of around 1.2-1.5 metres (4-5ft) and probably weighed around 30-55 kilograms (66-120 pounds).

Homo Antecessor:

Homo Antecessor is an extinct human species which died out approximately 800,000 years ago. Some scientists believe Homo Antecessor is actually the same species as Homo Heidelbergensis who actually inhabited Europe as little as 250,000 years ago. Even great scientific minds disagree but it is their disagreements and thoughts that eventually give us answers.

Neanderthals:

We have all heard about Neanderthals. People use the name as a derogatory term. To call someone a Neanderthal infers they are backward, rough and possibly thick.

Neanderthals were very closely related to us modern humans. They lived alongside modern humans and their fossils have been found in Croatia dating back to as little as 32,000 year ago.

Neanderthals certainly were not thick. They made and used advanced tools and lived in complex social groups. Some built dwellings out of animal bones. They were the top predators of their time but also cooked and ate vegetables.

Neanderthals obviously became extinct and again scientists disagree somewhat on how this actually came about. Below are a few possible factors.

1.   They died out because of climate change.

2.   They bred with modern humans and were therefore absorbed into modern human genes.

3.   They were wiped out by different volcanic super eruptions.

In their time Neanderthals were superb hunters, using their stone weapons and tools. It is thought that this hunting was to be a major contributing factor in the demise of the mammoths.

So what of our dinosaurs? ("At last we are talking about them," I hear you say.) Millions of animals have come and gone and millions will yet come and go so why is everyone, including me, fascinated by dinosaurs? The most fascinating of all has to be the great Tyrannosaurus Rex but there were many more. Let's look at their story.

Firstly, where does the word 'dinosaur' come from? It was first coined in 1842 by palaeontologist Richard Owen, and the word consists of *deinos* (Greek) meaning terrible and *sauros* meaning lizard or reptile. So dinosaur means terrible lizard. They were not terrible of course. All they did was live their lives as modern animals do today. Some were carnivores and some were herbivores. The carnivores did eat other animals but no more than do many animals now. Tyrannosaurus Rex was said to be a vicious killer but then so are lions, tigers, eagles and even wasps.

Dinosaurs are generally thought of as giant animals and this I think is probably part of their Wonderment but they did come in all sorts of shapes and sizes from giant herbivores such as the Argentinosaurus which measured 120 feet from nose to tail and weighed 100 tons (That's about the same as 15 good sized elephants) to the Microraptor which only measured a couple of feet in length and looked rather like a demented pigeon.

Sauropods and Theropods:

Sauropods walked on four legs and Theropods walked on two legs.

Sauropods were herbivores and Theropods were carnivores.

The word Theropod means 'beast-footed' and because of their exciting lifestyles they are the most easily recognised. They include the famous T.Rex and Allosaurus.

Some Theropods including Gigantosaurus and Spinosaurus were so large that we doubt their ability to actively hunt. These may well have been carrion feeders, scavenging carcasses wherever possible but not turning down an easy kill. It seems they probably did not attack their own kind but it is thought they ate the dead of their own kind. They were cannibals.

Sauropods were herbivores with long necks and long tails. They were among the largest land animals ever to exist but they had very small brains. Sauropods included Brachiosaurus and Diplodocus,

Ornithischia:

These dinosaurs were beaked herbivores. They were generally smaller than the Sauropods and lived in herds as do many herbivores today. Some commonly known Ornithischians included the horned or frilled dinosaurs (Ceratopsians) such as Triceratops, Brachyceratops and Diabloceratops.

Pterodactylus :

Pterodactylus were flying reptiles with wings composed of flaps of skin rather like today's bats but bats are of course mammals and evolved much later. Pterodactylus were carnivores and preyed upon fish and small animals. I say Pterodactylus but most people just say Pterodactyls which has become a synonym for Pterosaurs, Pterodactylus and Pteranodons. The largest species of Pteranodons had a wingspan of up to 30 feet. My mind boggles as I try to visualise such a creature flying. In Britain our largest flying bird is the mute swan but its wingspan is only around 5 feet. Try to imagine six of these flying wingtip to wingtip and then you can visualise what a Pteranodon must have looked like. Not easy is it?

The name Pterodactylus is derived from a Greek word meaning 'winged finger'. I can't actually put down the Greek word because I cannot understand it. It is all Greek to me.

Dinosaurs were a very successful group of animals and roamed the earth for 135 million years. When you think that us modern humans have only been on the planet for 200,000 years and are already ruining it I think the dinosaurs did very well.

So some dinosaurs were killers and some were just small, cute and cuddly. Some were just normal sized animals and some were absolute giants. They were a totally diverse and successful group. They were this and they were that but most of all they were totally fascinating.

Nothing was known of dinosaurs until the 19th century when fossils began to be found. Imagine the wonder in the finders' minds as they looked at their discoveries and thought "What the hell is that?" It opened up a whole new world of Wonderment, one which fascinates us still today.

After the Cretaceous-Paleogene event it was the mammals' turn to flourish and dominate and within 50 million years the earth had primates, modern birds, bats, camels, rhinos, tapir, sabre toothed cats, deer, bears, giraffes and kangaroos as well as many others I have not mentioned. 50 million years seems a long time but in the evolutionary span of life it is relatively short. Again, as I have said before, give life a chance and it will flourish.

Our evolutionary path has now led us from amino acids to aardvarks and from peptides to primates. Our next step has to be to the human race. We'll look into it in more detail.

Let's start with Lucy:

This Lucy is not my dear and cherished granddaughter but is the commonly recognised name given to AL 288-1. She is the part skeleton found in 1974 in Ethiopia. Her skeleton is about 40% complete and shows she was an Australopithecus Afarensis and lived about 3.2 million years ago. Her skull showed a brain capacity about the size of apes in general but her skeleton showed she was bipedal, a trait found in humans.

Lucy was 3ft 7ins tall and weighed around 64lb. She looked somewhat like a chimpanzee but her upright walking stance certainly made her a hominid. (Hominid definition: *A primate of the family Hominidae, of which Homo sapiens is the only extant species*). The length ratio of Lucy's humerus to femur was 86%

compared to 71.8% for modern humans and 97.8% for chimpanzees indicating that the arms of her species were beginning to shorten or their legs were beginning to lengthen or indeed both at the same time. She also had a lumbar curve which is a trait of upright walking.

One religionist lady asked me, "Where is the missing link between apes and human?"

As I have said before we are primates but Lucy can be seen as one link between apes and us but if you have a missing link there is only one link missing but if you find that missing link you then have two more missing links. Let me demonstrate. Let's say we are looking for the missing link between 5 and 9 and we find the link 7. We now have the missing link but have created two more, 6 and 8. It seems religionists will always be able to ask their question, one which gets more and more outdated as the years pass and science moves on.

There were several more Australopithecus species after Lucy but I will move on to the Homos. Homo Habilis, Homo Georgicus, Homo Erectus, Homo Ergaster, Homo Antecessor, Homo Heiledbergensis, Homo Neandethalensis, Homo Floresiensis and finally Homo Sapiens.

We have already looked into some of these so I am going to go straight to the final two on the list firstly Homo Floresiensis.

Homo Floresiensis:

The remains of an individual Homo Floresiensis were found on the Indonesian island of Flores, hence the name. It has been nicknamed 'The Hobbit' or 'Flo' and stood only 3ft 5in (1.1m) high. It is thought that this species existed until possibly only 12,000 years ago. Like Neanderthals they used stone tools.

Now onto the big one, Homo Sapiens or us:

So here we are at the end of this chapter and we end it with us. We are not the first or last animals to evolve but to us we are the most important.

We Homo Sapiens evolved about 200,000 years ago in Africa. Just like other human species at the time they hunted and gathered food and evolved to meet the challenges of life. We had a lighter frame than other species but had a large brain capacity.

With their brain capacity they developed stone and bone tools as did the Neanderthals and Homo Floresiensis but their brains allowed more intricate and complex tools to be made such as fish hooks and harpoons, bows and arrows, spear throwers and sewing needles. With the ability to think, invent and meet challenges we soon thrived and our numbers multiplied.

We have talked about single celled creatures and that makes me think. Corals at the bottom of the sea consist of a whole hoard or host of tiny creatures living together. They are creatures in their own right but when you look at them you only see one item. We consist of many cells. Are we the same? When we look into a mirror we see one creature but are we actually looking at many creatures working together in harmony? Is that silly?

About 70,000 years ago some Homo Sapiens managed to leave Africa and relatively quickly colonised the world. This act saw a great turning point for the world. It was now dominated by humans and over the next 70,000 years their numbers would grow to such an extent that the world could no longer really cope.

At first though all this was fine. Numbers grew but grew steadily. Believe it or not it has only been in the last couple of hundred years or so that things have really gotten out of hand.

The 1800s saw both the coming of the industrial and agricultural revolutions and vast improvements in healthcare. We had learned to overcome Mother Nature itself and still defy her wantonly without a thought for the future. We shall cover this in detail in another chapter.

So we have come from no life at all to life holding the planet to ransom. We have seen great bounds in evolution tethered with great periods of extinction. We are now entering another great extinction but this one is being caused by us.

Animal life wasn't made in a couple of days. It has taken billions of years to evolve. There have been great hardships and sacrifices along the way and only a few of evolution's animal species inventions or attempts have succeeded. What we have around us today is a wonderful and diverse amount of animal and plant species but it is only a tiny fraction of those that have walked, crawled, swum, slithered, grown or flown on earth before. The figure today is approximately only 0.1% of the total amount that have lived in the past. We are the successful ones but we have to remember that 99.9% of life forms never actually made it.

A while ago someone put a question to me. He said, "If we all came about by evolution, then why has evolution stopped?"

If you look at the world without thinking you may come to this same conclusion. The problem here was this person was not getting the simple gist of the situation. Evolution is still happening and will carry on happening forever but we cannot expect to see changes day by day, year by year, century by century or even through thousands of years. It has been happening for 3.5 billion years and will always keep happening.

I am about to leave this chapter and move on but I must first pay tribute to yet another great man, Charles Darwin (1809-1882). For it was this man who revolutionised the thoughts of scientists with his studies of animals both here in Britain and during his travels aboard HMS Beagle. He established that all species of life had to have evolved over time from common ancestors. For Victorian times this was a great step and one which he realised would appal those in the church. His thoughts even went against the beliefs of his own wife. He understood his wife's views though but withdrew from the church himself. He would walk his wife and children to church but then go off walking and thinking as they worshipped.

He wrote his book 'On The Origin Of Species' but put off again and again its publication. It was finally published 22 years later when someone else gave him the impetus by coming up with a very similar theory.

We evolved, we are here and that's that. Why not just enjoy it and revel in its simplicity.

Me.

6
The Wonder of Wonderment

When I was a small child, before we had a television, I used to have just a few tatty and damp old books. I particularly remember two of them. Both had lost their covers (Probably caused by me throwing them at my sister) but both were still spellbinding. I was fascinated by wildlife and although one of them was not really a wildlife book it did have an illustration on the first page of a lion raised up on its hind legs attacking a man who was wielding a long barrelled gun. I never thought of which one was about to be killed, I just marvelled at the size, power and prowess of the lion.

I was only about five or six at the time but the image of that simple but well executed illustration has stayed with me in my mind for well over fifty years. I do wish I had kept the book. If I had it may even have dried out by now. Our houses back in those days, especially upstairs, were very damp.

"We've got running water," my father would say. "Yes, running down the walls."

Anyway, I digress. I could go on all day about being hard up and having to wear my sister's hand-me-down clothes but quite rightly you would not believe me. I didn't have to wear her dresses because they were not my colour and didn't fit me anyway.

The other of my favourite remembered coverless books was a large book of British birds and their eggs. I would look out of the window and see house sparrows and hedge sparrows and blackbirds and song thrushes but in my book there were such things as grasshopper warblers, reed buntings, long tailed tits and common sandpipers. Even at that tender and innocent age I realised there was so much out there to explore and see, so much to look for, to study and to think about.

Of course there were no lions in Norfolk (Or are there? That is a debate in itself) but we did, and do, have an endless supply of our own wildlife to watch. Our hedgerows were full of nesting birds in springtime and soon my friends and I were old enough to search for them and then look up in my damp book what species they were. We would also watch butterflies and marvel at their bright colours. Of course we didn't know what kind of butterflies they were because I only had the one book on wildlife and that was full of birds. We couldn't afford anything else. "Aaaahhh Bless," I hope you are saying.

We were hard up in those days and life was not as comfortable as it is now but the one great thing we did have was freedom. I am talking about the very early years of the 1960s when even at the age of six or seven you could go out all day exploring without your parents having to worry where you were and what was happening to you. The roads were full of nothing then apart from the occasional slow delivery van or car or horse. The whole village knew each other and everyone kept an eye on you. We would be out all day and we never once thought that anything adverse could happen to us. They certainly were wonderful happy times, times of some austerity but times of true magic and simplicity.

Close to our house we had a farm lane which went out into the countryside for about a mile and a half. It had hedges, trees, shrubs, ditches and pits full of fish. The whole area was a complete haven for wildlife and much of our free time was spent there. Sometimes whole days would be lost to us as our knowledge of the world around us grew.

We had been taught at school and Sunday school about God and Jesus and Adam and Eve and Noah and his wife but at that time we didn't believe it all or disbelieve it all either. All that was school work but we were out. We were free and we were having fun. We often laid there on grassy banks in the sun looking up to the sky not thinking what was up there or who made it all but we did think of the hovering skylarks chirruping above us and the bumble bees buzzing close by. How great life was as a child, especially if you liked lying in the sun and thinking.

Life went on in this simple manner for some time but then it happened. A great event shocked me and changed my life. I came home one day to find my father had actually bought a 'Television'. It was there in our sitting room and I was amazed. Actually amazed is the wrong word. I was really shocked because my father never usually spent money. We didn't have much but he did usually like to keep the little he had. Televisions only had one channel then and the picture tended to scroll itself round and round occasionally but it didn't matter. I had looked at my picture of a lion a thousand times but before long there I was watching them on television. They were black and white in those days just like my picture but television's reality made me realise just how my picture's impression of a lion had been distorted for effect. The only other time I had seen pictures of lions was at Sunday school when they told us about Noah and these pictures were not too lifelike either but on television I saw them as they really were, gorgeous.

Before long (and he must be about 140 years old now bless him) I saw David Attenborough on the television for the first time. He introduced me to Africa with its Masai Mara, Serengeti plains and the Ngorongoro Crater. The Masai Mara and Serengeti were really something but why was I so especially enthralled with the Ngorongoro Crater? The place filled my head with wonder and although people of our ilk did not travel abroad in those days I vowed in my little mind to go there one day. How and when I did not know. I was a child and it was a dream. I never thought then about the practicalities of it all but I knew I would somehow go there one day. I was enthralled by these wildlife programmes. I had always loved wildlife and from then, thanks to David Attenborough, I was well and truly hooked.

A couple of years later we had a family return to the village from Rhodesia (today's Zimbabwe). They had lived there for a while and as none of us had ever travelled they put on a slide show in our local church rooms. Some people shunned this out of jealousy, calling the family snobs and would not let themselves be seen to revel in other peoples' good fortune but not me. I was there sitting in the front row and taking it all in. I cannot remember if my parents were with me but it would not have mattered if they weren't. I had to be there and probably did go on my own. In no way was I a sad child but I did sometimes like to be on my own and being able to think. I still do. Much time was spent on my own but most of it was spent with my sister. I always tell people we brought each other up because although my parents had us and fed us they never really interacted too much with us. In most households today things have changed thankfully but in most houses in our day it was them and us. We did not see it as a hardship though because we were happy. We were happy and free and didn't know anything different.

My father and I did spend time together when he took me fishing. This was a treat for me but to be honest we only had this time together because fishing was what my father liked to do. I knew he did not do it to entertain me but still I was grateful. What a way to enjoy the world around me, sitting on a riverbank watching wildlife and hoping to catch a big one.

Through my teenage years I kept budgerigars, parakeets and pheasants and bred them with some success. Again, it showed how little encouragement animals need to flourish. I was not great at what I did but just by giving my birds their shelter, food, water and a nesting box I saw reproduction. It was all so easy because life, no matter in which form it comes, wants to reproduce. The energy gained just from seeds enabled the birds to fly, sing, mate and breed and within just a few weeks tiny little helpless and featherless scraps turned into beautiful feathered delights. How can a few grains of seed and a few beaks of water produce everything needed to live, sing, see and procreate, such simple food producing so much? That's Wonderment.

After the death of my wife in 1998 I was, as someone very rightly called me, a 'lost soul'. She was gone, could never come back and I was alone with the knowledge I had to rebuild my life. I knew things could be good once more but the question was when. Those days were lonely and painful and although I had a lust for life, as should we all, I struggled to find a life to lust for. I felt like a bird without a song.

I had used the same travel agency for some years and on a visit to it again one of the girls suggested I should go to Africa. She said why dream about the place when I could make my dream a reality. How simple. Eureka! So there and then I took her suggestion on board and booked a trip to Kenya, Tanzania and Zanzibar and a few weeks later, one bitterly cold English February morning in 2000, I boarded a plane to Schiphol and then onto Nairobi.

Some people are frightened of flying but I have always been just the opposite. I am more relaxed than ever in the air. Chatting to your fellow passengers is lovely but I get totally spellbound just looking out of the window and watching the world go by beneath me. On this trip I was almost lost in a dream as I saw Italy, Malta and Egypt pass by beneath me. From earth everything looks good but from six miles up it is all a wonder. The sheer size of the Sahara alone is incredible and takes hours to cross.

A few days into the trip our Mercedes truck which carried twenty-three of us and everything we needed for self-sufficiency for three days at a time stopped on the edge of a great drop and our expedition leader, Nick, jumped out of the cab and announced, "There it is guys. The Ngorongoro Crater!"

As I looked down upon elephants and wildebeest that were so far below us they looked like insects, a huge lump came into my throat and privately I filled up inside. It had taken over forty years and the death of my dear wife but at last there I was with my dream stretching out below me. Reality can sometimes be a poor substitute for dreams but this reality managed to beat my dream hands down.

The following day, after yet another uncomfortable night in a tent, we drove down into the crater. This was the very pinnacle of my dream and I was almost dumbstruck with the complete awe and beauty of it. Someone asked me if I was okay because for once I was quiet. I was more than okay. For the first time in a good while I was starting to feel my old self again.

The Ngorongoro crater is a huge extinct volcano and because of its make-up it is rich in goodness and is home to hundreds of thousands of animals. It wasn't created in some heavenly whim. It has come about by many millions of years of geological changes that have shaped it into a vast paradise. If there ever could have been such a place as the Garden of Eden I'm sure this would have been a top contender.

I came back from the 2,500 mile slog absolutely shattered but I also came back a new man who was ready once more to look life square in the face and start again. On the new year's eve of that year I walked into a pub to meet my brother and his partner and a couple of my brother's friends. They were there and so was my brother's friend's sister Mags, who had also lost her partner to cancer. Within thirty minutes of meeting, she and I were together and we both still say today that if someone had offered to marry us on that first evening we would have gladly taken up the offer. I was no longer a lost soul and now we are growing old ungracefully together.

For our honeymoon we went to the Caribbean and while we were there we shared another great experience. We were fortunate enough to take a helicopter trip from Antigua over to volcano hit Montserrat. We actually sat at the very top of the volcano in the helicopter and watched as the volcano erupted.

I have never been a rich man but I have been lucky enough to travel but you do not need money or a love of travel or even any kind of academic intelligence to enjoy Wonderment. If we take a little time and imagination to look around us in our everyday lives we will see Wonderment everywhere. It is there for all of us to enjoy.

I remember talking to an academically minded and quite wealthy man once who perplexed me a little when he asked me what sort of bird it was in the garden a few feet away from us. I looked at him and realised he wasn't joking. It was black and it was a bird I thought, so perhaps it could have been a 'blackbird'? I thought this a little too simple for such an 'intelligent' man though so I told him it was a thrush. "Ah," he said. "Thought it was." So, as you can see, even wealthy academics can sometimes be thick.

Our world has evolved to such a point that Wonderment is everywhere. I have been walking just a few minutes from home and have seen a family of fledgling long-tailed tits just out of the nest and sitting in a row close together on a thin branch. They were so completely and utterly beautiful that no divine imagination no matter how great it was could ever have dreamed them up let alone made them. I watched from just a few feet away and they watched me without showing any morsel of fear. It seemed perhaps they knew they were too beautiful for anyone to harm. Who knows?

Keeping in my local area, I have watched a mother roe deer suckling her young. I have seen a cuckoo chick growing to an enormous size in another much smaller bird's nest. I have seen a peregrine falcon swooping over marshes and sending frightened birdlife hurtling in all directions and an amazing sight to see is the humming bird hawk moth. It looks like a humming bird, flies like one and is also about the size of a tiny humming bird but it is a moth. This creature is so weird that it could certainly not have come from anyone's mind.

In 1975 I was at the birth of my son Mark and I remember the nurse telling me to sit down so that I didn't fall if I fainted. I had none of it. To witness a real birth, especially if it is your own child is another wonder, and it is even more special if you are the father and not the mother. I don't know how much Wonderment I would have felt then if it was me having the contractions. Eventually all of Mark came out (He was a big lump even then) and I was thrilled. I looked at him and marvelled at being his father but also I could not help marvel at a minute single sperm swimming to reach a minute single egg and then nine months later turning into a Mark. Isn't life a wonderful thing?

We humans tend to think we are so much more intelligent than other animals but are we? Our brains are certainly relatively bigger than an ant but look at an ants' nest and wonder at all those creatures living in such close proximity to each other and working so well together for a common purpose. Many of us live together in cities and many of us do coexist peacefully but look at the trouble such close packed living can cause. Our equivalent to ants nests are usually full of problems and tensions and have to be policed continuously at a vast cost both in money and human resources yet the ants have the sense to live together in harmony just for life and the future of their kind. Are they the clever ones after all?

If we wish to travel abroad we drive or are driven to an airport, wait around in the departure lounge eating expensive food and buying things we do not need just because we are bored and then we clamber aboard a giant metal machine which takes us up and to where we want to go. What effort when swallows, cuckoos, house martins, swifts or chiffchaffs just do it on their own, such little creatures with such energy and sense of direction. How do they find their way over thousands of miles? You don't see them with little sat navs strapped to their heads do you? Mind you, the woman in my sat nav usually sends me the wrong way anyway.

The chiffchaff is a member of the warbler family and I always hold it as the first sign that spring is really here. We do have snowdrops to tell us spring is on its way but to me it actually arrives with the chiffchaff, this little bird, smaller than a sparrow, which manages to fly from Africa and arrive back in the same spot within a couple of days of when it did the year before. And we think we are clever?

The chiffchaff is named after its call which is just that, 'chiffchaff-chiffchaff-chiffchaff'. It is a wonderful sound when they first arrive at the end of March but it does get a little monotonous after a while. This bird is almost indistinguishable from its close cousin the willow warbler but this has a far better song in that it is a reversed crescendo, starting on a high note and warbling down to a lower one.

One more thing amazes me with this animal intelligence theme and it is this. If you look up at a huge flock of starlings or look down at a shoal of fish you notice they all follow each other's movements and form beautiful patterns in the sky or sea as they do so. How is this done? What sort of communication are they using and how do they decide which other animal to follow? I think in our arrogance of putting ourselves in the bible position of being above all other creatures we have lost the ability to see them for what they are and that is fellow creatures of the planet that sometimes have ways that even we cannot understand despite our brain size.

The African elephant, although far smaller than some of the dinosaurs, is today's largest land mammal. It is a great animal but if it had been made by a god it would have had to be seen as a mistake, a big mistake at that. Can you imagine its creator making it and then saying, "Oops! That was silly of me. How is it going to eat and drink? It can't reach the ground with its mouth. Oh, never mind. I'll just stick a long hosepipe thing on its nose. That'll do."

Of course, the elephant evolved like every other animal did and we have found fossils of various elephants with various leg lengths and therefore various hosepipe (I mean trunk) lengths.

And talking about God's mistakes, take a look on the Interweb or wherever and check out the following animal list and see what you think. Do you think any of them were designed rather than come about by evolution? They certainly are a weird bunch and it would have taken a weird mind to conjure them up.

Leafy Sea Dragon.

The Dumbo Octopus.

The Babirusa.

Pink Fairy Armadillo.

Blobfish.

Hagfish.

Axolotl.

Star-nosed Mole.

The Aye Aye

Naked Mole Rat.

Yeti Crab.

The above list just shows what wonders evolution can throw up. Some results are beautiful, others are weird and others are just plain ugly. What is ugly though? One man's meat is another man's possum as they say. All beauty really is in the eye of the beholder isn't it? Some people see warthogs and vultures as being ugly but I think they are gorgeous.

I have dwelt mainly upon animal life in its many and glorious forms. This is because that is where my interests lie. Of course though, we have so much Wonderment in our plant life as well and the first thing that will come to many minds is the 'mighty oak'. Some of today's oak trees stood, already as substantial trees, at the time of the Battle of Hastings. It is also a wonder that when we do eventually fell a tree we can tell the age of it but just counting its rings. Not only can we tell how old it is we can also tell when it first grew from a seed. This is done by looking at its various ring widths and checking those ring growth patterns against computer held records. We call it dendrochronology and use it today to date buildings and ship wrecks.

The mighty oak is only a plant but it takes in carbon dioxide and gives out oxygen for us and a single tree is home to hundreds of different animals.

Look also at a field of corn, barley or wheat. We drive past it when it first germinates and see small flecks of green in an otherwise bare field and before we know it we see a field of cereal which is knee high. Within no time it turns golden and is harvested to feed us. From seed to grain and field to mill in just a few weeks.

We need plants and could never live without them. The rainforests are said to be 'the lungs of the earth' as, like the oak, they take in carbon dioxide and give out oxygen. Plants give us the oxygen we need, they give us the food we need and these days so many are used in the drugs we take on an everyday basis.

We can wonder at an orchid or an orange or an elk or an elephant. Nature is an incredible thing in whatever form it takes.

As I write this piece I am sitting in a large bay window of a Victorian house which is perched on cliffs above Port Isaac harbour. To my left I have the sea, below me I have the harbour and to my right I can see the roof and chimneys of my next door neighbour, the surgery of television's Doc Martin. I am lucky enough to be his next door neighbour for the week although filming is not being done at this time.

Why I say all this is because from where I am sitting I can look down to the sea as it laps gently onto the harbour beach and in the harbour are herring gulls (some nesting and with young), lesser black-back gulls, fulmars, cormorants, hedge sparrows, jackdaws and the occasional swallow or swift.

It is June and the cliffs are covered in lush green foliage dotted with beautiful flowers which no one tends to but nature just lets them flourish on the meagre amount of soil available in the crevices of the rocks. The occasional fishing boat leaves the harbour to go out and catch food for the hungry residents and cars wind a difficult path up and down the extremely narrow but still two way traffic streets. Apart from the vehicles we seem caught in some kind of time warp.

Last night we had thunderstorms which lit up the harbour and surrounding area with vivid orange and violet light but this morning the sky has cleared and the sun is shining brightly. I gaze out to sea and my eyes come upon a flock of thirty to forty gannets and I watch as they busily find their breakfast. They have obviously come across a large shoal of prey fish and are taking their fill to set them up for the day. A hearty breakfast is good for us all, all apart from the fish concerned that is. But that's nature. We all eat to survive and because of it some have to die. That is the way of the world.

The gannets soar over the water and with eyesight far superior to ours they spot their prey from a height and then fold their wings back, stretch out their necks and dive in after them. They look almost like darts being thrown at a dartboard as they hit the water.

I have talked earlier of the humming bird hawk moth and as I look out of the window I can see one flitting from flower to flower along the steep narrow roadway of Roscarrock Hill which leads from the harbour past us and on up to the coastal path which leads to Port Quin. This almost weird moth is a rarity most years and to see one is a special treat.

Also from the window of our downstairs loo we can see the hillside which is covered in various plants from brackens to ferns to ivy and to cleavers, or sticky-buds as we used to call them. On the cleavers are many small globules of what look like spit. They are commonly called 'cuckoo spit' but are really the homes of the nymphs of a member of the superfamily called Cercopoidea. We commonly know them as froghoppers and they are called this because they can jump many times their own body length. The globule of spit is secreted for a number of reasons. It creates a safe home for the nymph, keeps the nymph at an almost constant temperature and also stops it drying out and dying in the sunshine.

This is not Africa or Mauritius or America or the Caribbean or the North or South Pole. This is just the south-west of England and it is beautiful.

I write this as an illustration of just how fantastic Wonderment can be when you can even just look out of a window at the simple but beautiful things nature has to offer and fully appreciate your surroundings. How much better is it to wonder at all this rather than wonder what harm or misery you can cause someone today.

I mentioned in my preface about my Lucy not being taught how the tides work. Sitting here overlooking the sea brings the tides to mind. Not only do they come in and out but in doing so they provide a vast amount of food both for us and wildlife.

As we have said, every single thing in the universe is held in place by gravity and the tides also are governed by it. The earth turns on its axis and in theory you would think the seas would just travel with it but in reality they are affected by the gravitational pull of the sun and moon plus the strength and direction of the wind.

The earth turns but the gravitational pull of the sun or moon holds back the sea so, in a way, the earth is actually moving underneath the water, thus making the water higher on that portion of the land. The land at the opposite side of the gravitational pull is then further away from the sea and therefore they experience a low tide.

A wind blowing from the land will help bring about an even lower tide and a wind blowing off the sea will help create a higher tide. So take in consideration the sun and moon in line together and therefore combining their gravitational force and then a strong wind blowing from off the sea and then we see really high seas or tidal surges as we call them. In 2013 the east of England suffered a major tidal surge which devastated a vast area of coastline.

The tide comes in and it covers and feeds the land and then it retreats to reveal that land. This makes tidal areas some of the richest areas in the world for wildlife. The earth beneath is filled with a myriad of different molluscs, worms and crustaceans, all there to feed a myriad of birdlife and us.

Without gravity there would be no tides and indeed no us. If we must worship something perhaps we should worship gravity. They say that Sir Isaac Newton discovered gravity but just as

Captain Cooke with Australia I'm sure it was there before. I jest as I'm sure they were both great men.

In their place all animals are wondrous creatures but we humans do have a nasty tendency to mix things up by introducing species that should not be there. They are put into an ecosystem that just cannot handle or tolerate the introduction. All life depends upon its environment and the other species within that environment to survive. All ecosystems are fragile. They have taken multi millennia to evolve and we can destroy them in just a few years. We have looked at the previous list as weird but wonderful creatures but the list below are not wonderfully weird, they are all wonderful but worrying.

The domestic cat.
The American Mink.
Muntjac deer.
Zander.
Coypu.
Grey Squirrel.
Signal Crayfish.

All of the above have been introduced into Britain's ecosystems and all have had quite devastating effects.

The coypu was wiped out in the 1960s and the zander doesn't seem quite so prevalent these days but it is still around as are all the rest. The mink was freed from fur farms by people who thought they were doing a good thing. Do good people, with the correct ideology as they thought, saw these poor creatures being bred just for their skins and thought they would be better off freed so that is just what they did. They broke into fur farms and freed all the 'prisoners'. The trouble was though, they did this as a knee-jerk reaction to the problem and acted without an inkling of thought as to the consequences. Maybe they were correct in thinking mink did not belong in cages and they were worth more than just the adornment of some posh person's coat but in no way were they or could they ever be part of our eco system. The mink were free but so much else was put in jeopardy.

Muntjac deer are very cute animals but their numbers are now so great they are eating too many young plants and trees while the grey squirrel has driven the native and much sweeter red squirrel out of most of England. The greys are larger than the reds and are more opportunistic feeders. Because of this they can eat and survive better than the reds in harsher times. The greys also carry a disease called squirrel pox. This is only 'carried' by the greys but it can be fatal to the reds. In my lifetime I have seen the complete change from woodlands being filled with just red squirrels to being filled with just greys.

The domestic cat is a pet that many people adore but most owners are blind to the devastation they cause. It has been calculated by those in the know that cats are responsible every year for the deaths of 250 million 'wild' animals.

"It is what they do," people say but what those saying it do not realise and appreciate is the fact that domestic cats are not natural wild animals and there are far too many of them for the ecosystem to cope with.

Do we keep animals that devastate the countryside just because "It is what they do"? They rip other harmless and defenceless animals to pieces because "it is what they do" Is that okay? We would not keep a paedophile as a pet and let him harm children would we? But then again "It is what he does". A little too simple an analogy maybe but believe me we should these days be realistic in our views and choices of pets. Cats are lovely fluffy purring animals but they are unnatural predators and are killing far too many other animals. The figure of 250 million is no exaggeration and cannot possibly be sustained. We need to open our eyes and minds as to what is happening in the world which has already seen drastic drops in the numbers of feline prey animals.

I am not advocating the killing of cats but what I would say is if you do lose one then please think twice about replacing it. We have too many humans in the world and those too many humans do own too many cats without giving a hoot for anything apart from their own wants, desires and comfort.

The Scottish wild cat is a natural species and because it is natural its numbers are only ever as great as the ecosystem can manage. The domestic cat's numbers run into the millions because they are not wild. They are fed, bred and cosseted and have no need to struggle, therefore their numbers have grown and grown. They may be domesticated, cosseted and fed but their natural killing instinct is still there and they follow it eagerly.

Our animal numbers have plummeted worryingly over the last few decades with some bird species down in numbers by 90% or more. Last year I only heard one cuckoo. In the past we have heard them almost continuously. Of course introduced species are not the only cause of this but we must think and do something. Many other factors come into play here as well and I shall cover them later. The trouble is that all the factors contributing to the massive decline in wildlife numbers all have humans as the basic root cause.

Wonderment does have its problems today but it is still there and we should all seek it. It isn't hard to find as it is on your doorstep, sometimes literally. Whether you are in England, Australia, South Africa or the USA or anywhere else, just sit on your doorstep on a sunny day and you will see all manner of wildlife from birds and butterflies in the sky to spiders, woodlice, snails and slugs actually on the step. Next time you sit there don't just look. Think deep and wonder what they are, why they are what they are and how they came to be. Imagine what their relatives were in the past and how they evolved. Imagine it all and not only will you learn but your life will be enhanced and your mind will be free.

Believe me fact is far greater than any fiction.

7

The Wonder of Superstition

Whether it is not cutting your nails on a Sunday or not putting an umbrella up indoors or Jewish people and others not eating pork or the practise of female genital mutilation, so many people's lives are shaped and blighted by superstition and no superstition has anything to do with reality.

My dear late mother lived her life by superstition. She would always say, "You mustn't cut your toenails on a Sunday or you will have the devil with you all week."

I couldn't work out why this should be but she insisted it was fact. I asked her why and how it worked but she could not answer. Although it made no sense at all she stood by the statement. It was all a bit nutty to me especially when she insisted it was true for every other day of the week as well. So have we all got the devil with us? We must cut our nails sometime otherwise our shoes wouldn't fit.

I witnessed an incident recently where someone had found a peacock tail feather and because she was fascinated by it she brought it indoors for others to marvel at as well. It was only a simple bird feather and we all saw the beauty but then someone else entered the room and I was gobsmacked by her reaction. "What is that doing in here!" she said with some panic and shock in her voice. "Get it out of here, now!"

We questioned why and she looked at us as if we were complete numpties. "Because they bring terrible luck!" she snapped. It seemed we should have known this. Of course we should.

I left the room without adding anything else to the conversation. What was the point in trying to explain?

How can cutting your nails on a day of the week which ends in Y or having a feather in a room suddenly turn your life upside down with all sorts of bad luck and misfortune? I may be stating the obvious here but 'It cannot happen!' It cannot happen and will never happen so why on earth do people live their lives by this idiocy?

I have been to antique auctions where lot number 13 has been missed out. I have seen rooms go from No1 to No12 and then to No12A before going to No14. In bingo they say 'unlucky for some 13'. Think about it for a while, a couple of seconds at least. How the heck can the number 13 be unlucky? It is a number, something written on a piece of paper or on a door. How could a number, whether it is 13, 113 or 113,000, ever possibly hurt anyone? If a child counts from one to twenty and doesn't miss out number 13 will that child have a bad future life? Come on! Thinking about it though, a child mentioning the number 13 could be unlucky but perhaps as the number 7 has to be mentioned before you come to 13 perhaps its luck outweighs 13's bad luck. I don't think so. Does a raffle ticket with the number 13 on it never ever win a prize? If it is so unlucky why do they even bother to print it? Does no one win the Lotto when the number 13 is drawn? What about those people with number 13 on their lucky dip? Do they just throw it in the bin even before the draw starts?

As you can see this type of thing does get me going. This is because it is rubbish and yet so many people let themselves be ruled by it all. If someone was to try and give you £13 million would you turn it down because it might be unlucky? And if someone told you to put your house on a horse in the Grand National which had a bad heart and only three legs but had been given the number 7, would you have a flutter? Of course you wouldn't. Also, when a child reaches the age of thirteen does he suddenly turn into an out of control monster? Yes, you are right. Many of us did didn't we?

What if someone told you if you walked round the town on a Saturday morning wearing nothing but a red carnation buttonhole God would put £100,000 in your bank account, would you? I doubt it, and why not? Because, A. You would get arrested. B. You know it would never happen, and C. Where would you pin the buttonhole anyway?

Another one. What if you were told if you gave all your worldly belongings to a quack religious sect it would guarantee your place in heaven, would you? Yes, come to think of it, you might. Many have fallen for this one haven't they? They have given their belongings, their money and even their bodies all for some false promise. How do people do it? How do they brainwash others to give it all? I'm sure if I tried I would be told very politely to go away.

Passing on the stairs:

I have come across this one frequently. Someone is coming up a wide staircase as I start to make my way down. There is plenty of room and I am not being rude and pushing my way past but suddenly the other person either starts to go back down or tells me to stop.

One lady said to me, "I have enough bad luck in my life without you doing your best to make it worse!"

Was I such an unthinking person? I was only trying to go down the stairs for goodness sake, not put a curse on her life. People cannot see just how their lives are held back by such nonsense and how their lives could be improved greatly if they managed to get over this and stop worrying about nothing.

Let's look at some more trivial superstitions:

Walking under ladders
Breaking mirrors
Giving an odd number of flowers
Giving red and white flowers
Friday 13th

Black cat crossing the road

Stepping on cracks in pavements

Toads causing warts

Sleeping on a table

Singing at the dinner table

Refusing a kiss under the mistletoe

Leaving through a different door to the one you entered

When a dog howls death is near

Dropping a dishcloth

Getting out of a bed on the different side to the one you got in

Rocking an empty rocking chair

Giving a purse or wallet as a present without putting money in it

Smelling dandelions makes you wet the bed

Seeing bats flying

There are supposed to be good superstitions as well:

Rabbits' feet

An apple a day

Four leaf clover

Horseshoes

Garlic protecting from evil spirits

Pot of gold at the end of a rainbow

So if I woke late to the sound of a dog howling on Friday 13th, got out of the bed on the opposite side to where I got in, rushed around and broke my wife's favourite mirror before seeing a black cat cross the road in front of my car and then I walked on cracks in the pavement and under a ladder as I entered my work building my luck probably would not be too good. Add to this I leave off work and buy my wife an odd number of flowers on the way home to say sorry for breaking her mirror, sing up the dinner table and then offer to wash up but drop the dishcloth and then look out of the window and see bats flying and can smell dandelions before I realise I've lost my best rabbit's foot, would I die that night after wetting the bed?

When we were children we were told that if you knock a nail in a church door at midnight and then run round the church three times a ghost would appear. Mad you might say but we found it fascinating. We talked and talked about it and then decided we would have a go although we quaked in our boots at the thought of it. We were scared stiff but we had to do it.

My father had a few old oil covered hammers in his shed so I borrowed one and a rusty nail and we went off to the church. Obviously though we were only children and couldn't be out at midnight so we thought we would do it at six o'clock instead, before it got dark. As we walked to the church we boasted about being the brave ones as other children would not come but really we half wished we had stayed at home as well.

At the church my friend did the deed with the hammer and nail as he was the tallest and then we looked at each other and began to run, once, twice around the church. As we reached the door for the second time we hesitated, looked at each other, started on our third lap, and then turned round and ran home leaving the nail in the door and the hammer on the ground. I don't suppose this superstition is any more true than any of the others but we did not prove it one way or the other and luckily my father never did mention his missing hammer.

Before I move on to more serious superstitions let me take a little of your time to talk about three that have always amazed me.

The first is a subject that not everyone feels comfortable with and I feel this is the problem. The act concerned is masturbation which although perfectly harmless and totally innocuous is often frowned upon and therefore the superstition has arisen that masturbation will make you deaf or blind or both. Please don't tell anyone but I am wearing glasses while writing this. Masturbation is frowned upon openly but in private (the best place really) everyone has done it and why not? Men when they are young have hormones raging around inside them like a herd of buffalo. I know I did. Masturbation in those puzzling years is the only thing that stops them exploding and I presume the same factors apply to women as well. There is absolutely nothing wrong with it and no, you will not go blind or deaf. Pardon?

The second superstition I would put in this category is why some religionists do not eat pork or shrimps or crabs or lobster. This is because they are not classed as 'kosher'. For an animal to be kosher it has to have cloven hooves and must chew the cud. Therefore a pig must not be eaten. It does have cloven hooves but does not chew the cud. On the fish menu crustaceans are banned because only fish with fins and scales may be eaten, but why? We have looked into this a little before but let's look at the reason.

Here is a translation from Deuteronomy.

And the pig because it has a split hoof but does not chew the cud. It is unclean for you. You shall neither eat its flesh or touch its carcass.

These you may eat of all in the waters; all that have fins and scales you may eat.

But whatever does not have fins and scales, you shall not eat, it is unclean for you.

Is it saying they are simply unclean and that is that or are they unclean for reasons such as because a pig roots around in the ground and eats all sorts of things and crabs, shrimps and lobsters feed on the bottom of the sea and eat detritus? Is this why they are classed as 'unclean'? I don't know. It is all a bit silly to me.

It is understood that these laws may not seem logical but people follow them because it is God's command and they say there are moral lessons to be learned as well. They seem to be frightened that the negative characteristics of the animals concerned could be absorbed into their bodies. For religionists to follow this is their concern but isn't it taking it a little far when this practise has been carried on for so many years just because of a small passage in a book? What negative characteristics can a poor old pig or crab or lobster have? Haven't any of these people ever tasted a delicious bacon butty on a Sunday morning or a gorgeous piece of crispy crackling with their roast? I'm glad I'm not Jewish, my mouth is salivating as I write. What about a fresh crab from the seaside or even a big fat juicy lobster? I have eaten all these in abundance and am perfectly healthy. Will I be condemned to hell just because I have eaten a prawn rather than a Pollock or a little shrimp rather than a lemon sole? Life is too short to live by illogical rules. I feel we should all lighten up. If God loves these people will he love them less if they chew on a shrimp? If their god is so benevolent and understanding would he really give a damn? No, of course he wouldn't.

Praying:

Praying is a superstition. We are told to pray and God will listen and help us. Does God listen to every one of the seven billion people in the world and all at the same time? And why should God give everyone all they need just because they ask for it. When I was a kiddie and before I knew better I did once ask for the chance to kiss a pretty girl in our street but when I tried to she just smacked me across the face. I didn't know at the time but obviously God was busy that day.

I am going to be a little naughty here and quote from a brilliant article I have found on the Interweb. The author of the piece is unknown to me and I cannot therefore ask his/her permission to quote it but it is such a well thought out and constructed piece I feel by publicising it I shall only be heaping praise on the individual concerned. My thanks go sincerely to

143

the author and I hope this person will forgive my cheek. If I ever meet him/her I shall buy them a drink.

Quote:

"Let's say that you were to create a far flung news network, and you somehow had the capacity to observe all of the inexplicable tragedy that occurs on earth each day.

All of the murders
All of the car wrecks
All of the rapes
All of the mutilations
All of the tortures
All of the miscarriages and still births
All of the disease
All of the starvation
All of the destruction
All of the terrorism

Let's say you had a news feed that delivered this all to you in real time. Just ten minutes with this news feed would be unbearable. Thousands of tragic heart-wrenching events would impinge themselves upon you every minute. It would make you vomit over and over and over again until you passed out in exhaustion and despair.

In other words the amount of gut-wrenching anguished tragedy in our world is unspeakable.

Meanwhile, there is a housewife in Pasadena who firmly believes that God answered her prayer this morning to remove the mustard stain from her favourite blouse. She prayed to God to help with the stain and after she washed it the stain was gone.

Praise Jesus! There are tens of millions of people in the United States who firmly believe that God is personally helping them each day with their trivial prayers like this. They believe that they have a personal relationship with God, that God hears their prayers each day and that God has time to reach down and remove the mustard molecules one by one. They believe it with all their hearts.

It makes you wonder: If God has the time and the will to answer these trivial prayers, then why does he have no time for the millions of other massively serious problems that arise on earth every day?

Simply look at the world we live in. All around us we have murderers, rapists and robbers, child molesters, terrorists etc. How do they do their deeds? If God is all-knowing and God answers prayers! Then we have to believe that:

God watches them as they murder! Rape! Molest and terrorise other people. Millions of them every day! But he does nothing to stop them.

God watches the victims as they are being murdered! Raped! Molested and Terrorised! But he does nothing to help them.

God completely ignores the prayers of the planet to eliminate murder! Rape! Child molestation and Terrorism and allows these atrocities to continue unabated.

This sums it all up I think and so I have little more to add except for quoting Carl Pilkington's character Dougie in the Channel 4 sitcom Derek.

"Praying? No. I don't bother. No one listens to you anyway do they? What's the point in praying? No, I just have a moan instead. That's my way of getting it out. That's what it is. It's a posh moan, praying."

So, in essence, I would sum praying up by saying if you do believe in a God and do feel you need to have a posh moan please think of others first. Give God time to work on the real needs of the world and let your washing machine get out that mustard stain as it probably has done before and will again, all by itself.

The above superstitions do control some peoples' lives but they are all what I would term 'trivial superstitions'. They may seem stupid and unbelievable to people like me but the only people they actually harm are those silly enough to be ruled by them. There are others though which really do blight lives and some really harm those concerned, both humans and animals. I have joked so far but superstitions can become serious for many.

In some countries it is commonplace to eat dog meat and although I have absolutely no desire whatsoever to try it I can see little wrong with it. I have never eaten a rat or hedgehog but some people say they are delicious. Surely a rat, a dog or a hedgehog is no different to a chicken or rabbit but one thing about eating dogs does really rile me and that is the practise of beating the poor things to death. I watched a television programme once where, I think it was a Korean man, stated quite openly and without any remorse that he killed dogs for meat by hanging them up and beating them to death with a stick. He said this transferred the strength of the dog into him. What? How pathetic can you get?

People also believe the same goes for eating ground up tiger bones or rhino horn. Surely with the brain capacity we humans have this should never enter into anyone's mind at all let alone have the person actually go through with it. Bones and beatings can hold no magical, mystical or miraculous power. If we must kill let us do it for food not for any stupid superstition.

Killing properly brings me onto another section. If I was in my shed or kitchen and I had an animal hanging alive and conscious upside down and I was about to slit its throat when the police or RSPA walked in I would be prosecuted. I would hold out my hands and say, "It's a fair cop guv." It would bring punishment to me and justice for the poor animal concerned but only because I am not religious. If I was religious and because of over-zealous superstition, the government of Britain, in their infinite wisdom, would condone my actions because this is the

'Halal' way of killing meat, the method of which is just as I have described. An animal is strung upside down and has its throat cut while it is totally aware of the immense pain and trauma it is suffering. It is then left to die in agony as its blood drains. How can stunning the poor wretched creature first be so against anyone's religion? What religion condones suffering of this magnitude and what government of a supposedly moral country condones it also? I am no vegetarian and I do even hunt my own food from time to time but everything I eat I can morally justify. To torture an animal in this way can never be justified to satisfy anything let alone just religious superstition.

Circumcision: (Male)

Millions of boys and men have been circumcised. Let's try and look at why:

Genesis Chapter 17 (King James Version)

And when Abram was ninety years and nine the Lord appeared to Abram and said unto him, I am the Almighty God; walk before me and be thou perfect.

And I will make my covenant between me and thee, and I will multiply thee exceedingly.

And Abram fell on his face and God talked with him saying,

As for me behold my covenant is with thee, and thou shalt be a father of many nations.

Neither shall thy name any more be called Abram but thy name shall be Abraham; For a father of many nations have I made thee.

And I will make thee exceeding fruitful, and I will make nations of thee, and kings shall come out of thee.

And I will establish my covenant between me and thee and thy seed after thee in their generations for an everlasting covenant to be a God unto thee, unto thy seed after thee.

I will give unto thee, and to thy seed after thee, the land wherein though art a stranger, all the land of Canaan for an everlasting possession; and I will be their God.

And God said unto Abraham, thou shalt keep my covenant therefore, thou and thy seed after thee in their generations.

This is my covenant, which ye shall keep, between me and you and thy seed after thee; every man child among you shall be circumcised.

And ye shall circumcise the flesh of your foreskin; and it shall be a token of the covenant betwixt me and you.

And he that is eight days old shall be circumcised among you, every man child in your generations, he that is born in the house or bought with money of any stranger, which is not of thy seed.

He that is born in thy house, and he that is bought with thy money, must needs be circumcised: And my covenant shall be in your flesh for an everlasting covenant.

And the uncircumcised man child whose flesh of his foreskin is not circumcised, that soul shall be cut off from his people; he hath broken my covenant.

And God said unto Abraham, as for Sarai the wife, thou shalt not call her name Sarai but Sarah shall her name be.

And I will bless her, and give thee a son also of her: Yea, I will bless her, and she shall be a mother of nations; kings of people shall be of her.

Then Abraham fell upon his face, and laughed, and said in his heart, shall a child be born unto him that is an hundred years old? And shall Sarah, that is ninety years old, bear?

And Abraham said unto God, oh that Ishmael might live before thee!

And God said, Sarah thy wife shall bear thee a son indeed; and thou shalt call his name Isaac: And I will establish my covenant with him for an everlasting covenant and with his seed after him.

And as for Ishmael, I have heard thee: Behold, I have blessed him, and will make him fruitful, and will multiply him exceedingly; twelve princes shall be beget, and I will make him a great nation.

But my covenant will I establish with Isaac, which Sarah shall bear unto thee at this set time in the next year.

And he left off talking with him, and God went up from Abraham.

And Abraham took Ishmael his son, and all that were born in his house, and all that were bought with his money every male among the men on Abraham's house; and circumcised the flesh of their foreskin in the selfsame day, as God had said unto him.

And Abraham was ninety years old and nine, when he was circumcised in the flesh of his foreskin.

And Ishmael his son was thirteen years old, when he was circumcised in the flesh of his foreskin.

In the selfsame day was Abraham circumcised, and Ishmael his son.

And all men of his house, born in the house, and bought with money of the stranger, were circumcised with him.

I am thinking hard here. This is the story of how God made Abraham and all other men he knew become circumcised, but why? Is this why so many millions of people have been circumcised since? In the bible it just says God told Abraham to do it and he did, just like that. Would he have cut off both his arms without question if God told him to do so? I suppose he may have struggled with the second arm (Think about it). Abraham was 99 years old and you'd think he would have become a little attached to his foreskin by then. Why didn't he even ask why? There is no reason given at all.

Was this the first time circumcision had been practised? If so Abraham would not even have known what it was let alone be able to perform the operation. In the text God didn't explain. If it was not the first time it had happened and everyone knew what it was and what to do then what was all the fuss about between God and Abraham? And why did God suddenly change their names, Abram and Sarai to Abraham and Sarah? What difference did that make?

In this bible extract, again we are reading that God said this and God said that. As I have said before, if there was a God no one could possibly ever know what he said. There are no records of his speech apart from the fact 'it is written'.

Also, if God was such a fantastic, all-powerful and all-knowing creator and didn't want men to have foreskins why did he invent the things in the first place? And why do we just circumcise a certain sector of society? Surely if it is such a necessary thing we should all have it done. If it is not such a necessary thing then why does anyone have it done?

None of my family members or even family's members have been circumcised. Are we to be stopped at the gates of heaven by someone shaking their head, rubbing their chin and frowning, saying, "Oh no mate, you can't come in here. You've got a whole willy."?

So many are taking notice of this bible text and so many are believing every word they read and living by it but how probable is the story? It isn't is it? Abram, or Abraham was 99 when he was to father a child. That didn't happen did it, so why have so many boys and men been mutilated just because of a story in a book that doesn't really make any sense at all?

I cannot see why male circumcision is necessary apart from for any medical reason. To my mind it is simply carrying on with an age old superstition and tradition. Isn't it also unjust? I think if someone was going to take a knife to my penis I would like the chance to say "No thanks!" People are baptised into a faith before they have the chance to make a choice and this is bad enough so surely unnecessary surgery like circumcision being performed without consent on an infant has to be wrong and most probably against their human rights.

If a boy grows into a man and that man then wishes to be circumcised then why not. I wouldn't but then I would never have my body pierced or tattooed. Circumcision by choice does not sit comfortable in my mind but at least it would not be forced upon anyone.

God said to Abraham that those who would not be circumcised would be 'Cut off'. I think I would rather be cut off than cut off. Anyway, do people shun you just because you have a foreskin? I've never had a problem. How would they know anyway? Do circumcised people feel the need to go into a pub and drop their trousers to prove they have been circumcised before being accepted into the darts team?

So is this all there is to it? For centuries boys and men have been mutilated because of a highly improbable story? Am I missing something which others can plainly see? If so I am sorry and hope someone will explain to me what it is but I have read various articles on the Interweb and can find nothing more. Everything I read seems to come back to the same reason, God talking to Abraham. It just happened that God was supposed to have told Abraham to circumcise people but what if God had told Abraham to make sure all men wore tall top hats and walked on stilts? Would we have just accepted taller doorways as the norm? At least you could see they were following their faith while they were still wearing trousers.

What harm has any foreskin ever done to anyone? What harm could it possibly do? Why are some men supposed to be better off without one? If slicing off flesh could somehow make you wiser, or more academic or even a better husband perhaps there could be something in it but (Again, correct me if I am wrong) it doesn't. Circumcision does nothing to enhance a person at all. All it is is a token to say a person is of a different sect. Am I being too simplistic here in suggesting people could just wear a badge saying 'I am a Muslim', 'I am Jewish', 'I am a Christian', 'I follow Hare Krishna' or 'I believe in reality'.

Do we even need a badge? Why can't we all just be ourselves.

Mrs Brown's Boys again:

Winnie McGoogan
"What do they call that useless piece of skin on the end of a willy?"

Mrs Brown
"It's called a man."

Female Genital Mutilation:

I do not personally believe in male circumcision but Female Genital Mutilation (FGM) is something that to my mind no one should ever believe in. The practise is horrendous. With most things, whether it is religion, porn or parsnips, it is possible to have an opinion either way but how can anyone think this practise is correct? Whatever abomination of a human ever thought of it and how did they ever talk others into having it done? Removing a male child's foreskin is bad enough and should be illegal but what they are doing to girls hardly bears thinking about at all.

This is sometimes performed with a religious intent but unlike male circumcision it is not necessarily anything to do with religion at all but just because of a very weird and long held tradition. I'm sorry but to explain just how horrendous the practice is we will have to look at it in detail.

Female Genital Mutilation is sometimes called Female Genital Cutting or just Female Circumcision but whatever it is called it still makes me feel a little sick inside just to think and write about it.

It is said to have originated in the Horn of Africa (Egypt and Sudan) at around 2,200BC, before the birth of Islam and some historians say, rightly or wrongly, that it was started by one Pharaoh who cut all his women so that he could control them. It is widely performed in African countries as well as in the Middle East and parts of Asia. It is also performed in Great Britain although it is totally illegal. Many girls are taken back to their mother countries to have it done but it seems there is a rising trend to have people come into the country to perform procedures en bloc. This saves the expense of individual travel costs. I wonder if the authorities scrutinize and police it with the fervour and vigour it deserves?

Before we actually go into the procedure of FGM let's look at some of the reasons why it is carried out:

It can ensure virginity before marriage.

It can ensure fidelity during marriage.

It can increase male sexual pleasure.

It can decrease female sexual pleasure.

It can ensure a good marriage for the recipient.

It can stop a female's clitoris becoming large.

Female genitalia is considered by many as being unsightly.

It will help keep a female's body clean.

It is an important part of a girl's journey into womanhood.

It is an important tradition.

So after reading and studying the above reasons for at least half a second we come to this conclusion. All the pain, trauma, discomfort and disfigurement a female goes through is purely for the pleasure of a man and the woman gets nothing out of it in the slightest. Yep! That's it! Is it all down to the fact that insecurity in men makes this come about? Do men feel inferior if they marry a woman who isn't a virgin? Do they worry about the fact that someone has had intercourse with her before? For normal people this is not an issue and it is a good job too. FGM is supposed to promote faithfulness as well but if these men didn't treat their women as pieces of dirt then perhaps there wouldn't be anything to worry about. The need for unfaithfulness would disappear. My wife is faithful to me, but not because she has been mutilated. She is faithful to me because I treat her with love, kindness and the due respect she deserves.

The procedure seems to heighten the man's desires and reduce those of the woman. How ridiculous! Why should a woman's desires be reduced? As I have said before, this harks right back to biblical times when women in Genesis were not even worthy of being given a name. Women are worthy and men should be worthy of them. They are not the property of men. They never have been and never should be allowed to become so.

We have looked at a brief history of FGM and why it is performed but we must now look at the procedure. I would call it an operation but I think an operation is something that is performed to help a person. This barbaric nonsense certainly doesn't help and doesn't warrant such a title.

There are different forms of FGM:

Sunna Circumcision:

This is where the tip of a female's clitoris is shaved off thus decreasing its sensitivity and reducing her level of sexual feeling.

Clitoridectomy:

In a clitoridectomy either part or the whole of the clitoris is removed together with the labia.

Infibulation:

This is the most drastic of the procedures and not only involves the removal of the clitoris and labia but also involves bringing together the skin from each side of the vagina and sewing them together, leaving only a very small hole through which the person can urinate and menstruate. I have read in my studies that sometimes the vagina can be opened up again just before marriage or sometimes it is even left as it is and entry is forced by the husband's penis. I am at a loss really to know if both or either of these are true but how absolutely disgusting it is. It is also said that if a husband has to go away and leave his wife for any length of time she is sometimes sewn up again until his return.

When the person is sewn it is either done with thread, cat-gut or even thorns and then her legs are bound together for between 2 and 6 weeks so that the wound can heal.

If you were to have your tonsils out or have a stent put into your artery you would be doing it to reap the operation's rewards. With this tradition there are no rewards for the woman whatsoever. All she can look forward to are a few of the following.

HIV.

Tetanus.

Septicemia.

Hepatitis.

Pain and trauma.

Blood loss.

Psychological damage.

Painful periods.

Problems in pregnancy.

Infertility.

Acute urinary retention.

Acute urinary infections.

Incontinence.

Post-traumatic stress.

I could go on but having any, all or even just one of the above is totally unnecessary. It all comes about by absolute human stupidity. This practise should be totally outlawed throughout the world. That was a quick and just statement that I just made but how the hell do we achieve it? Basically we don't, at least not in any hurry. The trouble is it is an ingrained tradition and belief no matter how bad the practise is. Going back to the lady arguing with me about not crossing on the stairs, she would never listen to reason even in such a simple superstition and will always think and do the same thing. I know a lady, one who is in my family and whom I love dearly, who says it is going to be a hard winter because there are berries on the trees. Even if the winter turns out to be the mildest on record she will still say the same thing again the following year and again the year after. Of course there are berries on the trees. 'It's Autumn'. All these things are so ingrained that even the silliest will never be accepted as rubbish let alone the worst ones but can we possibly stop this one? I don't know. It is the women who receive the mutilation and it is women who perform it but perhaps we should not start with them but with the men. We should teach them the worth of their partners and teach them just how much more enjoyable life can be if we treat our women with respect and dignity. To have a loving and doting wife must be far better than having an object which is all wives are to them at present.

Even sexual intercourse has to be more enjoyable when both partners are lost in their sensual and sexual feelings. Get this through to men and then perhaps the women will follow. Will they though? Who am I kidding? No, of course they won't, and why? Because no matter what you say and no matter who you say it to, no one ever listens. They will never listen and therefore they will never learn. Life is as simple as that. It is but it doesn't have to be. Why don't we all start listening now? Perhaps by listening we could change things. Is it impossible?

I have read stories about girls from Britain undergoing FGM and thought I would finish this chapter off with a story I have put together myself from what I have read:

A young English girl is enjoying life. She is approaching her teens and life is fascinating for her. She is at school, has many good friends and is doing well in her studies. It is approaching the summer holidays and the sun is shining as she walks home with her friends. They look at boys on the way and giggle as they imagine all manner of things as their minds race because puberty is only just around the corner.

As she enters her home she is greeted by her mother who tells her, with a big smile on her face, that she has some good news. They are going back to their mother country during the summer holidays to visit long since seen aunts, uncles and cousins.

Of course our young lady is thrilled with this. Summer in her home town would have been fine but the thought of summer in another country with all her own family made her feel ecstatic as she danced to her bedroom to change.

The weeks went by and then they boarded an aeroplane, left England and soon found themselves far away in the company of family and friends. Celebrations started and all was wonderful but then someone dropped a little hint that something was going to happen to her but she was quickly reassured that it was only something minor and it would bring her into womanhood. Womanhood? That sounded exciting.

She was reassured to such an extent over the following days that she was feeling quite relaxed as she was eventually driven to a stranger's house and was led into a room where many women were standing. She just had time to calmly ask what was happening before she was forced onto a table, pinned down and had her undergarments removed. Her lovely holiday (and life) were both suddenly ruined in seconds as she was forcibly cut without a single thought for her feelings, wishes, dignity, rights or extreme pain and trauma.

The rest of her holiday was spent in agony and shock and when she returned home she withdrew deeply within herself. Her sparkle, her lust for life and her whole being were gone. She tried to look at herself but found the affected area revolting so she then found herself revolting too. This wonderful child then turned into a teenager. Not into one who felt she had worth and a fantastic future but into one who hated herself, her family and life in its entirety. Her life had been shattered by superstition.

I know this story is so sad and sombre and perhaps it is not the kind of story you really like to read. It is not the kind of story I particularly like to write but believe me it has something over Wuthering Heights, Harry Potter or Pride and Prejudice in as much as the contents may have been cobbled together from other stories but in its context it is true.

When discussing male circumcision I did, rightly or wrongly, joke very light-heartedly about the subject matter. Many other people before me have seen some perversely comic side to the practise. I don't know why it happens but it does. With Female Genital mutilation though I have not joked and neither do other people. This is a superstition which is way beyond any sort of humour. It is totally perverse, disgusting, inhumane and wrong and should be frowned upon by every individual from every sect in every country until somehow it is banished to history and women are treated with the same dignity that men demand and usually get.

There is something else I have noticed about the bible and superstitions:

Adam and Eve were shocked when they found themselves naked.

Noah's grandson was persecuted when his father saw his father's nakedness.

Lott's daughters seduced him.

People 'knowing' this person and that.

Genesis 38 "That I may come in unto thee."

Genesis 29 "That I may go in unto her."

God told Abraham to cut off male foreskins.

And although FGM is not a wholly religious practise, it is carried out in some religions.

Again, I could go on. Why are there so many obsessions in religion which are to do with sex or sexual parts? It is all quite perverse.

8
The Wonder of War

'War, huh, yeah. What is it good for? Absolutely nothing.'
Edwin Starr song 1970.

Absolutely nothing! Yes. That sums up the whole chapter really and I could stop here but let's look at war and try to understand why human beings, (Remember, they're the ones with the huge brains and intellect), seem to just love going to war. They kill and maim each other at the drop of a hat, have always done so, still do so and more than likely will always do so. The 1st World War was supposed to be the 'War to end all wars' but of course it wasn't. To human beings that would be far too boring and sensible. Where would the fun be in that?

I have called this chapter the 'Wonder Of War' but believe me there is no 'wonder' in war. My only wonder is why? Why on our tiny little planet set in such a vast universe, do we have to go to war all the time? I wonder why we cannot just get along together, celebrate life and spend our energies looking out into that universe to see what else and who else is out there.

In my mind I have imagined a group of highly evolved and intelligent aliens coming to earth and asking me to be their guide around the world. They are inquisitive and ask questions. They ask why the people of this tiny planet insist on and have long insisted on dropping bombs onto towns and cities without the slightest thought of how many children they are blowing to pieces. They are puzzled, to say the least, at why our race seems to relish war and why our leaders seem to rush into any war with such enthusiasm. They ask why these leaders send so many young men to their deaths but always stay safely at home themselves. They ask why there isn't money to feed the starving but there is always an abundance of money to buy bombs. They ask why humans have never learned anything from the wars they have managed to conjure up apart from how to do it more efficiently and cause more harm the next time. They ask why people are tortured and raped in war as a matter of course. They ultimately ask where all this horrendous hatred comes from and of course in my daydream I am dumbstruck and devoid of any answer at all.

I have been to the cemeteries of the poppy fields of France and have seen the thousands of graves of young men. You stand there, look down at all that is left of their bright lives and if you have any heart in you at all you weep inside for them and also for the poor families at home who waited in vain for their return. I found it impossible to stand there and not think of what a diabolical tragedy their shorts lives had become and what a diabolical thing war is. I and those with me felt the same but if we were to ship all the world's leaders out there and get them to stand in the same spot that I did would they think the same as well? Do you know? I actually think they would. They would actually grieve for those soldiers as I did and they would grieve right up until the time they got back to their own countries to plot more wars just as they always have done before.

I have set myself a little challenge here. I am going to list a number of wars which come into my mind. I shall think of them without hesitation and when I do have to hesitate I shall stop listing. I am no war historian so this will give an idea just how many wars there have been and just how prevalent wars are. Here we go:

Trafalgar.
Hastings.
American civil war.
English civil war.

161

WW1

WW2

Crimean war.

The crusades.

Boar war.

Korea.

Afghanistan.

Iraq.

Syria.

Northern Ireland.

Vietnam.

Spanish civil war.

30 years war.

Napoleonic wars.

Rwanda.

Spanish Amada.

Wars of the roses.

Williamite war.

Falklands.

That's 23 without hesitation and after doing this I have also just had a quick squint through the Interweb and have found way over 100 listed wars and insurgencies just in my lifetime and I suppose there would more if I cared to look hard enough.

So what is it that makes man go to war at the drop of any old hat? Maybe we can think awhile and come up with a few answers such as:

Sheer greed.

Ideology.

Religion.

Religious extremism.

Oil.

Land grabbing.

Revolution.

Power.

Another thing I have thought of is something I mentioned in the previous chapter regarding teaching men to value their wives and partners and why I felt it likely they would not learn? It is simply because they will not listen! So often even in everyday life we meet people who will not listen. Even if what you say makes perfect and perfectly simple clear sense they seem to find it an affront to listen. I once worked for a firm and came up with an idea which could have possibly saved lives in the event of an emergency. I was told to mind my own business. I was only a minion and those above me would have been demeaned by listening. Do folk all feel demeaned by listening? Lives in this case were left at risk. What is wrong with listening? If a person or group or country will not listen then conflict soon rears its ugly head. Whether that conflict comes just in the shape of an argument or in the shape of a fight or even a full-blown war depends on who and how much dogma is involved.

As I shall explain fully in the chapter The Wonder Of You, every human is different and therefore we all have different views. I have heard someone say that western women are allowed to wear mini-skirts and therefore all the morals of that culture are completely wrong and war should be waged upon those countries.

In the countries governed by the spokesman's religion many women are forced or coerced to wear hijabs or burkas (burqas, burkhas or bourkhas). In the west we accept the mini-skirt while Muslims may accept the burka. Maybe the mini- skirt could be seen as being too revealing to some but on the other hand the burka reveals nothing. Surely it does not matter what women wear as long as it is worn out of their own personal choice and

163

it is acceptable in the society they live in and come from but I can't help a thought or parallel coming into my mind. In early bible stories, women are given no names and little significance and couldn't the same be said for ladies wearing burkas. We see them and they are there but the burka they wear does hide any character or significance.

Really, the point of writing this is to say that we do all have different and widely varying views. It is only natural that we do but what we must not do is assume without thought that our views are correct and every other view is totally wrong. We must enjoy our views and the lifestyle they bring but we must also be totally mindful of the views of others. We must certainly never go to war just because others do not think in exactly the same way as we do.

The person or country causing any argument, fight or war will always justify it in their own mind and no matter who gets hurt for whatever stupid reason that person or country will always be right no matter how wrong they are.

Another thought is that ordinary everyday people could not just sit down and make a bomb, gun or missile. This takes very clever people. They must have brains and intellect but if so why do they use them to destroy others? They make their bombs but do they care who is killed by them?

Look at Adolf Hitler. His ideology saw the downfall and death of tens of millions of people throughout the world but did he care? No, of course he didn't, he went to his death by his own hand no doubt thinking he was right. We will shortly look at him and his ideology. I shall talk about facts and give facts but I shall also put down from my own mind what I think led to him being the way he was and therefore what led him to do what he did. As with my view on religion please read and accept these are my views. Read them, think and then draw your own conclusions. Remember, this is totally what the book is about.

Adolf Hitler was only one of the world's many tyrants, crackpots, dictators and despots, all of whom have caused the death and hardship of so many. We could go into the lives of

Saddam Hussein, Robert Mugabe, Idi Amin, Lenin, Hirohito, Ho Chi Minh, Kim Il Sung, Pol Pot, Stalin etc. etc. but Hitler is probably the most renowned and prominent of them all. Let's look at him in detail and see what we can deduce.

He was born in Austria on 20th April 1889 to parents Alois Hitler and Klara Polzl and was one of a family of six children although only two of these, he and a sister survived into adulthood. Adolf's sister Paula lived until 1960 but his other siblings all died as young children. They died between the ages of three days to six years. His early years were hard because his father was very abusive towards his family. His father was fifty-one when Adolf was born and he was strict, exceedingly short-tempered and unrepentantly brutal. He had a son, also called Alois, from a previous marriage. This son had been sent to jail for theft and although this alone did not make his father such a brutal person, it certainly did help. Having your son in jail, especially in those days and to such a proud man, must have been felt as quite a disgrace and maybe some of the brutality thrown towards young Adolf was an unconscious effort to stop him going down the same road.

In my mind offspring of abusive parents can often develop into characters that are just the opposite of that parent or they can develop the same characteristics and become copies of their parents or worse. A child can grow into an adult and positively decide their parents were wrong and therefore go a totally different way or they can grow up thinking the way their parents were was the norm and therefore they would continue in the same vein. Obviously Hitler, knowingly or not, chose the latter.

I talk about 'the way their parents were' but in this case it was not both parents who were abusive. Adolf's mother really doted upon him which I would presume, would raise jealousy and anger in his father even further. I have read an account of Adolf receiving a severe beating in the attic of their house and when his mother felt she had to step in she then became a joint victim. It is said that Adolf Hitler carried a photograph of his mother with him wherever he travelled.

Alois Hitler senior was a respectable civil servant and wanted Adolf to follow in his footsteps so was therefore shocked that Adolf spoke of his desire to become an artist. I can imagine how Adolf must have felt at this stage because my father loved aeroplanes and the RAF and desperately wanted me to join. He then thought of me as worthless because this was not what I wanted. Unlike Adolf Hitler, at that age I had never even contemplated what I wanted to be but my future certainly would not be in the RAF.

Adolph Hitler went to school but had few friends. It seems he had some potential but was lazy and eventually lost his place in the school's top class and you can imagine the shame and anger this brought upon his father. His father had always tried too hard to get Adolf to do well but in his harshness all he had achieved was to drive Adolf to rebel.

His father died when Adolf was 13 years old and this left Adolf to go much his own way with his doting mother supporting him whichever way he was to turn. He continued at school but did so in an ill-disciplined, bad tempered and argumentative way and left with no qualifications.

His father was gone and although at that age he had chosen no real career path apart from his artist dream he was, at least, free from his father's tyranny but a huge blow was to come from just around the corner when at the age of 18 his dear mother died of cancer. Witnesses have said that he spent hours beside her deathbed just staring at her and drawing sketches.

So here we have someone who is not even properly a young man yet but who has endured much. He has come from quite a tragic family which was ruled by a tyrant, had suffered many serious beatings, had not really been accepted by his peers at school, and the only person who had really held his life together, his mother, had just been cruelly taken from him. It doesn't take too much of a philosophical mind to work to out how he must have felt. He was only 18 years old and had seen little in life apart from pain, loss and heartache. We have all had times in our lives where all we felt was emptiness and at this point he surely must have felt that in abundance.

So we see him, at his dead mother's bedside, a little lost teenager, one who we can only, at this point at least, feel sorry for. How then did this sorrowful soul become, in just a few short years, one of the world's most infamous and reviled individuals?

He decided to attempt to follow his inkling of becoming an artist but again rejection came when he was denied access to the Vienna Academy Of Art and ended up living in a doss-house with tramps. Can you feel his anger and resentment rising? With much spare time on his hands and in his rising anger and despondency his mind started to wander to unsavoury thoughts such as it was a Jewish professor who had rejected his entry to the Academy and it was a Jewish doctor who had failed to save the life of his dear mother.

These thoughts and others manifested so strongly in a mind that, in his life state, saw no argument or reality and thus his hatred of the Jews began to multiply.

His life carried on in a sorrowful fashion until when in February 1914 he decided to try and escape it by joining the army but failed his medical. His rough life and lack of nutrition had led to poor health.

In August of that year though World War 1 broke out and he decided to cross the Austrian border into Germany and join the army there. It was now war and soldiers were needed and so the medical was not quite as stringent as it might have been so he passed and joined. He went to war and became a regimental runner carrying messages, very often through lines of enemy fire, from the front line to officers. These acts were seen as being exceedingly brave and he was awarded six bravery medals including the Iron Cross. At last he felt he was something, someone but he ended his war in hospital after being caught in a gas attack at Ypres.

Germany lost the war and he was devastated. You can imagine his feelings. Here was a young man whose childhood had been devastated by hate, fate and ill-fortune. In his early years he had found nothing to celebrate apart from the love of his mother who had then so viciously been taken from him at an early age and his chosen career as an artist had achieved little. The war had been his salvation and in this he had achieved so much but even that had not ended the way he wanted and had fought bravely for. He had fought for Germany and now felt much a part of that country.

As I say, the war had been his salvation but it had not ended in his favour. Was the second world war, in part, a chance to rectify the matter? It would give him chance to indulge in his new passion again and hopefully this time he could bring his country out on top. Was this in his mind from the moment the war ended or was the seed planted then and it manifested itself fully as the years passed? Let's look at how it came about.

His rise to power did not just happen overnight and neither was it brought about by any single event. His rise didn't even start due to factors just within Germany.

After the war he was determined to enter into politics and in 1919 he became the 55th member of a small anti-Semitic party called the German workers party and soon became its leader. He then created the red background, white circle and Swastika emblem of the party. In 1920 the party's name was changed to the National Socialist German Workers Party (i.e. *The Nazi Party.)*

He made several rousing speeches to gain support and finance and then in 1923 he headed a coup to take over the German government. The coup failed and he was sentenced to five years in Landsberg prison. It was in Landsberg that he wrote his book Mein Kampf (English. *My Struggle).* In the book he painted a much rosier picture of his early life than the one which had led him to where he was at that time.

He actually came out of prison after just nine months and was determined to build the Nazi Party in order to take over the German government legally.

In 1929 the U.S. suffered its great depression and felt the need to call in all its foreign loans. To achieve the payment the

German government had to cut spending, cut wages and had to cut everything else that was at all possible. Unemployment rose quickly to six million and bitterness grew within the country. Hitler capitalised on this, was granted German citizenship in 1932 and in the elections of that year his Nazi Party gained over 37% of the vote making it the controlling party in Germany.

At the end of January 1933 he was appointed chancellor and used his high rank to gain absolute power over Germany. This finally happened after the death of Paul von Hindenberg in the August of 1934. Hitler then took on the title Fuhrer and Reichskanzler (Leader and Reich Chancellor).

So in a few short years Hitler had risen from a down-and-out artist living in doss-houses to being the most powerful man in Germany. If this were any normal person we could all cheer and shout "Well done Adolf!" at the top of our voices as this in any normal person would have been one almighty achievement but in Adolf Hitler this was to be ultimately no good thing, not for Germany, for Europe, for the rest of the world, for the Jews and even, in the end, not for him himself.

As Germany's dictator Hitler had the strength and desire to increase Germany's power and territories. The Treaty of Versailles which had ultimately ended WW1 was ignored as in March 1938 Hitler annexed into Germany his old home country Austria without even a single shot being fired. He followed this by attacking Poland in September 1939 and because the rest of Europe could not just stand by and do nothing, WW2 started.

I could go on and on about WW2 and all its troubles and wickedness but will relatively quickly sum it up and therefore sum up Adolf Hitler after first paying tribute to the poor Jewish folk that he persecuted to cruelly.

As you will probably have realised by now I am not a religious person but whether you are or not, no religion or faith should ever lead to any tiny amount of hatred or persecution let alone the extermination of so many.

Hitler's attitude towards and hatred of the Jews soon began to raise its ugly head now that he had the power to do something about it. By various means, and ending with gas chambers and incinerators, Hitler and his henchmen somehow managed to murder six million Jews and just because of their difference by religion. The rest of the world was at war and powerless to do anything about it as they suffered and died.

The death toll in WW2 was so widespread and vast that no one really actually knows just how many people died. Educated estimates though put the figure at somewhere between 50 and 70 million. Was all this suffering just because of Hitler's upbringing and life? I do feel we are what we are when we are born but our lives are also certainly moulded and transformed by events during our lives. All of us have problems through our lives but fortunately not many of us let these problems become this great and need this great a solution. Hitler was a lost soul but felt he found himself in war. In his childhood he had no power but yearned for it and in war he found it. The only way he could feel fulfilled was to make others suffer as did his father before him. He didn't like Jewish people but he didn't just say so or feel perhaps his dislike was his problem. Instead he murdered them in their millions and no doubt thought he was right in murdering every single one. He thought he was right in invading Poland etc. and he thought he was right in causing the deaths of so many innocent people, men, women and children. He thought he was right in torture, rape, beatings and starvation and no doubt, as I have said before, he thought he was right, right up until he pulled his own trigger to end his wretched life. I wonder how many of his followers and staff thought they were right all along too or how many of them actually thought what they were doing was wrong but were afraid to say so for fear of retribution?

No one would say every one of the 50+ million deaths during WW2 could possibly be personally blamed on Hitler but I find it absolutely incredible that they were all killed basically because of problems in one troubled man's mind. It also troubles me greatly that despite these 50 million terrible deaths we are all as a species so keen to do it all again. What is wrong with learning and why do we not do it?

For some reason the 1950s war in Korea fascinates me. Probably because it happened around the time I was born although it finished when I was just a five month old and I cannot therefore remember any of it. It probably fascinates me more though because of the sheer pointlessness of it all. Let me try to explain.

The Korean war 1950-1953 was a war between North Korea and South Korea. Korea was ruled by Japan from 1910 until the end of WW2. In 1945 Russia declared war on Japan and, by agreement with the US, occupied the Northern part of the country above the 38th Parallel. US forces then occupied the South and by 1948 two distinct governments had been formed, a communist government in the North and a right wing government in the South. This sounds all well and good but as with all humans they were not satisfied with their lot and each government laid claim to the whole of the country. This brought about a conflict of words which went on until it escalated sharply into open warfare when the forces of the North, aided by the Soviet Union and China invaded the South.

The forces of the South were overwhelmed and suffered huge casualties in the first couple of months of the conflict but then they were joined by twenty-one member countries of the United Nations and an amphibious counter attack was launched which cut off many of the Northern forces while others were forced back north. The whole of the North Korean forces were pushed back as far as the Yalu River which lies at the Korea China border and fearing the war spreading to their country the Chinese crossed the Yalu and fought with Russia in pushing the Southern forces back again into their part of the country. For the last two years of the war a stalemate ensued until on 27th July 1953 an armistice agreement was signed. The agreement set out the border between the two halves of the country almost exactly where it was before the fighting erupted so the whole thing was, as is all war, utterly futile. But what suffering did this futility bring?

US data shows that:

The United States suffered 33,686 battle deaths and 2,830 non battle deaths with another 8,176 said to be missing in action.

South Korea suffered 373,599 civilian deaths and 137,890 military deaths.

The PVA (People's Voluntary Army) suffered 400,000 deaths and 486,000 wounded.

The KPA (Korean People's Army) suffered 215,000 deaths and 303,000 wounded.

Recent studies say a total of 1.2 million people lost their lives during the conflict and all for nothing and have we learned a thing from it? Of course we haven't. Let's not be silly.

We have in recent years entered Afghanistan, have killed many innocent people and are now trying to leave. We rushed in without too much thought after the 9/11 bombings and did it without an exit strategy and now we have to leave with no clear resolution. It is said that Afghan troops and police will take over from us once we leave but do we actually have confidence in them achieving this? I don't think those doing the organising do believe it. I think they accept quietly in their own minds that the Taliban will take over again from where they left off when first pursued. I think their amazing laws and subjugation of women will again take over and all the thousands of lives lost and ruined during the war will be for nothing. Well nothing apart from man's love of war.

Gt Britain is currently building a pair of huge warships, weapons to go out and kill people, and how much are these ships costing? Only a mere six billion pounds. Six billion pounds? That's six thousand million pounds and we are all contributing greatly to the pot when many are struggling to pay simple things like gas and electric bills and buying school shoes for their children. In the world we have today we may well need these ships to defend us but in a real world with people actually thinking we could have saved that six billion pounds and put it towards good causes.

Talking of good causes, wherever I go and no matter what person I speak to I am endlessly hassled to give money to charity. I can't afford to give to everyone, and have in fact stopped giving to anyone. Not because I am a skinflint but because I am contributing a fortune already to bolster the government's war coffers. It is all so futile.

The twin towers of 9/11 were so futile too. Those responsible for the atrocity were, just like Mr Hitler, convinced in their own minds that what they were doing was the right thing to do completely. No doubt they cheered loudly as each tower fell but although they could justify it totally to themselves in no way could it have been the correct thing to do. Let's say their feelings towards the west were justified for some reason and they did have a grievance. In no way was that grievance the fault of any single one of the three thousand people who died on that day. Had any of the firemen, cleaners or office workers actually harmed anyone beforehand? In any war why is it the innocent that suffer? I liken this to bullying. Bullies always pick on the innocent.

Talking about the innocent, we all talk about war but what of the legacy of war. We fight and fight because that is what humans love to do but as I have said before so many totally innocent people get maimed and killed. This applies in wars but it also carries on long after the final shot has been fired. Landmines have been left everywhere with absolutely no regard which child later steps on it and either loses a leg or their lives. War is more important than children.

During the Vietnam War vast amounts of napalm were used to destroy everything it touched. Napalm is a mixture of petrol, or other fuel, which is mixed with a thickening agent. It sticks to whatever it touches and causes severe burns and was invented by human beings. We naturally think about napalm being used in the Vietnam War because that is where it was used most and where it received the most publicity but it was also used in previous wars. 32,000 tons were dropped during the Korean War and 16,500 tons were dropped on Japan but they say a total of almost 400,000 tons were dropped on Vietnam. It is difficult, painful and horrendous to even try to imagine the suffering caused both to combatants, civilians and also to other animals.

Another legacy of the Vietnam War is a chemical called 'Agent Orange'. To my mind the name actually sounds sinister and it is. Vietnam is a forested and jungle area and the 'great minds' at war thought if they could kill off the foliage then they would be able to see the enemy more clearly. Their thoughts were correct of course so they devised the chemical called Agent Orange which is a mixture of two herbicides. It was used at will, did its job and allowed more of the guerrilla enemy to be killed but even today, approximately forty years later we are still seeing its effects as many children are being born with highly serious defects and many of these end up in orphanages as their parents are very poor and cannot stop work to look after them. All this suffering has come about because 'intelligent' world leaders thought it would be a good idea. In much the same way as in sport these days it doesn't matter how we win as long as we do.

Every war has to be fuelled by people and people make the decisions on who to kill and when. The leaders of those countries give the go-ahead to shoot and bomb. All those leaders are supposed to be educated and many of them are supposed to be religious so how can these so called religious and educated people give the order to kill children? How can they justify this in their minds?

I think back to the 'shock and awe' of our invasion of Iraq and can still clearly see in my head the massive explosions in Bagdad. Huge weapons blasting innocent people. How in these leaders educated and religious minds did they justify it, knowing children and even babies would be killed maimed and torn to pieces? I know Saddam Hussein was not the nicest chap in the world and had not been for many years. Maybe he deserved being ousted from power but his ignorance and arrogance were not the fault of the people of his country were they? We rushed in there and aimlessly killed thousands because of his massive stock of weapons of mass destruction and how many did we find? Oh no, we didn't find any did we?

The Japanese treated their captives with almost unimaginable cruelty, men in Rwanda raped women with sticks, Nazis beat captives senseless and worse and other unspeakable atrocities have been mercilessly carried out by people from all manner of countries. How many of these perpetrators have actually enjoyed what they were doing? How many got a kick out of it all and why?

Why can't the leaders of warring countries just sit down in a room and talk things over? Perhaps there should be an independent adjudicator, a judge, who decides who is right and who is wrong. Wouldn't that be a terrific and simple idea? It would be a wonderful idea if we were not humans because being human our judge or adjudicator would always come down on the side of the party that gave him the biggest backhander. We do not talk and we do not listen and we do not play fairly. What is then left apart from war? As we shall see in the chapter 'The Wonder Of Future Dilemmas', in order to survive as a species we do have to start thinking and learning. There is no place left for war, just survival.

"Look at your young men fighting
Look at your women crying
Look at your young men dying
The way they've always done before"

From the song Civil War by Guns n Roses

9

The Wonder of Illness, Love and Loss

'The Greatest thing you'll ever learn is just to love and be loved in return'

From the film Moulin Rouge.

'We are born and we die but what lies in between? The only thing we can be sure of lying in between is the fact we will have to pay taxes.'

There are so many wars and so much hatred but what of love? We do have war films and we do have war songs but we do have a far greater number of films and songs based around love. Even many war films have a love theme running through them. In my chapter on war I listed the wars I could think of without too much hesitation. Let's do the same with love songs. Perhaps you could do the same before reading my list and then you could show me yours and I will show you mine as it were. Forgive me if I was a little crude then and forgive me if some of the song titles are not quite correct. Here we go.

Love is all around.

All you need is love.

Love lifts us up where we belong.

Part time lover.

When I fall in love.

I can't help falling in love with you.

The power of love.

When a man loves a woman.

Dream lover.

What's love got to do with it?

Loving you.

Endless love.

Silly love songs.

I want to know what love is.

It must be love.

I just called to say I love you.

I will always love you.

Have I told you lately that I love you?

This guy's in love with you.

Greatest love of all.

You've lost that loving feeling.

I make that 21 songs against 23 wars but I was careful to only include songs with the word 'love' in their title. If we count actual love songs without the word love in the title there would be far far more. So it seems we do love to love just as much as we love going to war. Why can't we just live with each other and love each other and forget war completely? We have a big enough fight just to preserve life and our planet and fight against illness without fighting each other as well.

If we think of illnesses the first one that will immediately come to mind is cancer, or the 'big C' as some call it. I think they find the word cancer hard to say but the 'big C' comes easier. I have not had cancer but I have witnessed it closely and very devastatingly personally so I do have a decent insight into it. I shall talk about it at length soon but first let's look into illness.

What is an illness?

Basically an illness is something that does nothing for us at all apart from make us feel rough. I jest but it is true.

One illness we have all suffered from is the common cold. We have all had so many colds that we are all experts in our own right.

The cold is a 'viral infectious disease of the upper respiratory tract which affects mainly the nose although it also affects the throat, the chest and even the eyes'. Cold symptoms are horrendous and we all get through boxes of tissues, packets of cough and throat sweets and plenty of paracetamol based tablets and powders but it isn't the actual cold virus which causes all the symptoms. It is our own bodies reacting to the virus and trying to rid us of it. Our bodies are doing their best but in doing so we have to suffer for a while. We are the same with food poisoning. Our bodies become infected and through diarrhoea and sickness we eject the infection. When I was on my third honeymoon I ate a large piece of infected chicken and boy did that give me the knowledge to talk about it? I was hungry, or greedy, and took the much larger of the two pieces offered. My wife had to make do with the smaller piece but at least hers was cooked through and therefore stayed down, or in. You know what I mean.

Getting back to the common cold, there are around 200 different cold viruses and you can only catch a cold once. Once you have had a cold you will never catch another one? That sounds great doesn't it but remember there are 200 versions of it so although you will never catch the same strain again there are still another 199 left floating around for you to suffer from. So that is an average of two to three colds per year for the whole of your life. If you are unlucky enough to get six colds in one year at least that means there will be fewer or even a cold free year later.

As I have said, the common cold is caused by a virus but what is a virus?

Viruses are obviously very common and can cause many diseases ranging from common and relatively harmless diseases such as the cold, flu, chicken pox, measles and cold sores right through to Ebola and AIDS.

They say viruses 'straddle' what we see as the definition of life. They contain some but not all of the structures that would be seen in what we class as organic life. One thing they lack is the ability to multiply which, if you think about it, raises a question. If they cannot multiply then how do they survive? What happens is they invade a 'host' cell and then force that cell to make thousands of copies of itself at an extraordinary rate. So this is what happens when we catch a cold, we breathe in a cold virus, it forces us to create copies of itself, we get ill and our nose produces loads of gunk in order to rid us of it.

A cold is 'common' as its name suggests and very rarely does it cause serious problems but it is still a bloody awful condition isn't it? It can lead to other complications such as pneumonia but even in its basic form it can cause sheer misery from days to weeks for both those suffering from it to those having to put up with the moaning individual who is suffering. Does everyone become a festering moan machine when they have a cold or is it just men? Or is it just me?

Last year I was boasting I had not been ill for some time and then caught an absolute belter of a cold on one of my first days of a walking holiday in the Yorkshire Dales. I climbed up Malham Cove with a stick in one hand and a handkerchief in the other.

This brings me to another thought. Catching a cold on a walking holiday is not exactly a drastic happening but if I look into it more closely I can see a connection and a possible reason for getting it. I am in my early sixties (very early I will add) and before I went on that holiday I had been felling trees and cutting them up for firewood. With this, work and other activities I was shattered. I remember my wife asking me if I felt well enough to go on holiday and inside, no I didn't. For my age and having suffered a heart attack a few years ago, I am quite fit but all I had done before getting infected had wiped me out. Was this why that cold virus had readily and easily been able to infect me? My system was down and vulnerable.

I also had a bout of Clostridium Difficile once and reading up about it I was amazed to see that the virus of this can lay dormant on a dry surface for up to three months without dying. I caught that too while my system was down due to yet another cold and sore throat.

In a while I shall talk about the love and loss of my second wife Chrissie but although I have no real belief in reincarnation I do sometimes think my Mags is Chrissie who has come back to haunt me. They are so much alike. They are both short and short-tempered. Sorry girls.

It is probably because of the loss of Chrissie that I have named this chapter 'The Wonder Of Illness, Love And Loss'. All three are inexplicably linked in my mind, so I am going to indulge myself and tell you Chrissie's story in the hope that you can either learn from it or relate to it. It is a story that may one day be told in its own book but I will try to do it justice here in a few paragraphs so that I can illustrate with feeling the title of this chapter.

I was a driving instructor in 1979 when I met Chrissie and she was a pupil. She lived just around the corner from me and she booked me for lessons. She did need to pass her driving test but she also did it because we had first met while taking our children to school and she liked me. She was obviously easily pleased.

My marriage was on the rocks which is, (unknowingly when I typed it) quite an apt phrase as two weeks after Chrissie began to take lessons I had sat on a rock at Prawle Point in Devon and decided my marriage could not carry on. I was at an extremely low point in my life when I returned home but found comfort in Chrissie's smile and also found solace in the fact she was in exactly the same situation. Before long we were a couple and after much of a struggle we were together. Without putting any blame on either my first wife or Chrissie these were hard times

180

and although I did love Chrissie things were not as rosy at first as I had dreamed they could be. My trouble is I am a very romantic person and wanted everything to be perfect but things were not. I could go into it all at length but I will jump forward a few years.

Firstly though, I never had a good relationship with my father but when he became ill at a relatively young age he realised he needed me and we did get along well in his last couple of years of life.

Chrissie was just the same. She was never a bad wife and perhaps I was more at fault than she was but in 1989 she developed rheumatoid arthritis which quite quickly took hold of her. As with my father she suddenly needed me and I remember her saying so, so passionately and eloquently as she sat on the edge of our bed clasping her painful hands together to try and get some relief from her affliction. From that moment forward we had the most beautiful relationship imaginable and luckily now with my Mags I have found the same.

Chrissie's arthritis progressed and she would lie on her sofa and I would spot her crying with the agony but was powerless to help. She was given a drug called Sulfasalazine to help with the pain but a nasty side effect of this was the fact it gave her the serious symptoms of meningitis which almost killed her. Things went along and progressed and then one day she lay in bed while I went to get us breakfast and when I returned she said worryingly that she had found a lump in her right breast. Despite the thought and realisation that it could have been anything simple, our lives fell apart there and then.

The lump was breast cancer and within a couple of weeks it had been removed. She had the operation and came home the next day to be away from the hospital and to be with me. This was a brave move but that completely summed the lady up. All through her illness and eventual death she was so brave and pragmatic.

For the next three years life went on with us spending most of our time either at doctors' surgeries or hospitals. My mother became seriously ill and this was a shock but another shock was about to hit us as well. We had a new car and Chrissie came home in it and said the brakes were faulty as she had almost failed to stop at some local traffic lights. She was a little annoyed when I doubted her by saying it was a new car and the breaks could not be faulty but she insisted I was wrong. When I took the car out to test the breaks they were, of course, perfect. This left us puzzled but then a couple of weeks later I was in my small workshop at the top of our garden when I heard her shout. She was hanging out a small amount of washing and had fallen over. Something was obviously wrong but we didn't at that time connect the past breast cancer to it.

I then had real problems. My mother was now dying and my wife was seriously ill. Two doctors came in to assess Chrissie and halfway through their assessment the telephone rang to say my mother had passed away. My head was all over the place and I still feel very guilty that I was almost relieved (no I was just plainly relieved really) that my mother had gone because that meant I could concentrate my mind and efforts on my wife. I took Chrissie to Addenbrookes in Cambridge the following Friday and was told she had multiple brain tumours and they hinted strongly that she was not going to survive. So my mother had died and my wife was diagnosed as being terminally ill both within two days. It was not the best week of my life.

I took Chrissie home and nursed her twenty-four hours a day for the next five months. She had been given the drug Dexamethasone to help with swelling in her brain but this ruined her pancreas. During those five months this nearly killed her more than once.

That woman was frightened, quite naturally but she quickly accepted her fate and became so strong she deserved a medal for gallantry. I remember lying beside her one night at about two am and realised she was awake and when I asked her if she was okay she said in a completely stoic and pragmatic way that she was fine and was, "just planning her funeral." I couldn't talk any more. I just cried my heart out but somehow kept it to myself. I could not let her hear me.

Soon I lost her completely but first I lost her as a wife. She had many moments when she was still completely compos mentis but she also had moments of talking gibberish as the condition took hold of her and this was distressing for all of us. Her deterioration hurt me just as it did her.

She died just five months after my mother and they both lie side by side in the graveyard.

Towards the end Chrissie lost the ability to even talk but one of my greatest memories in life is the fact that just an hour before her death she did manage to sum up the strength to look at me in a beautiful way and mouth the words, "I love you." These were her greatest and last words. They were by far the greatest words I never heard. For years she had been in my arms and that is where she ended her life. I could not save her but I did give her all the comfort and support that I could. I bless her completely.

I have taken a little breather here because even after all these years and after finding another superb wife the above words and happenings are still very poignant and they bring me both the memories and joy of a great lady but also they bring back to me the pain endured during those times. I have shed a few tears but have managed to put down my tissue now so I can carry on typing with a finger on each hand instead of just one.

Chrissie did plan her funeral that night and she did get every one of her wishes but why, at the age of just 45 did she have to die? She was young and of course many who die are even younger. It cannot be fair and it is certainly not due to some great god taking them for sunbeams or moonbeams is it? It is all to do with nature and evolution and cannot just be at the behest of someone's or something's wish or punishment.

Chrissie spent a few weeks in hospital when she was very poorly and she was visited by a religionist one day who sat at her bedside and told her, her a woman in great pain, torment, anguish and dying of cancer, that God would not test her any

183

more than he had to. Test her? Why would any god want to test her? I visited to find her extremely upset by this and when she told me what had happened I quickly left the ward in search of the woman responsible. Luckily I did not find her. I was an angry man and I didn't know exactly what I would have said to her. When I calmed down I just accepted her ignorance had been instilled in her mind by someone stupid and she was too stupid to think differently for herself. She is probably still saying the same thing to other poor half-dead individuals as you read.

Another lady in the hospital annoyed me as well although I ignored her because in her way she did mean well. She spoke well (I mean with a plum in her mouth) and when she saw Chrissie being wheeled into the X-ray department, obviously very ill and with no hair, she turned to me and in a very condescending and patronising way she said, "You have my deepest sympathy." She did sympathise. I could see that but 'deepest sympathy'? This is what you say 'after' someone has gone. What was on that hospital bed was riddled with cancer and was nearly dead and anyone could see it but what was on that bed was still my wife, a wonderful person who was still a loving and caring human being. I felt however my wife was and whatever she looked like it was her business and nothing to do with any toffee nosed woman who felt she had to stick her nose in. As I say though she did mean well and at the time I was angry with it all. Giving sympathy in such times is a kind reflection of your feelings but when doing so you have to be aware of just what you say and what the recipient is going through and is feeling.

One night I left the hospital with the usual dark demons in my mind and turned on the CD player in my car only to hear these words from a Rolling Stones song. They went, 'And I won't forget to put roses on your grave'. Those few words put everything in perspective.

My brother is not the most tactful of men to say the least. He visited Chrissie at home shortly before he was to go on holiday to Tenerife. It was a hot day and I asked him jokingly to bring me back a nice cool beer. He said he would but to my astonishment he went on to say to Chrissie it was no good thinking about bringing her back a gift as a keepsake. I was stunned and could not believe even my idiot of a brother could say such a thing but Chrissie's little face just beamed at him and with a huge laugh she called him something I dare not write here. This joke, bad taste or not, kept her smiling for the rest of the day.

Cancer is a terrible thing and no god would ever have invented it. If God was so clever to have made the world and everything in it then why would he have invented cancer?

I have read an article on the Interweb written by a religionist and in it the author tries to explain why God allows people to suffer from cancer. It reads something along these lines.

God did not create cancer. It is the result of people falling prey to an evil world. We live in an evil world and to understand why cancer has gripped you, you have to understand that world. You have to be shown the differences between right and wrong and believing in God is a must in order to survive.

The world is governed by Satan and he is a great deceiver and corruptor of the world. God has given us the Holy Spirit to guide us when we face uncertain times. God takes the pain of cancer and helps us live through it. He makes us an example of what God can do. Sometimes it is God's choice that we are healed and sometimes it is his choice that we die. All things work for the good when he is in control.

It goes on to say that God hates cancer and it is all the doing of Satan. God is ready to help us fight cancer even if that fight should eventually lead to death. God promises us he will reward us in heaven for the pain we have endured. It goes on to say if we all believe in God then cancer will go away.

So God did not create cancer. It was the work of the devil. How convenient! Where does it stop? It is said that God made all the animals. Did he make tapeworms, bot flies, malaria carrying mosquitos or plague carrying rats or were they all made by Satan? Of course they weren't. Tapeworms, bot flies, mosquitos and rats are all creatures that have evolved into what they are. They are animals just the same as me and you. We just do not see them that way. Cancer is not anyone's invention. It is a condition that has evolved alongside us.

As I said in an earlier chapter, God was supposed to have made the world from absolutely nothing. There was nothing existing so where did this Satan chap pop up from? God must have made him as well. So if Satan made evil and God made Satan then God made evil. Is it as simple as that?

It says in the article that cancer is the product of people falling prey to an evil world. I have known many people who have died of cancer and they were all good people who have harmed no one. How did they 'fall prey' to an evil world?

'God takes the pain of cancer' it says. What! In the article the author of this piece says she herself is actually suffering from cancer at the time. Is God taking her pain away?

Ultimately, although it says it is the fault of the devil when we get cancer it states that it is God's choice whether we live or die. How does he decide?

The article makes no sense but in writing about it I do feel greatly for the author and hope she has survived and thrived. Cancer is not caused by the devil and it is not the choice of any God whether we survive or not. It has evolved like the rest of us and is an utter monstrosity of an illness and no one should suffer from it. My heart sincerely goes out to this lady and her family. She may be misguided but she does not deserve cancer.

Of course people do not all just suffer and die from cancer although it is the single largest killer of humans. It is many years now since cancer research started and still we have made little progress. We still have to treat it in quite a barbaric way such as cutting out lumps, cutting out lymph nodes, performing mastectomies and using chemotherapy but things are improving all but slowly. One day another Eureka moment will happen and cancer will be sent to the recycling bin together with all the other diseases we have conquered.

There are many thousands of things we can die from and I am not even going to try and list them without hesitation because I could be here all night but it does amaze me that why, with so many things that could go wrong, are we even here and healthy at all?

Just thinking about myself I have had the following:

Cold.

Chicken pox.

Chest infection

Clostridium Difficile

Flu.

Measles.

German measles.

Norovirus.

Tonsillitis

Glandular fever.

Osteoarthritis.

Sickness and diarrhoea.

Hay fever.

Sciatica. (That was a pain in the bum)

Heart attack.

There may be more but I have fought them all off and am here to tell the tale. What gets me though is just how hard you have to work to be healthy. My mother died of diabetes and my father died of heart disease. She was 68 and he was 58. All I ever really inherited from them is a tendency towards both of these so I have to strictly live a life that keeps them at bay. I have to exercise, which is no bad thing but I also have to keep myself on a strict and healthy diet and weigh myself constantly. Death does not hold any fears for me at all but I do not want to go for a few years yet and I certainly do not want to go and leave behind those who love me and rely upon me. I could eat chocolate, cakes, takeaways and other unhealthy items all the time but I don't. I do eat them occasionally and when I do have them it is as a special treat. I could sit around all day but I choose not to because exercise keeps me slim and helps my heart.

There are so many people who do eat anything and everything and then sit around doing nothing. They just get fat, lazy and unhealthy. I have seen people puffing hard when all they are doing is walking slowly. It is a lifestyle choice and that choice is theirs. When you think about it what is the best thing to do? Do we struggle hard to follow a strict regime or do we die earlier because we have pleased ourselves? I have not chosen the latter, maybe because I have flirted with death through having a heart attack and have learned.

Before I had my heart attack I used to get very tired. I ate reasonably well and took some exercise but I also smoked three or four cigarettes each day. I am now six feet tall, just over thirteen stone, need far less sleep, am a total non-smoker and can walk fifteen miles without getting puffed in the slightest. I may still be the same person psychologically but physically there is no comparison to my pre heart attack days. It is not an easy lifestyle though, very rewarding but not easy.

I am a very caring person and I do really care and feel for all those concerned but something that fascinates me are the dilemmas in care and nursing. To some illnesses and incidents there is no real answer and that is what fascinates me. As an example I give the story of Michael Schumacher, a man who in his motor racing years I followed with fervour. He was a hard driver but his results reflected his brilliance behind the wheel. I never met him but admired him both as a driver and a person. He won the Formula 1 championship seven times and earned millions or even billions. He was a young, successful and very wealthy man when he fell during a skiing holiday and banged his head with such a force that it very nearly ended his life.

Now here lies the dilemma.

This great and lovely man is now (at the time of writing) lying in a hospital bed months later with only the briefest of interludes of consciousness. We do not know just how he is because nothing is being reported. For something to be reported it has so be sensational which his accident was but after the accident we have only been given slight and spasmodic information.

He is alive and we do have to cling onto that and of course his family love him dearly and want him back but in what state will they get him back and what would Michael himself want? I do not know what the outcome will be but will he be anywhere near the old Michael he was? Will he ever again be the same husband and father he was? Would Michael himself rather had not survived than be in some vegetative state?

The dilemma is huge and my heart goes out to him and his family. I sincerely hope he can regain some form of normal life and I hope he can be what his family had before the accident. I use Michael as an example because we all know him but there are many families throughout the world who are facing such similar dilemmas.

Michael Schumacher became greater than the sport itself and it has now changed forever. It had to change to try and beat him and it has changed so much that it is now, to my mind, almost laughable. I do hope Michael can survive in a better shape than the sport he did so much to shape in his hay-day.

I have seen medical programmes on television where a child has to be operated on to save their life. We can all see why the operation is necessary but the operation is sometimes certain to leave the child with brain damage. At what point do we say no. Can we say no? Is life so sacrosanct that we must save it at all costs? We can save a child's life but leave them without a life. How do we decide which path to take?

I lost my Chrissie and it was hard but from the moment she drew her last breath she was suffering no longer. When the doctors and specialists found her brain tumours they realised immediately they could never have operated upon them but what if they had come to me with the following dilemma?

"Your wife has three brain tumours and we can remove them and save her life. The trouble is there is no way in which we can possibly do it without leaving her without sight or speech. She will be in a wheelchair for the rest of her life and will be doubly incontinent. We can certainly save her life but in the event we will leave her breathing but without a life."

Do you know, I am glad she died as she did rather than me have to make such a choice. How can anyone make such a choice but some people do have to. With these dilemmas to handle it is no wonder doctors and surgeons earn such a good salary.

I watched a programme one night which featured an absolutely stunning little girl. She had intelligent and loving parents and also had a great lust for life but then cancer got hold of her. She went downhill fast but doctors thought there was a chance for her survival. They worked hard with her but had to pump her full of chemicals. Her pretty little face soon became bloated because of the drugs she had to take and then her beautiful character was gradually eaten away. It was heart-wrenching to see her suffer. The doctors worked hard and did everything they possibly could as she suffered but it was all to no avail. That beautiful little girl lost her battle and struggle for life and she passed away.

From this quick, emotional and devastating story we can only deduce that if there is a God he is totally unfeeling. Even if we foolishly believe that the devil causes cancer we have to accept that it was God who did not take away her suffering and it was God who chose to let her die. What so called great and merciful being could do that? Do we go to church and sing and praise at the top of our voices to someone who is capable of causing all this anguish? Why do we pray and believe? Is it just because we are afraid not to?

When we realised there was a 'New World' to the west of Europe we had to go, invade and take over their lives. There was land to be grabbed and money to be made so off we sailed. Of course we knew it would be better for the natives of these countries to be converted to Christianity, wouldn't it? Strange really when they had managed quite well without it for thousands of years.

We went out there with our 'we know better' policy and took Christianity to the 'heathens'. I'm sure they were far better off for it. We gave them Christianity but we also gave them smallpox, typhus, measles, cholera and whatever else. These were all illnesses they had no immunity to. When Cortez entered today's Mexico City in 1520 he found half the population infected with smallpox alone.

We cannot blame the invaders for all this as they simply did not understand disease and immunity as we do today. Half the population died but at least they died as Christians.

So we are all born, we pay our taxes and then we die. This is what life is all about but what else lies between is totally up to us. In my chapter 'The Wonder Of You' I shall expand greatly on what we should put in between and how it is up to us to fill the 'in between' with as much love and laughter as possible but in this chapter let me talk further on love.

Falling in love can be wonderful but falling out of love can be downright painful. Some people can give tons of love and others cannot. Some people fall in love at the drop of a hat and others do not fully understand what it is. Some people cannot fall in love at all because they know falling out of love can hurt so rather than get hurt they avoid it altogether.

Love is not finding a person you can live with,
It is finding a person you cannot live without.

This is a very romantic and true notion but as we have discussed sometimes we do lose the one we love and do have to live without the one we love. We lose someone and suffer the pain in doing so but ultimately we have to realise that life is for the living and we have to forge another life out of what is remaining. I have lost my parents, my wife and other people I know and have eventually bounced back but how do you bounce back when you lose a child? The answer is you do have to. Love can be great but it can also hurt badly. The good thing about it though is it doesn't matter how rich or clever or tall or short you are love is for everyone and it is completely and utterly free. Don't be afraid of it.

My mother did love us but she only found the strength to say it just a few days before she died and even when she did say it the words were hard to find and yet Lucy, my granddaughter, at just eight years old, tells me all the time. My granddaughter Phoebe does not just come out and say it but conveys it with things like a drawing or just a gorgeous smile. Love is love and I have thought that the love for one's wife is exactly the same as the love for one' granddaughter but it is also totally different. Having a wife or partner to love is special as this person should, in a true relationship, be the one person in life you can rely upon above all others and that person is there to listen to all your thoughts, concerns and worries ('a worry shared is a worry halved'). This person is truly the other half of you whereas a granddaughter's love (or that of any other child) is completely special because this person isn't there to listen to you or your troubles. They simply snuggle up to you because they totally love the person you are and trust you in every way to love them, care for them and protect them just for who they are. I melt completely when they do. Just recently I grabbed Lucy tightly and said "Granddad does love his Lucy." She looked me straight in the eyes and said, "And I really love you because you are a very special Granddad." Now that is reality and what more can anyone ever ask for or need?

I have heard some say that they do not need love and are quite happy living without it but are they? Is it just me who would be and have been lost without it? In the period between losing Chrissie and meeting Mags I was lost without it. To me it is the greatest thing in life and as I say it is free. To wake up in the morning beside a loving woman while the sun is shining and the birds are singing is, to me, what life is all about. The best things in life certainly are free.

'Love is finding someone you care for more than yourself'. From the film Starman.

We are born and then we die but what is death and what happens to us after it? It is amazing that some people can die of very little and yet others seem to have everything and still carry on. Some people die instantly and others linger for far too long. Any religionist would say that we die and go up to heaven. The bible says heaven is the space between the ground and the clouds so are we all there? If we are then we must be nothing because if you look up you don't see anyone. Even if your spirit does go to heaven we still have to dispose of the body. Even the most fervent of religionists would agree that our bodies don't go to heaven. They are disposed of usually either by burial or cremation and more often than not as part of a religious ceremony but let's be totally honest here and say they are not burned or buried because of any religious belief or tradition. They are all burned or buried because otherwise they would begin to rot, smell and disease would set in and spread. Any dead body does give off a horrendous odour.

Some funeral ceremonies are religious and some are humanist. Chrissie's was a humanist funeral which was important to her. The whole ceremony was totally about her and not about some god giving life and then taking it away. She even had her own special songs played instead of having everyone sing 'All things bright and beautiful' which seems to be played at every funeral, wedding and christening I have to go to.

Chrissie's songs were 'The first time ever I saw your face', 'Songbird' and the Iris Dement song 'There'll be laughter even after you're gone'. She had always planned to play this one at my funeral but it turned out to be the other way around.

'Songbird' was our song and 'The first time ever I saw your face' came from her making plans with me from the first time she ever saw my face. Bless her, she really was easily pleased.

So if we die is that it? How will we ever know? If there is nothing after life then we will know nothing and if there is something we will be gone and will never be able to tell anyone.

People do make a living out of talking to the dead and some are convincing. I must say that although I am hugely sceptical I do have to say the late medium Colin Fry did seem genuine and he did seem to give some people some comfort. Are there billions of dead people floating around the ether or was he a fake? He seemed too genuine to be a fake but if he was he did it very nicely indeed.

I have sat in on a couple of sessions with three other people. We had letters cut out and laid around the table and we all put our fingers on an upturned glass. I only did it for a laugh and found no fear in it whatsoever. It didn't frighten me but it did amaze me as some of the things that came up did actually happen to be true. I would like to dismiss it all as a complete load of rubbish but I can't because I have seen some proof.

But what are mediums like Colin Fry tapping into? Is it the thoughts of long lost dead people or is it a kind of library of the past. I once read about something which someone had called Anima Mundi which the theorist said is the history of everything that has ever happened in the world. It has happened and is therefore there to be tapped into. As I say, it is a kind of library or Interweb. Is there something after death? Is there such a thing as a library of everything? I don't know but my mind is open. As with religion please prove it to me and I shall believe.

What about if we all do go to heaven (or hell) and meet up again? I could eventually be surrounded by all my wives and my father would still be there moaning because I had not lead my life exactly as he would have done. I could even meet some of my old teachers who would have to admit I haven't tuned out too badly after all.

And what of ghosts? Many say they have seen them but what gets me is why are they all Victorian? As with other 'life after death' I have no real belief in ghosts but if there are such things I would love to see one. Everyone seems so frightened of ghosts but why? If they do exist then they are only the remnants of people who are dead. Why should they be harmful or frightening? I remember a cousin of mine losing his father when he was only a teenager. He wanted to see his father but was frightened. His father's doctor was there and I remember him putting his hand on my cousin's shoulder and saying, "He didn't harm you when he was alive so he certainly will not harm you now he is dead." His words were true. Why should someone who has died suddenly turn into some kind of horror story.

Are ghosts real or are they just figments of someone's imagination? Are ghosts likely to appear in certain places or are certain places likely to instil ghostly thoughts? If a house is old and old fashioned you may feel it ghostly but if that same house is completely modernised would the same feeling still prevail? A bunch of us stayed in a house in Keswick once and all the women were scared stiff. The men, however, felt fine. Was it because we were men and were stronger or was it because we lacked enough imagination to feel the ghosties? One of our party said she looked in the mirror in her bedroom and saw someone looking back at her. I've done that several times but the person I have always seen looking back at me was me.

We have laughed about it several times since but one thing was unexplainable. Our Lucy was there and was only a toddler at the time. She had taken her blow-up princess bed with her to sleep on but halfway through the holiday she refused to use it. She loved that simple little bed but even when we returned home she would have nothing to do with it. That did make me wonder.

There are several things we do not understand. Do people really converse with the dead? Are there ghosts? What about the time I was driving along and I knew for certain I was going to come across a fatal accident and five miles later I did and how did one of my dogs years ago used to know when I was about ten minutes from home? Evidently he would start to get excited and wait at the door. I certainly do not understand but I do keep an open mind.

We can choose to be in love but we cannot chose when we are born or when we die. The best we can do and what we must do is thoroughly enjoy that bit in between.

1 0
The Wonder of Drugs

I had thought of including the topic of drugs within another chapter but as I began to think about the subject thoughts seemed to come to me from such wide angles and on such varied matters that I quickly realised the subject was vast and I had to devote a whole chapter to it.

When we talk about drugs we have to consider such a wide range. They go from 'over-the-counter' drugs to help ease a cold and those which help with things like hay fever, sore eyes or constipation through to prescribed drugs such as antibiotics, steroids and anti-inflammatory pills and creams and then on to tobacco and alcohol and through to illegal drugs such as amphetamines, cannabis and heroine. We may take an Aspirin for a headache or rub on some cream for a sore back or we might be of a mind to take an 'upper' or a 'downer' or maybe even something which will knock us sideways but they are all drugs. Let's take a while to look at their history.

Someone once asked me how people knew what to take to heal themselves in the days of prehistory. Just like us and everything else it all evolved.

In the early days of human civilisation medicine relied largely upon people such as witchdoctors and shaman and in some societies today this is still the case. I know that in places like Haiti these things are still widely practised. In many cases these people would go into a trance and try to drive evil spirits out of patient's bodies. I have even seen a chicken being sacrificed and its entrails pulled out. The shaman or witchdoctor would then study the entrails to see what is wrong with the person they are treating. It is much the same as reading tea leaves really but in either case I would not hold out too much hope for success.

Trepanning is a practise that amuses me in an ironic way. This is the practise of drilling a hole into someone's head to let the devil out. That little rascal gets everywhere doesn't he? This procedure was carried out as long ago as Neolithic times and the hole drilled was up to 50mm or 2 inches in diameter. Can you imagine the pain and trauma inflicted and for no good scientific reason as we have to remember this was done thousands of years before the invention of any anaesthesia.

The evolution of drugs came about by pure chance and word of mouth just as everything else has done since. We'll use another little story to illustrate it.

Yug was an early human who woke up very early one morning feeling rather rough after eating a piece of mammoth steak the night before which had been hanging around in the pantry a bit too long. His wife had told him not to eat it but Yug was hungry and the only other thing sitting in the larder was a few berries. He was a man and a meat eater so, despite his wife's sound advice he tucked into the mammoth rib-eye and by bedtime he had completely sated himself and settled down for the night. His stomach rumbled for a few hours and the family cave began to smell none too sweet until Yug finally had to get up quickly and ran out to the communal latrine. This went on for hour after hour but whilst spending a few painful and uncomfortable minutes there on one occasion for some reason he picked at the leaves of a plant and ate them. To his surprise he soon began feeling better and could only put this down to the plant leaves he had been nibbling so when his fellow cave dwellers awoke he told them of his good fortune and henceforth they had a cure for the disease they named 'mouldy mammoth middle'.

As you might have guessed this story is not wholly true but is was how medicines first evolved and the same went for food. It is how early humans knew which foods were good and which were bad. If you were a Neolithic human and someone told you not to eat a certain type of mushroom because their mother had eaten one and had died a horrible death then you would certainly think twice about eating one yourself wouldn't you?

Someone once told me that boiling nettles and then drinking the infused liquid as a kind of tea was a great cure for arthritis and they were right. I drank the liquid several times and it did help my joints but the problem was that it had side effects and the worst one was it affected my lungs and I developed a cough which was quite severe. Thinking about it logically though perhaps the nettles didn't help my arthritis at all, maybe it was just the cough being so bad that it took my mind off the pain.

Today we have literally thousands of drugs to treat thousands of ailments and I thought I would talk about the one which is probably the most commonly used, Aspirin. Like all other drugs the Aspirin does have side effects but it is a tablet used very successfully by many people for a variety of conditions. Some use it for headaches, and period pains while I and many others use it for keeping our blood thin to help our heart.

The active ingredient of the Aspirin is taken from the bark of the willow tree so if our Yug had been suffering from a headache and had chewed some willow bark he may have invented the Aspirin rather than Imodium. The use of willow tree bark was actually discovered by Edward Stone from Wadham College, Oxford in 1763 but Aspirin was not synthesised until 1897. Most of us have relied on Aspirin for one ailment or other and it is said that there are up to 40,000 tons being taken every year. Not by the same person I would add as this would make for quite some hypochondriac.

Antibiotics are another very widely used type of drug. They work by either killing or inhibiting the growth of microorganisms. The term 'antibiotic' was first used in 1942 although the discovery of Penicillin was attributed to Sir Alexander Fleming in 1928. Penicillin is the name given to a group of antibiotics derived from a fungi called Penicillium.

Penicillin antibiotics were the first drugs to be successful in the treatment of illnesses such as infections caused by staphylococci and streptococci. Staphylococci species are mostly harmless and some reside on the skin of humans and other animals while others live in soil. Some staphylococcus toxins though can be relatively to considerably harmful and can cause food poisoning, boils, skin abscesses, septicaemia, or endocarditis which is an infection of the lining of the heart.

Streptococcus A is a bacteria which can cause sore throats, scarlet fever, impetigo and cellulitis while Streptococcus B can cause blood infections, pneumonia and meningitis in new born babies and urinary tract infections, blood and skin infections and pneumonia in adults.

As you can see, both of these can be quite nasty but both have been treated for some time with antibiotics. In recent years though a problem has developed in as much as some bacteria are evolving to become resistant to antibiotics, hence the appearance of MRSA or Methicillin-Resistant Staphylococcus Aureus which is a bacterial infection causing havoc in our hospitals today. The fight against it is being fought hard and with some success but it can be devastating.

Staphylococcus Aureus is a common type of bacteria and is often carried on the skin or in a person's nose or throat. In this state it is harmless enough but if it manages to enter a wound or break in the skin it can cause life-threatening infections, hence the spread of it in hospitals.

As I have said before most drugs used to treat illnesses do have certain side effects. I was told by my GP that it may be possible for me to be given the drug Metformin which would stop me developing diabetes which was what my mother died of. I was told to reduce my weight and exercise well and if I did perhaps the Metformin would not be needed.

It all sounded good and I knew, one way or another, that I should not suffer as my mother had done. If I lost weight I probably wouldn't need the tablets but if I didn't lose weight I could rely on the tablets to do the job for me. 'Everyone was a winner' until I looked on the dear old Interweb to see if Metformin had any side effects. Below is what I saw.

'Metformin side effects':

Disturbance to the gut

Nausea

Vomiting

Diarrhoea

Abdominal pain

Loss of appetite (That would have helped with the weight loss)

Taste disturbance with usually a metallic taste in the mouth

Elevated levels of lactic acid in the blood (Lactic acidosis)

Decreased absorption of vitamin B12

Skin reactions such as rash, itching and flushing

It then goes on to say if you want to find out more about side effects, you should talk to your GP. I didn't want to find out more. What I found on the Interweb was enough for me. I just decided to diet hard and exercise vigorously and luckily enough it is having the desired effect so far and the Metformin can stay on the shelf.

We have talked about legal drugs which can either be bought over the counter or can be obtained from a GP on prescription by what of other legal drugs? I mean alcohol and tobacco. These are drugs which none of us need but how many of us have never indulged in taking them? I know I have and still do to a certain extent. I am not a smoker these days but I do enjoy a glass or three of wine after a hectic week or a bottle of cool beer on a hot day.

Alcohol and nicotine are legal drugs because in moderation they do relatively little harm. I don't suppose two or three units of alcohol each week is going to kill you and I suppose the same may be said for two or three cigarettes in the same space of time but it is when these drugs are taken in excess that the problems start.

Drink and smoking are both things that are there for us to enjoy. I have indulged in both and have certainly enjoyed both but as I said in my previous chapter it has to be us ourselves who dictate how much we smoke or drink and it has to be us ourselves who need to say when enough is enough and they are starting to harm us as both of these drugs can and do cause serious harm and eventually death to those who do not keep their indulgences in moderation.

Just imagine the damage you are doing to your own body by inhaling the smoke from ten, twenty or even more cigarettes each day. It cannot possibly do anything to you other than cause harm. And what about the price of the things? I was asked to get some for someone who could not get to the shops himself and was astonished by the cost. They were over £7 for a packet of twenty. I remember years ago a friend and I saved up to buy five Woodbine cigarettes just to try them. We were about seven then and they cost us ten and a half old pence which is today's currency relates to approximately 4p. Even then they were a waste of money because I took one puff, inhaled it and almost coughed my heart up.

The trouble with nicotine is it is very addictive and, believe me, it does get you hooked. I have not smoked anything for about seven years and yet I must admit the urge is still there. The thought of what cigarette smoke is doing to you inside your lungs makes me sure I will never smoke again but it does not take that urge away.

Just what is cigarette smoke doing to you? Let's see with another list.

It robs you of some of your good cholesterol.

It raises your blood pressure.

It damages your circulatory system and increases the threat of blood clots.

It impedes good breathing and therefore also impedes exercise.

It causes a build-up of fatty substances within the arteries.

It heightens the risk of strokes.

It curses chronic obstructive pulmonary disease.

It causes cancer, emphysema, tuberculosis, bronchitis, asthma and pneumonia.

It can also affect your sexual organs causing erectile problems and can lead to infertility.

Women who smoke during pregnancy are more likely to miscarry, have a baby with a low birth weight or have a premature or still born baby.

Babies with smoking parents can be more likely to succumb to sudden infant death syndrome.

The stomach and kidneys of a smoker do not perform well.

To cause all these problems it is obvious that cigarettes must contain a few harmful chemicals so I have looked the matter up on the Interweb again and to be honest I am shocked. I am shocked by the sheer amount of harmful chemicals and I am also shocked that with these present I ever smoked one. I feel another list coming on.

Cancer Research UK lists the following.

More than 70 cancer causing chemicals including:

Tar (A mixture of dangerous chemicals)

Arsenic (Used in wood preservatives)

Benzene (An industrial solvent derived from oil)

Cadmium (Used in batteries)

Formaldehyde (Used in mortuaries and paint manufacturing)

Polonium-210 (A highly radioactive element)

Chromium (Use to manufacture dye, paints and alloys)

1,3 Butadiene (Used in rubber manufacturing)

Polycyclic Aromatic hydrocarbons (A group of dangerous DNA-damaging chemicals)

Nitrosamines (Another group of DNA-damaging chemicals)

Acrolein (Formerly used as a chemical weapon)

Other poisons in cigarette smoke include:

Hydrogen cyanide (Used as an industrial pesticide)

Carbon Monoxide (Found in car exhausts and used in chemicals manufacturing)

Nitrogen Oxides (A major component of smog)

Ammonia (Used to make fertilisers and explosives)

Thinking about this in any realistic way is terrifying! So why do we smoke at all? It seems it is as futile as going to war but we do it. We do it because, as with war, we love it, are addicted to it and do not have the discipline to stop.

I have been with a group of people at a wedding and have seen them being desperate to reach the church so they could light up. They were then desperate to get out of the church, desperate to reach the reception venue and then desperate to finish their meal just so they could do the same thing again. They may have enjoyed the wedding but their enjoyment was over dominated by their addiction to fags.

I know giving the things up is difficult but more are doing it and I say well done them but if you are a smoker be realistic, look at the cost to both your body and your pocket and then join the 'give up gang'. It has to be done because every time you light up a cigarette all you are doing is killing yourself and that is the simple and realistic fact.

It has been said by some in the know that a small amount of alcohol can actually be good for you and I do hope so because I do enjoy it in small amounts. A glass of Shiraz with a meal can be wonderful and having a quiet drink with friends can be very enjoyable and entertaining but the tendency lately has been for people to binge drink to such an extent that they make themselves ill, stupid or violent or all three.

The big question I have always asked myself is this. "How would I feel if all alcohol was banned?"

Luckily I can easily answer the question with the totally true statement that "I wouldn't give a damn".

The trouble is that for many they could not possibly answer with the same statement. They are then caught in the horrible state of being an alcoholic. This is somewhere I have never been but I do know people who either have been there or are still there today and believe me, from what I have witnessed, it is not a great place to be. We know that smoking ruins your body and your life so does alcohol do the same thing? Of course it does. Let's make yet another list.

Alcohol causes:

An increased risk of cancer of the throat, oesophagus and or larynx

Breast cancer in women

Strokes

Heart disease or an irregular heartbeat

High blood pressure

Liver disease such as cirrhosis and liver cancer

Pancreatitis

Infertility

Again, why do people do it when all they are doing is ruining their lives?

Obviously the need for drink is great and history tells us so with what happened in the 1920s in the US. Alcohol was banned and all this did was create a huge underground trade in which illicit alcohol was made and illegal drinking joints popped up. Instead of the trade being run by breweries and the government it became run by gangs who went to war with each other and the authorities and many lives were lost.

It is easy to say no one needs to drink heavily when the person saying it is living a good life without worries and strife but I know not everyone has this luxury but drinking will never solve anyone's problems. It will only mask them for a short while and the drinking will only add to those problems eventually and make life even worse. I'm afraid if anyone has problems in moderating their intake of alcohol they simply (or not simply) have to give up completely. Despite help being available, in the end it has to be our problem and the solution has to be in our own hands. There may be genies in lamps in pantomimes but you'll never find one at the bottom of a glass.

Addiction to legal drugs is bad enough but what of the addiction to illegal ones?

In my experience the 'drug scene' exploded in the 1960s but drugs were being taken long before this. As with trepanning, it is known that Neolithic people used to take opium and they lived thousands of years ago. I have had to study and research the drug problem and what illicit drugs people take because although I was a child of the 1960s and have seen the problem of drugs go on into the next and then the next generation I have never really seen illegal drugs and have certainly not taken any of them. If you don't mind I shall stick to the theory side of research rather than do the practical bit.

In the mid-1800s Europe was importing a vast amount of goods from China but the market for western goods in China was virtually non-existent due to Chinese self-sufficiency and the access to China's interior being denied to foreigners. The Chinese emperor also banned the importation of most European goods anyway which left gold and silver as the only available payment. This caused a shortage of silver in the west but a way round this was sourced when we found something the Chinese really did like and that commodity was opium. As we know opium is highly addictive and this did not go un-noticed by successive emperors and the trade was banned but it carried on with smuggling becoming rampant.

Chinese officials made an attempt to hinder the opium supply by confiscating 20,000 barrels of opium which upset the British who decided to use military force to redress the situation.

There were two opium wars, 1839-42 (20,000 casualties – one for each barrel confiscated) and 1856-60 (50,000 casualties). As this book illustrates, we will go to war over anything.

People 'do' drugs to try and escape from reality but I'm afraid reality and the Wonderment around us is all there is. Anyone who tries to search for anything else is only heading for trouble.

Forgive me if I mention this again later but is a totally true and important statement.

The 1960s saw a great leap for freedom. The world was fed up with the legacy of the Second World War and it seemed they suddenly realised the need not to live, dress and think as they had done in the 40s and 50s. We all rebelled and out went the 'short back and sides' haircut and in came long hair. Out went hobnail boots and in came winkle-pickers. Out went browns and greys and in came flowery patterns and tie-dyes and out went Glen Miller and Vera Lynn and in came the Beatles, The Stones and psychedelic rock. We had seen the Teddy Boys who were probably the first group to be seen to rebel and then these were followed by the Mods and Rockers and Hippies. 'Flower Power' and 'Free Love' emerged but I didn't find too much of that.

Young people escaped the drabness of the times but to them this was not enough. They also wanted to escape life and reality so they took drugs to 'enhance' their lives. No lives are ever truly enhanced by taking drugs though but did they care? They became 'high' or 'spaced out' and to them the world was great although, in true reality, they were only kidding themselves.

Back then it was all seen as a bit of a joke. Hippies stood out a mile and people would treat them with a light contempt. Everyone knew the lives they were leading and as they were not hurting anyone else they were largely left to get on with it. It all seemed a little silly and futile but it was only the few who were indulging. Pop stars were doing it and others followed them. The authorities saw it as being serious and as the habit began to spread we all had to adopt the same viewpoint.

The drugs issue has gone from the small scale it was in my younger days to being a massive problem today. It is no longer a silly habit of the few but is a rampant and vile parasitic habit which is feeding off so many. The authorities fought against drugs in the 1960s and lost. They are fighting ferociously, tooth and claw, against them today with exactly the same outcome.

"Difficult as it may be to face one's problems, the consequences of drug use are always worse than the problems one is trying to solve with them".

Quote from the website of 'Foundation For A Drug-Free World'.

The above quote is simple and succinct and yet it says it all. So why do people take drugs when it doesn't take too much of a brain to figure out that in the scheme of things they can only ever bring pain and problems?

Let's do another list.

People 'do' drugs because:

Peer pressure

The need to fit in

Curiosity and the desire for experimentation

Depression

The need to escape from life and reality

The need to rebel against life or society

To relieve boredom

To seem cool and grown up

To mask abuse

Maybe we can illustrate this with yet another story.

Donald is approaching the age of sixteen years and was born into quite a large and poor family. His upbringing has always been on the same huge social housing estate in a large city. His family consists of his father who has always been in and out of prison, his mother who, in recent years, has become an alcoholic and his two brothers and three sisters. Donald is the second oldest and does try his hardest for the family when his father is not there and his mother is incapable. He feels for his family and although he tries hard, his attempts never seem to bring any great rewards. His family is living on social benefits and much of this is spent on alcohol and tobacco.

Donald is, as with all children, supposed to attend school on a daily basis but the pressures of his family life often mean more to him and he stays at home with his mother not being bothered either way whether he is at school or not. At first he misses school out of necessity but the necessity soon begins to become a habit and he leaves home in the mornings and loafs around with a few friends who have fallen into the same routine.

They meet in a disused shed on what was once an allotment plot but has been left to revert back to nature. In the shed they are away from the realities of life and here they do manage to laugh. His friends laugh even more when one of them brings out a couple of cigarettes which are laced with cannabis. They light them up and pressure Donald into trying it. He doesn't take too much coercing and puffs keenly. Soon he feels better about life and his laughter becomes strong. At last he is feeling good.

As the days go by Donald and his friends meet up regularly but his friends soon question why Donald is doing his share of the smoking but is not contributing to the pot.

Donald realises what they are saying is true and does something about it. He has no money and no prospect of getting any in any legal way but does find ways illegally. He begins to shoplift and is surprised just how easy it is.

With his new found wealth the cannabis is plentiful but he then begins to wonder just what else he can try. Maybe there are things out there which can give him an even greater high. One of his friends said he could get some cocaine so they all eagerly club together and buy some. It had the desired effect but, as with the cannabis, they felt they needed to experiment further so the next step was heroine.

By now Donald had changed as a person. The young lad who had before devoted so much time and love to his family became withdrawn from them and the only family he felt he needed were his friends and his brothers Cocaine and Heroin. While he is on his heroin he feels intense pleasure and therefore escapes totally from his normal life but he has to try his hardest to put aside the other effects such as a dry mouth, his loss of appetite, his weight loss, nausea and vomiting, slurred speech and drowsiness. He is totally addicted, his health is suffering and he is having to commit more and more crime to feed his habit. A habit which is becoming worse and worse because as he takes more drugs his state of health decreases. He feels bad with all the drug's side effects and he knows the best way to escape these feelings is to take more drugs and the whole thing becomes self-perpetuating.

Soon his habit is so bad he starts to fall asleep anywhere and everywhere, his nausea and vomiting become worse, he feels an almost constant need to urinate but finds it very difficult to do so, he begins to feel cold all the time and his mind cannot concentrate on anything. He was using so much that his friends could not keep up with him and he often went to the shed by himself to get his fix.

It all took time but eventually Donald was using so much heroin that he either came across a bad batch or his body could no longer take the abuse he was giving it and he passed away, aged nineteen, alone in that small tattered allotment shed with only spiders, earwigs and woodlice as witnesses.

Sad isn't it and of course I have made the story up. It is a story but it is also completely true to life. It is what happens these days. Donald was not a Hippie who took a couple of pills just to enhance his 'free love'. He was basically a kind hearted person who was born into a hard and harsh life. It was a life where drugs were the only means of escape. He was approaching adulthood but what prospects were there for his future? He felt there were none. All he could see was the life his mother and father were leading and who would wish that upon themselves?

In no way was he going to go to Oxbridge, or become a judge, accountant or politician. He even felt in no way was he even going to be able to secure a job which was going to make it worthwhile leaving home. Most of the work in his area paid so little that it was not worth leaving home to do it. Many jobs just paid the minimum wage or even less so he could understand why so many whole families stayed unemployed through choice. Why work when you can get paid virtually the same amount of money by staying at home? It all made sense and yet it all made no sense as well.

Donald saw drugs as his means of escape and to a certain extent his plan worked but no drugs just bring euphoria. They all, even prescription ones, have side effects and Donald's side effects eventually brought him death. In the end I suppose he did manage to escape. He managed it totally and forever and the saddest thing is there would have been very few who would have missed him to any great extent.

This is so often the way these days as the drug scene bites harder and harder. Donald's story is only made up but I feel sad for him because his story is indicative of so many today.

Here we will get away from Donald's tragic story and will explore other drugs that have become so popular with today's population.

Cannabis.

We mention cannabis in Donald's story but only briefly so I want to look at it here in more detail. If you ask someone if they have ever used drugs the first one they will always own up to is cannabis. I call it cannabis but it is also known as weed, pot, ganja, grass, skunk, hashish, hash oil, reef, bang, herb, gangster or boom. I must admit I have had to look many of these up as I had little idea there were so many names.

There are so many names but it is still the same plant, the same drug and it does the same things to you. Smoking cannabis can make you relaxed, chilled and very happy. It can give you the giggles and make you talkative. It can bring on hunger pangs and it can also heighten the user's senses.

Looking at it all quickly it all looks fun and innocuous and the effects seem very similar to those of alcohol but as with all drugs, as we have said, there must be side effects, otherwise we would all be using them. Cannabis can cause paranoia, panicking and anxiousness. It can affect your concentration and can also cause a higher heart beat which can lead to high blood pressure. It is said that it can also lower a male's sperm count and therefore lead to infertility.

As with drinking alcohol, cannabis does have its effects and some of those effects can be joyful but its side effects certainly make it something to avoid.

Cocaine.

I find this drug curious to say the least. In Donald's story we saw why he became addicted to drugs and his plight was quite obvious and understandable. In the long run it caused his death but we could see just what took him along his chosen path. Cocaine (or White Lady) is not just a drug used in some abandoned allotment shed. It is actually fashionable among the rich and famous and so-called celebrities. Those that seem to have everything still 'do' drugs which, in reality, shows that fame and fortune do not always bring happiness and contentment. Nobody can truthfully say, "Look at me. I am rich so I can afford to buy and take the best drugs possible."

The only reason they are snorting cocaine is because, to some extent, their lives are blighted just like Donald's. They seemingly have everything but they are still trying desperately to escape from reality and we must remember that, in the end, reality is all we have.

Cocaine too has its effects and side effects.

It causes a short term high. This high is quite intense but then it is quickly followed by the opposite, an intense low which brings with it depression and edginess. It isn't hard to see here that the low following such a high only serves to make the user wish for more of the drugs in order to get back to that high. The drug affects the brain and leads to a greater and greater need for more and, again, the user becomes an addict.

All drugs are a poison of some kind and cocaine is no different. It can make the user hostile towards others and it can cause paranoia, anger and anxiousness. If regularly taken, as it mostly is because of its addictiveness, it can also cause sleep deprivation, loss of appetite and then on to cardiac problems, seizures, respiratory failure and sudden death. It has been widely publicised that cocaine can ruin your sense of smell and even physically ruin your nose completely.

Methadone.

In Donald's story we explored the effects of heroin. Donald did not survive but many heroin addicts do and if they can own up to their addiction they can be helped by being given methadone. It is very similar to heroin and can be prescribed. It lasts longer in the body and can be a great help in quitting the use of heroin as it helps greatly to reduce any withdrawal symptoms. There are no quick fixes to coming off heroin but methadone certainly helps although it is still no easy answer but it does help you feel better about yourself and can help you get away from the drugs scene that caused the problem in the first place.

Amphetamines/Speed. (Billy, Whiz or Phet)

Legally, amphetamines are used to treat narcolepsy and ADHD (Attention Deficit Hyperactivity Disorder) but illegally if they are taken they can 'screw up your head'.

'Speed' comes usually as a white powder which the user either swallows, snorts or injects. It all sounds to me just as futile as it really is.

About half an hour after being taken it starts to make you feel really awake, bright, chatty and euphoric but you will suffer a loss of appetite, will feel warm and will develop sweaty palms. As I have said it can screw up your head and can also make heart attacks more likely as well as bring on epileptic fits and bad mood swings.

Magic Mushrooms. (Shrooms, Mushies or Magics)

Magic mushrooms or psilocybin mushrooms contain the psychedelic drugs psilocybin and psilocin. They are one of the most commonly used 'recreational' drugs as they can either be found growing in the wild or can be cultivated relatively easily and with little outlay. They are so commonly found that it is said about 10% of the whole of the US adult population has tried them.

I am going to group magic mushrooms together with LSD as their effects and side effects are quite similar. Both are psychotropic drugs and both act on the central nervous system and both send the user on 'trips' although the magic mushroom is milder and its 'trips' are shorter. Both of these drugs distort in the mind the perception of actual objects. I have been told that the user sees his/her worst fears but those fears are magnified while their feelings and emotions are intensified. The whole being of the user is changed and time can speed up, slow down or even stop. Someone once said he had put magic mushrooms in his tea and the next thing he knew was he thought he was God.

Magic mushrooms are not generally considered as being addictive but they can cause the usual symptoms of nausea and loss of appetite as well as causing dizziness, muscle weakness, stomach problems and numbness.

I know I am a boring old codger and neither would I ever try any drug or recommend the use of any. This one though (taking away its side-effects) does seem fun. Don't do it though! It is not worth it!

Ketamine.

Ketamine is a tranquiliser used in veterinary medicine and can be used on animals as big as horses so why do people use it? They do so to get an out-of-body experience which makes your mind feel detached from your body and reality. It can be injected, snorted or swallowed and makes you feel floaty and dreamy while larger doses can give you hallucinations. The user can feel he/she has left this world for another and can lose the concept of life completely. They can truly feel they have become supernatural beings.

What a place to be in but what of the consequences?

Ketamine can cause blackouts or even if you are not totally blacked out you can lose the ability to walk, talk or feel totally awake. Because ketamine is a tranquiliser you could severely hurt yourself and not know.

This drug causes bladder problems, abscesses, blood clots and even serious mental health problems.

Crystal Meth.

This is an extremely powerful form of Speed and its effects can last for up to 12 hours. It comes in the form of small crystals and is highly addictive. The reason for taking it is because it gives a 'rush' but on the flip side of this is the fact that its comedown effect will leave you feeling totally flat and washed out and the more of the drug you take the more flat and washed out you feel. The side effects are much the same as for Speed and Cocaine.

Mephedrone. (Meow Meow, M-Cat, Drone or Bubbles)

This is a powerful stimulant and belongs to a group of drugs that include Amphetamine, Methamphetamine and Ecstasy. Again, it can be swallowed, snorted or injected. When used it brings on feelings of euphoria, alertness and affection toward others as well as a feeling of heightened sexuality and restlessness. The problem is it can overstimulate your heart, your circulation and your nervous system. It was classed as a 'legal high' until 2010 when it was then made illegal. Other side effects include headaches, heart palpitations, nausea and blue or cold fingers.

Ecstasy (E, XTC, X, Adam, Roll, A or 007)

Ecstasy is a stimulant drug which can cause hallucinations. It is seen as almost being 'fashionable' by youngsters who go to clubs or raves. Because it is a stimulant it does help people to keep going while dancing the night away but youngsters are impressionable and while they are dancing and 'looking cool' they are also damaging themselves. This drug has been the cause of many people ending up in hospital and even some ending up at the funeral directors.

Ecstasy can cause a dry mouth, blurred vision, chills, sweating, nausea, anxiousness, paranoia and confusion. It can also cause direct damage to brain cells and we must be mindful of the fact that the vast majority of those who take ecstasy are young people who need those brain cells in order to develop into adults who can cope with what can become a trying adulthood even if all a person's brain cells are present.

Glue Sniffing or Solvent Abuse.

I have been into hardware stores to buy glue but there is none to be seen. It is all on shelves behind the counter because, "So much of it has been stolen by Glue Sniffers," I have been told. I think we have all had an inadvertent sniff of glue and it does make you feel weird but why sniff the stuff on purpose? I have seen youngsters on television with glue in a plastic bag and they are breathing in and out of it. They are getting no air in their lungs at all only noxious fumes from the glue. It isn't hard to see they are damaging themselves but what exactly is happening?

I say 'Glue Sniffing' but in this section we will also include gasses and aerosols as they are all quite similar in as much as they all contain volatile substances and it is these which, when breathed in, give the user a certain 'high'. They can make you feel euphoric and uninhibited but they can also damage your heart and cause sudden death.

If someone takes a tablet it is not easy to think of the side effects it may cause but breathing in the toxic vapours of glue is easy to see and it is also easy to imagine just what damage a person is doing themselves.

I remember a true story from some years ago about two lads who went into a garage and bought some engine oil and then went outside and drank it. Whatever did they think it was doing for them apart from lubricating their motions?

OxyContin. (Hillbilly Heroin)

OxyContin is a prescribed drug which when used properly is a wonderful treatment for the relief of chronic pain but in recent years it has fallen into misuse together with others. Taking OxyContin makes you feel good and the more you take the better you feel which makes it easy to see why so many have fallen into the trap of taking it on a non-prescription and illegal basis. When used, the drug stimulates the nervous system in the brain and spinal cord. It can give a feeling of great euphoria

OxyContin is an opioid drug which means what it says. It is based on opium and is highly addictive.

Taking the drug by tablet gives a slow-release mechanism but drug users do not want this so they tend to chew, snort or inject it so as to receive an almost instant hit and intense high. Frequent use of the drug can make the user become immune to its effects so as time goes by larger and larger doses are needed in order to achieve the necessary desired result.

The side effects are nausea and vomiting, dizziness, confusion, constipation, respiratory problems, unconsciousness, increased risk of cardiac problems, coma and even death.

So as we can see, all drugs can do some good. Even the illegal ones can have a fleeting advantage. When used correctly, a prescribed drug can be highly beneficial and can even save your life but no illegal drug will ever enhance your life or change it in the slightest let alone save it. Taking illegal drugs is a pathetic thing to do and will, in a very little time, only add greatly to the troubles you are trying to escape from in the first place. As I have said, all drugs are a type of poison and all must be monitored by those who know. If a GP tells you to take a drug then take it. Take it as it is prescribed but if a so-called friend tells you to take a drug, decline the offer immediately and in no uncertain terms.

Never succumb to peer-pressure to take drugs and never think these people are big or cool. Believe me they are only doing so because they cannot cope with life. You are better than that.

So what of our friend Donald in the story? Was he wrong to take drugs and eventually kill himself? Of course he was but look back at what made him do it. He didn't become an addict because he wanted to be cool or look good did he? He did it to escape from a world where he saw little for himself then or in the future. His life was, in his mind, a waste of time and what other means was there of escaping from it? Even those who sold him his drugs were only doing so to try and earn a little money in order to better their lives.

In today's world there are many many people in the same position. They are lost and disaffected by the world and its 'Self' attitude. They feel, quite rightly, that they are being let down by those who should be there to help. They feel that those who are governing the world are turning a blind eye to them. Those who govern are raking in their huge salaries and that is all they care about. A few pounds are put their way in the form of help centres or charities or a little more methadone but anything such as this is only a token gesture.

So are those with the power doing enough? More could be done it has to be said but the trouble with drugs is now so rife that it can never be stopped. We can raid houses or pick up drugs in traveller's luggage but we will never ever make even the slightest dent in world trade. Our culture is such that there will always be drug-takers and where there are drug-takers there will always be suppliers. It goes back to the economic theory of supply and demand again.

In most trades there are those who benefit but in the drugs trade no one ever wins, as even much of the money made at the top goes towards funding terrorism and wars. We all lose out as well as it is our hard earned wages that fund all the policing it takes just to try and keep things under any sort of control. We do try but it doesn't work. So due to illegal drugs some lose their lives and others lose their liberty but in the end we all lose totally.

11
The Wonder of Future Dilemmas

When you read this chapter you may well think I have gone from being someone who likes a joke to someone who is some kind of miserable prophet of doom. We live in a world of Wonderment but that world must soon change drastically if we are to keep the Wonderment that we know. If we want to salvage some of life as we know it someone somewhere has to make huge decisions but who will ever be brave enough?

Why do these decisions have to be made?

70,000 years ago man managed to leave Africa for the first time and began to populate the globe. There were only a few of them and it all took time but the human population did grow although their lives were tough and not many managed to see any kind of old age. They had no hospitals or medicines and nature was their ruler.

For the next 70,000 years the human population grew very slowly and steadily and the world coped well but then in the mid-1700s things started to change drastically. The industrial revolution and advances in medicine saw a population spurt that is still prevalent today although the spurt has turned into more of an explosion.

People of the lower classes of the 1700s and 1800s probably would not accept that their standards of living were getting better as their lives were still hard compared with the lives of those above them. What was actually happening though was a revolution in industry and agriculture. Up to the 18th C people had lived off the land. They had toiled for existence with the seasons and weather ruling their lives but people had started having Eureka moments everywhere and change was afoot.

In industry, water and steam power would become more advanced as would the machinery that actually produced goods that water and steam powered. Transport was becoming more efficient as well with better links between cities and between cities and ports. Thousands of miles of roads, railways and canals were built.

Gt Britain had been powered mainly by wood and this was becoming a harder commodity to find. As forests were felled wood had to be carried further and as we know it is a heavy and bulky thing to transport so therefore its cost rose sharply. Coal was the fuel which kick-started the revolution and luckily for us we had it in vast quantities. It was a fuel that was readily available and one which burned hotter and for longer than wood. Pound for pound it actually gives about three times more power.

As with the rest of the world Gt Britain had been built by horse power but then in 1712 a gentleman by the name of Thomas Newcomen built the first commercially viable steam engine. It worked well but needed a vast amount of coal to fuel it. This was why it was mainly used at pit heads to draw flood water from the mines. It needed vast amounts of fuel and the pit heads were where that fuel was in abundance. The machine was an atmospheric steam engine and to put it simply steam was used to push a piston along its cylinder and then cold water was injected into the cylinder to condense the steam, lower the pressure and therefore bring the piston back. To see such a machine in action is almost comical compared to engines we see today but in those days it was a total advance. It did the work of up to twenty horses.

Other notable machine advances come to mind from my time over forty years ago when I studied social and economic history. I wasn't too good at it then but have remembered some. There was Hargreaves spinning jenny, Crompton's mule and of course Stevenson's rocket.

In agriculture too advances were being made and the following list gives some idea of what was happening.

The Norfolk four-course crop rotation system was adopted.

The Dutch plough was used.

Enclosure.

Intensive farming.

Land drainage and reclamation.

Transportation infrastructure.

Selective breeding.

We will quickly look at these one by one.

The Norfolk four-course crop rotation was brought about by the realisation that different crops took up different amounts of different chemicals from different depths of soil so each field would grow a succession of different crops. E.g. a turnip has a long root and would feed off chemicals at a depth deeper than corn. It is also known that disease builds up in soil which is used to harvest the same crop year after year. Changing the crop each year eliminates this problem as well.

The Dutch plough was originally adapted from a Chinese plough and consisted of an iron tipped blade, a better mould board and an adjustable depth. It was more efficient and easier to pull. This was a great advance in its time but look in a field now at the huge tractors and multi-furrow ploughs. I often wonder just what those people of the 18th C would think if they could see it all today.

Enclosure was a boon to farmers as it meant the enclosure of common land and bringing it into farming production. In the early days of farming it was carried out on what was called the traditional open field system. Farmers farmed strips of land within fields. Enclosure was the act of bringing this land under direction of one farm and farmer and therefore less labour and less costs were needed to produce food. Many farm labourers had to move to the cities to take up employment in industry while others, including some from my own family, decided to take the gamble of emigrating to the new lands of Australia and Canada to seek a better life and avoid starvation.

Intensive farming saw agriculture go from small farmers keeping a couple of cows and pigs mainly for their own food to large scale production of meat for sale to everyone who could afford it.

Land drainage and land reclamation had the obvious effect of bringing more land into production.

Better transport infrastructure meant that all the extra food these advances were creating could be sent to various markets quickly while they were still fresh.

Selective breeding, which was a very simple idea, saw far better farm animals reared and the better they were the more meat they produced. The man largely responsible for this was Robert Bakewell who, in his lifetime, it is said managed to double the size of ordinary farm cattle.

All of the above saw huge improvements in the quantity of food produced and we now had a market flooded with goods. As well as studying social and economic history I also studied economics and one thing that was drummed into my head was that 'law of supply and demand'. This basically says that the more goods there are the less they will sell for and the less goods there are the more they will sell for. For example, if I tried to sell ten cars and no one wanted them I would not get too much for them but if everyone wanted a car and I only had one for sale then the price would be much higher. Here in the agricultural revolution we now have a surplus of food. It is wanted but there is no great population to buy it so the price has to be low. The population then had cheaper and therefore more plentiful food. Their health consequently increased and as it increased they became able to live longer and have more offspring and the whole thing became self-perpetuating again.

This was not yet the end of low population though as many people still died young and so many children died before reaching adulthood. I have studied my family tree and have a direct line of ancestry back to 1715. In those days some of my family were extremely wealthy although the money has long since disappeared. I have not worked out where it went but I think my wife spent most of it on boots, coats and handbags.

Anyway, getting away from frivolity, even the wealthy among my family were losing children at an alarming rate. I have a couple of grave sites nearby where you see the mother and father buried alongside a number of their children. It must have been heartbreaking for them to live with either losing their children or knowing that at any time one or more of them could be taken from them.

The industrial revolution planted the seed of population growth but it took advances in medicine to allow it to achieve its goal. For many years we knew nothing really and people with illnesses died with only their faith for support. There was bloodletting of course which had been sworn by for generations but this did no real good. From 1750 we saw the advent of the following:

Benjamin Bell, the first scientific surgeon of Scotland published his book 'A System Of Surgery'. His 'save skin' adage led to huge advances in wound healing after amputations,

John Bell became a surgeon who made great advances in the knowledge and surgery of the vascular system.

John Priestly discovered nitrous oxide which would later be used as an anaesthetic.

In 1736 Claudius Amyand performed the first successful appendectomy. Can you imagine that without anaesthetic? Blimey!!!

William Withering discovered the use of digitalis (foxglove) in treating dropsy.

Edward Jenner developed the smallpox vaccine method.

Humphrey Davey announced the anaesthetic properties of nitrous oxide.

Rene Laennec invented the stethoscope.

Joseph Lister fathered modern surgery with the use of antiseptics.

James Blundell performed the first human blood transfusion.

Louis Pasteur and Robert Koch established the theory of germ disease.

Within a space of three years vaccines had been developed for cholera, anthrax and rabies, tetanus and diphtheria.

All these had been achieved as the industrial revolution took place and suddenly, although people were still not living as long as we do today, they were living. Infant mortality was still high but it was not so great and of course the more children that survive the more of them there are to breed. This self-perpetuates again and we see an explosion in population numbers.

In London the percentage of children who died before their fifth birthday was around a shocking 75% in 1750. This figure fell to less than half that percentage by 1850 and subsequently in the 200 years between 1700 and 1900 the population of Europe rose dramatically from 100 to 400 million people. From 1900 to 2000 the population of England had doubled to 60 million and the population of the USA had grown from just 76 million to 300 million in the same time.

Here we are then. We have travelled through years of stable and steady population growth right up to the rapid and unsustainable growth we have today. We have heralded all the changes in agriculture, industry and medical advances but they have led us into a highly precarious position. I have seen estimates that show the earth can support somewhere between 4 and 16 billion people. Arguments I have listened to and agree with put the actual number at around 5 billion. If my memory is correct the person I heard saying this first was Sir David

Attenborough and even if he said the world was made out of a giant coconut filled with pineapple yoghurt I would believe him. 16 billion is a wholly optimistic and unrealistic figure because if you look at the world today you see signs all around you of overpopulation. We are running short of fuel, we are ruining the atmosphere that we breathe, we are creating global warming, we are deforesting the planet, we are causing the extinction of many animals and we are gradually seeing more violence within society.

It has often been said that if overpopulation occurs in any species then nature will find a way of bringing those numbers down to a sustainable level. For all other species I think there is a lot to be said for this theory but remember we are the ones with the huge brains and intellect. We are the ones who are defying nature at every turn. We are the ones who have conquered nature and are the ones whose population has already risen sharply to 7 billion which to my mind and others is too great a number for our planet to sustain. Remember, our planet is all we have. If we get short of money we can go to the bank to borrow more but if we get short of planetary resources there is nowhere else to borrow them from. We cannot just pop out to another planet and get a few more buckets full of oxygen or electricity can we?

We have a huge dilemma on our hands. Our population is growing out of control and it cannot be sustained but how do we tackle the problem? Come to that who is going to tackle the problem? No politician is going to suddenly stand up in the houses of parliament or the US Senate and say "We must lower the population by 2-3 billion in the next 50 years and keep it there". No one is going to do it because it would make them extremely unpopular. No one will do it because we all bury our heads in the sand and hope it will go away but it will not.

I will use my 'hungry lion' analogy to explain.

We are walking through the grasses of the plains of Africa and we come across a hungry lion. It looks at us, salivates and licks his lips at the thought of tasting a nice piece of juicy human flesh. It is no good us closing our eyes and ignoring it because when we open them again the lion will still be there and he will still be hungry but he will also be much closer.

We are the same with overpopulation. We ignore it now at our peril and the longer we ignore it the bigger problem it will become.

Above I have listed some of the problems that have occurred because of over population. Let's look at them individually.

We are rapidly running short of fossil fuels. A sudden knee-jerk reaction has taken place and we see wind farms popping up everywhere. The problem here is that although scientists are putting every effort into designing them they are still so inefficient that vast forests of them have to be built to supply any kind of percentage of demand. We have an abundance of hydrogen in the atmosphere and this is a flammable gas. It could well be used commonly as power but the technology is not there yet. We do need something though because it takes little thought to realise the consequences of running out of fuel. We live on a planet which is absolutely packed with energy from wind, waves, rivers, the sun, natural gasses and even volcanoes but we cannot seem to successfully harvest any of them. Apart from nuclear power which is inherently dangerous we are still relying on fossil fuel as did the Victorians.

We are ruining the atmosphere by our actions. We are all to blame here. Many a time I have driven down a motorway and my senses have been shocked by all the cars, vans, lorries and coaches around me all spewing out vast amounts of noxious fumes. My senses are then brought to reality when I realise I am driving a vehicle which is doing exactly the same thing as the rest of them. I have driven the M25 several times and have sat in lane after lane of traffic, often stopped and with literally hundreds if not thousands of vehicles around me all poisoning each other and the planet. This is only the M25 but multiply this by all the motorways in the whole of the world and you see we have a giant problem.

It is not just the roads which are to blame. Drive up the M25 between the junctions for the M3 and the M4 and you will see plane after plane taking off from Heathrow. To me it is a wonderful sight and I do quite enjoy being stuck in traffic there just to see them but imagine the amount of fuel a jumbo jet is burning and the amount of fumes it is producing. These planes are taking off almost continuously and not just from this one airport. Again we have to multiply this by all the airports in the whole of the world.

Our houses and factories all have to have power and we are building more and more of them in order to cope with the population. If the population of the USA is 300 million and we can average four people per household this give 75 million houses that have to be heated and powered. It would make an estimate of 15 million houses in England alone.

Global warming is quite a contentious issue these days and people love to think it isn't happening. Of course, if it isn't happening then we do not have to do anything about it do we? The trouble is despite everything the sceptics say it is happening and it is happening at an alarming rate. I think most people would agree that the climate is changing but then some would rather hope it is happening naturally. I'm sorry but it isn't.

Since the industrial revolution we have been burning fossil fuels at an alarming rate. These fuels are coal, gas and oil. Even if we did not heat our houses or drive a car we would still be consuming too much fuel because even the mass produced food we eat is fed with artificial fertiliser, it is packed in plastic and it is transported using fuel.

Artificial fertiliser is made from oil. Packaging is made from oil. Plastic carrier bags are made from oil and, of course all transport relies upon oil.

Fossil fuels are just what they say they are by description. They are fossils of once living creatures or plants. Coal, for example is just the remains of fossilised trees. Fossil fuels are made largely of carbon and when we warm our feet in front of the fire we are burning coal and releasing that carbon into the atmosphere. All well and good you might think but wait and think a little more. If we release carbon into the atmosphere what happens? It mixes with the oxygen in the atmosphere and what do carbon and oxygen make when mixed together? Yes, you've got it, its carbon dioxide, CO_2.

I have a small greenhouse in my garden as I like to grow my own tomatoes. They are so much tastier than shop bought ones but how does my greenhouse work? It lets in heat but some of that heat then becomes trapped inside making it the warm environment that tomatoes love. Tropical animals would not survive in our climate but they would stand a good chance in my greenhouse.

In our atmosphere the carbon dioxide acts the same as the glass in my greenhouse letting heat in but not letting it radiate back out. This is why it has been dubbed 'The greenhouse effect'.

With greater heat comes greater evaporation from the earth's surface and this then puts more water vapour into the atmosphere. This, in turn, causes more storms and floods so this is why we are seeing a greater number of floods and storm damage. Some people will say there have always been storms. We all know that. Just ask poor old Noah. The difference is that bad storms and flooding may have always been there but they are far more frequent today because of global warming and their frequency will only intensify as time passes.

Our climate is changing and we are responsible for it but I am not saying we as individuals should all drive electric cars to save the world because even that electricity is probably produced by burning fossil fuels. We as individuals should be concerned but our actions alone will not help. Even my old favourite sport of Formula 1 has sold out and does not allow enough fuel for the drivers to race each other with. Actions like these will solve no problems. We need a strong government who will have the bottle to stand up and say "Enough is enough". Today we have the Green Party whose promises are to look after green issues. Would even they be strong enough to stand up and say what needs to be done? I doubt it because if they did it would alienate them totally from other parties. Let's face it, the party that does stand up and say what needs or has to be done will be shunned by everyone and that would be no vote catching idea would it?

We are deforesting the planet at an alarming rate. I have heard it said that the equivalent of an acre of rainforest is being cleared every minute. That is a lot of trees and a lot of trees that are no longer taking in the carbon dioxide we are creating. They are not taking in carbon dioxide and they are no longer giving out oxygen. The rainforests are said to be 'the lungs of the earth'. Just like someone who smokes twenty cigarettes each day we cannot expect to destroy our lungs and still survive. Although we do not have rainforests here, Gt Britain is not innocent in all of this. As I have already said, our forests were cut down for fuel (and shipbuilding) and we do still buy timber from felled rainforests. Much of the trade is illegal in this country but you can be sure some gets through.

I have talked at length about my love of wildlife and have commented upon the pressures we have put on different species. This is another huge problem. In the chapter 'The Wonder Of Evolution', I talked about previous mass extinctions. The world is witnessing one now and it is being caused by us. With nature being as resilient as it is it will eventually recover from whatever we do to it but we really ought to stop doing it now. It is estimated that, due to the activities of human beings, the extinction rate of other animals is somewhere between 1,000 and 10,000 times higher than any normal rate. We are having a drastic effect on our planet. If my earlier given estimate of 8 million different species is somewhere near correct we could actually be seeing somewhere between 8,000 and 80,000 species becoming extinct each year.

A once common and very attractive British bird, the turtle dove, is now almost extinct in Britain. Just a few years ago its 'tur-tur' call was heard as a sweet but nothing extra special sound above our fields but today if we even see one we are asked to contact the RSPB or the BTO. If I had rung them a few years go and said, "I have just heard a turtle dove 'tur-turring' on a telegraph post," they would have thought I was a bit of a nutter.

The cuckoo is another casualty of human activity. Last year I only heard its call on one occasion. Those in the know are saying because of global warming British birds are nesting earlier and the event no longer coincides with the arrival of the cuckoo so when they arrive to find host nests in which to lay their eggs it is too late. This may be a factor but other human factors such as hunting and eating cuckoos in Western Africa are all not helping.

And talking of Africa, African vulture numbers have fallen by 60% in just the last ten years. Some would not care but this is caused by the human population and it is horrendous. Vultures are my favourite birds and not only are they wonderful but we have to think of how they live and what they do. What do they do you ask? They only eat dead meat don't they? They do and you are right but what does the eating of that dead meat mean? It means cleaning up everything before disease sets in. Now, with only four out of every ten birds left in existence we only have two fifths of the meat being eaten. The other three fifths rots, becomes infected with bacteria and those diseases spread to other animals including us. We may be poisoning these great birds but in the end what we are doing is inadvertently poisoning ourselves. How many times do humans act first and then think later?

When I was a youngster the house sparrow was the most common bird in England and they were shot as pests because of their great numbers. This cute little bird has now declined in numbers by over ninety percent. The only birds which are thriving are those which have capitalised on our activities. The wood pigeon is probably our most common species today as it lives well from our farming and birds like crows and magpies live well off the carrion we leave on the road as road kill. Our love of the household moggie has, as I have said before, led to a

231

great loss of birds and also small mammals which are normally there to feed natural predators such as owls and hawks.

We had all the very rapid advances in medical science during the time of the industrial revolution but the speed of these advances has increased dramatically in recent years. We have fought and beat many diseases and are now looking into stem cell treatment and gene therapy. This just shows what brains and intellect we do have but all this is also having a huge detrimental effect on population growth. When medicine was in its infancy any step forward just brought forth cheers but now any step forward must be counterbalanced by the worry of overpopulation.

Also when I was a youngster I remember my old Nan saying, 'Well, he may be gone but he lived a good life and he had his three score years and ten."

Three score years and ten. That's three times twenty plus ten which is 70 years. That back then was the life expectancy of a human being. It was far higher than at any time before but look at us now. We are lasting well into our eighties as an average. The problem is although we are living much longer our brains are not surviving quite as well and we are seeing an almost overwhelming number of cases of dementia. In the future we will probably come to yet another Eureka moment and will find a cure for dementia as well but then there will be still more people to house and feed.

Women who cannot conceive naturally are being given (or sold) fertility treatment and premature babies are surviving being born earlier and earlier. I am not giving an opinion here but again we are going against nature. Who is going to stop fertility treatment and who is going to let those babies die just to keep the population down? The trouble is many of those poor premature babies have not developed enough to survive properly and do have consequential problems all through their lives. There comes that word dilemma again.

I have talked about the dilemma of illness and this is the kind of dilemma we all have to face, huge dilemmas which will take super human courage and conviction to overcome. Can we stop people having fertility treatment? Can we stop fighting to save premature babies? Can we stop advances in cancer research? Can we stop any potential progress in medicine? Can we stop looking into heart disease and diabetes and dementia? If someone is ill do we let them die? If someone has an accident do we let them die? If someone is old do we let them die? If someone cannot look after themselves with just the bare basics of help do we let them die? Question? Question? Question?

An increase in violence within society will come. Our government is trying to tell us that violent crime is dwindling and yet even on our local news I see stabbings being reported on a daily basis. Where the government is getting its figures from I do not know but they certainly do not reflect any news I have seen. As we get more people more pollution and less natural resources it is plain enough to see we also get strife. Let me give you another of my analogies, the *'Mr and Mrs X Syndrome'*.

A husband and wife, Mr and Mrs X, are locked in a normal sitting room but the room has only one very small window which opens. This is their only source of fresh air but it is adequate for them. In the middle of the room is a huge Harrods hamper full of food and they have all the usual comforts of life including two chairs, a two seat sofa and a television. Water is also provided for them but it is limited. Mr and Mrs X are quite content. They are comfortable, do not have to go to work and have all they need and desire within their space but then the door opens and in walk another couple, Mr and Mrs Y. At first Mr and Mrs X are okay with the situation. Perhaps it would have been nicer for them to have had the space to themselves but now they had company, other people to share the time with and get to know. At first the two couples get along quite reasonably but burning in the back of their minds is the fact that the food and water is now being shared by four people instead of two. A couple of days go relatively peacefully by and then the door opens again and in walk Mr and Mrs Z. Now the trouble really starts.

Mr and Mrs X and Y were getting along okay but Mrs X did notice Mr Y was eating more than his fair share of their food and Mrs Y didn't like watching Coronation Street and moaned constantly while it was on. Now Mr and Mrs Z were in the room as well the whole thing became strained. Firstly, there were only two chairs and a two seat sofa so arguments started as to who was going to sit on the floor and then Mr Z wanted to watch the footie all the time and Mrs Z smoked like a factory chimney with the small window not allowing enough air in to clear the fumes. What had started out as a nice little experiment for Mr and Mrs X soon degenerated into anarchy and as the food and water started to be greedily consumed by everyone actual fights broke out between the three couples. Mrs X was fighting Mrs Z and Mr X got into a fight whilst trying to break them up. They soon came to a war situation and what were once normal everyday couples turned into couples consumed with anger and hate. This hate was generally vented towards the other couples but in time the couples even started to hate and fight their own partners.

This is just another of my silly little analogies but it is what will happen when we get too many people living in too little space with too few natural resources. Wars will break out. We have had many wars and we are already seeing much more rioting and war throughout the world than we ever have before. Wars do prevail today but believe me as Bachman-Turner Overdrive used to sing "B-B-B-Baby you just ain't seen nothin yet!"

So as a conclusion what do we do?

The only way we are going to save our species and that of many others in a world anything like we know today is to drastically reduce the human population. The only way we are going to save our planet as we know it for our grandchildren is by not having grandchildren. Something has to be done but the only way it can be done is by stopping medical research, by stopping reliance on fossil fuels and returning to the days of the distant past where we lived as either hunter gatherers or existence farmers.

This idea to my mind would be quite romantic, getting up when the cock crowed (if he wasn't already in the pot), toiling in the fields during the day and sitting around the fire in the evenings talking to each other rather than watching inane things on the television just because it is there. We could go out hunting and bring back fresh wild meat from the fields, meat that had not been ill-treated and stuffed full of chemicals. We could once again breathe in deeply without wondering just what we were inhaling and we could eat vegetables from our fields that had not been sprayed a dozen times with more chemicals. Our only transport would be a horse and cart and that would produce nothing any more noxious than manure for our rhubarb.

To tell you the truth I would be the kind of person who, on a romantic level, would love all that but I would not be one of the few chosen to survive would I? I am an old codger and only the young would be given the chance. I would have to be killed off or left to die with the rest of the dross.

I have been to Mauritius a couple of times and have fallen in love with the place. It is beautiful and the people are smashing. I have daydreamed about living there but I know, in reality, it would not be good. In England we have top quality doctors, dentists, surgeons and hospitals and I know I would miss relying upon them as I would have to in Mauritius.

It would be the same for living as we did back in olden times. The romance would certainly be there but the advantages would not. So what do we do? No one is going to suddenly say we have to stop breeding, are going to stop all medical research and we are going to kill everyone who has had their three score years and ten are they?

What we are going to do, is just what we are already doing and that is talk about it and make a few token gestures but not have the guts, determination and commitment to face the problem head on. Our eyes will remain closed ready for that hungry lion to pounce.

Our population will rise and rise from today's 7 billion through to 10 and 12 billion until the earth cannot possibly sustain it any longer and then we will fight ferociously for the few crumbs left on the table. Only then, once all resources are depleted and we have massacred each other will our population drop to a level which can be sustained. We will take with us perhaps millions of other species but some of them will be left. Some of us may be left as well and then the whole cycle will start again. We as a race will rebound but that will be good as the advantage then will be that the previous population, (us) will have used up everything from the planet that can be harmful to it and they will have to evolve with a much simpler lifestyle, perhaps like the romantic notion I have given above. They will be living a simple farmer or hunter gatherer lifestyle but this time without any choice in the matter and without fossil fuels they will probably have to stay living that way which will be tough for them but very easy on the planet. Is this what religionists say is the 'second coming'?

Even if the human race did manage to kill itself off and take all other life with it would it matter? No, in the huge scheme of things, it wouldn't. As I have said before, we are living on what is just a tiny speck of dust in a vast universe. If we disappeared it would not matter in the slightest. The world would go on and other planets in other galaxies would evolve. We would be just a tiny lost part in the long history of a great universe.

12
The Wonder of Humankind

We have talked about war and the horrors of it but I thought I would leave the biggest horror of war until this chapter to really define the depths that humans will plummet to in order to harm each other. I am talking about the nuclear bomb.

Nuclear bombs have a massive destructive force and work by either fission or a mixture of fission and fusion. Both methods release a huge amount of energy from a relatively small device. A thermonuclear bomb which weighs just a little over one ton can produce an explosive force as great as 1.2million tons of TNT.

I am not going into the workings of various nuclear bombs. It is all very complicated and in the context of this book, thank goodness because I do not fully understand myself, it is not necessary to do so. What we are looking at here is why? Why, again on this tiny planet, do we need to even think of making such totally insane machines?

America dropped two such bombs onto Japan towards the end of World War 2. One, codenamed 'little boy' was dropped onto Hiroshima on 6th August 1945 and three days later another device codenamed 'fat man' was dropped onto Nagasaki.

Firstly, it seems a little absurd to me that such vile weapons were given the trivial names of 'little boy' and 'fat man'. There could have been no triviality in dropping them could there? And what of all the people involved? Did the designer give a cheer when the bombs exploded? Did he feel exalted that his theory and work had been proven? Did the person who gave the order for the mission give a cheer as the many thousands of men, women, children and babies were vaporised? And did the pilots cheer as they successfully completed their mission and flew home? I would genuinely like to know.

It is said that over 100,000 people died in the two explosions and the same amount again were injured. Take a little time here to imagine '100,000 people killed'. What does 100,000 dead bodies look like? Of course though, many of the victims were not even left with bodies were they? And what sort of people were they who died? Probably most of them did not even have an educated view on or any involvement in the war anyway. I have seen film of a young girl, probably about ten years old, running in complete panic and naked down a road with her flesh severely burned and I have seen a picture of a concrete doorstep which still had the faintest of outline of someone's bottom on it. The person had been instantly vaporised and the doorstep where he or she had been sitting was just that slight amount less charred where their body had been.

What makes us, sorry but here we go again, large-brained and intellectual beings want to do this to others of our kind? What makes us lustfully revel in killing?

The first thing we have to admit was yes, there was a war on and the Japanese were not the nicest of people themselves in times of war. Abominable atrocities were committed by Japanese forces throughout Asia, either during occupation or in POW camps or along the Burma railway. Thousands of allied troops and civilians were tortured or raped by them and we will talk about that in a while but despite the terrible horrors the Japanese forces committed it was not the fault of that lovely innocent little ten year old or the person sitting nonchalantly on that step was it?

I remember an English lady telling her story of how she was working as a nurse in a hospital in the Far East when the Japanese invaded. She said the very first thing they did was rape the women, including her. What made the Japanese soldiers think this the first thing they had to do? It wasn't necessary was it and how did it promote their war? It was just terror set in the depraved minds of the soldiers, soldiers who obviously had a craving for war, power, lust and brutality.

On the Burma railway they say that one POW was killed for every sleeper laid. POWs were treated as sub-human because they capitulated. The Japanese thought their prisoners had lost all honour and in the minds of the Japanese this made them far less than human and therefore they could be treated without any morsel of respect, dignity, pride, comfort or concern.

In an interview on television one former POW said a Japanese soldier had made sexual advances towards him and because he refused them he was severely beaten all that night, all the next day and then again through the next night. He may have kicked the soldier between the legs in the denial of the advances but no one could possibly ever have deserved his punishment.

In a book I read entitled 'One for every sleeper', it stated that one POW was held down, had his mouth filled with salt and then his lips quickly stitched together. The salt made him sick and when he was sick he tore his lips apart. Were his perpetrators actually human at all?

Yes, the Japanese did commit terrible atrocities and yes, the war was ended much earlier and many more lives were saved by the dropping of 'little boy' and 'fat man' by why were we at war to start with? War and all the above incidences are pathetic and obscene.

At the time of writing the powers that be are searching for 200 schoolgirls who were kidnapped in Nigeria by a group called Boko Haram. Boko Haram are said to be fighting to overthrow the government of the country in order to create a Muslim state. To them it is wrong to educate girls and they have therefore been kidnapped to sell off as wives. Sell off as wives? How can one person in the 21st century even consider selling off another and what sane individual would consider purchasing one?

Also at this time I have heard of a lady in Sudan who has been imprisoned and sentenced to 100 lashes and then death by hanging and what was her heinous crime? Was it infanticide, regicide, large scale genocide? No, it was none of these. Her dreadful crime was to marry a Christian and refuse to convert to Islam. It seems her father was Islamic and those who have imprisoned her expect her to follow her father's ways. She has had her second child while in jail but, again, what is she in jail for? Marrying a man? Did she seek him out because she wanted to marry a Christian and cause herself trouble? Of course she didn't. She married him because she fell in love with him and what can possibly be wrong with that? And why is all this hate being vented towards an innocent woman? Oh yes, it is totally down to hatred coming from religion again isn't it? Take away the religion factor and those two people would be allowed to do what we all do. Fall in love and be together. How can it possibly matter what sex, colour or religion they are? All that matters is they are decent human beings which is totally opposite to her tormentors and torturers who are willing to do anything they feel like to her just for kicks whilst hiding behind religion. How can she be so bad for just falling in love and yet the person whipping her can be seen as good? How can getting married be a capital offence and yet the whipping and hanging of an innocent young woman be lawful? I know Sudan is not the most modern of countries in their ways or thinking but how can anyone ever think this situation is right and just? They cannot unless they are totally insane.

(I would add in retrospect that due to pressure from other countries, this lady has been released in the time it took for me to finish the book. There is some sense after all but why would anyone other than an idiot ever even consider it in the first place?)

We have also at this time had a Malaysian airliner brought down by a surface to air missile with the loss of almost 300 lives. The plane was brought down in the Ukraine and obviously all those killed were totally innocent including 80 children.

War is raging in Gaza as well and I have just seen the headline that two brothers have been killed and one of them was just five years old. Were these lads soldiers? I don't think so.

And what of women who are stoned to death for committing adultery? They are placed in a hole in the ground with just their heads showing and then people throw stones at them until they are dead. The ironic thing is the next hole is seldom occupied by the man who she committed adultery with. He is probably off having sex with the stoners' next victim.

Another article I have read told the story of a young lad who was very naughty and stole a loaf of bread, a crime he had, quite rightly, to be rebuked for. The trouble was he was not rebuked. Under Sharia law he was held down while someone drove a car over his arm. He and his family were probably hungry so he took the action of stealing a loaf of bread. Of course what he did was wrong but did he deserve losing the proper use of his arm for the rest of his life?

And talking about Sharia law the following laws come to mind for their absurdity:

A man can beat his wife for insubordination.

A man can marry an infant girl and consummate that marriage when she is 9 years old.

A man can divorce his wife without her permission but she needs his permission to do the same.

Testimonies of four men are needed to prove rape against a woman.

A woman who has been raped cannot testify against her assailant or assailants.

All of these show the degree of regard in which women are held.

Another incident comes to mind is the story I once read in a hospital magazine while waiting for my late wife as she underwent radio therapy. It was the story of two women in the Middle East who went to the police station to report the fact that one of them had been raped. She was rightly upset and aggrieved that this appalling thing had been done to her so she went to the police station with her friend there for support. They entered the police station and gave their report and what did the police do? Did they take them into a private interview room, make them a cup of tea and listen intently to the lady's story? Did they let them talk to a lady police officer to make things a little more comfortable? Were they treated with all the due respect, honour and kindness they deserved? Of course they weren't. The so called police officers just laughed loudly as they raped both women themselves. It seems the woman who had been raped must have 'deserved' being raped and by talking about it she deserved even more. Her friend was seen as being just as bad by supporting her. What? The story went into absolutely horrific detail of just what was done to them but I will just leave this paragraph.

It is strange really but when I think about the hatred, abuse, injustice and general wickedness of the world, without meaning to, my mind goes to religion again and again. The above set of Sharia 'laws' and injustices are laid down within religions, and what of all the abuse within the Catholic Church? Priests abusing youngsters in their care and those above them knowing full well it is happening but keeping it quiet for fear of their church getting a bad name.

We have had a massive run in recent times of celebrities being accused, (and some being found guilty) of child abuse, molestation and rape and this is bad enough but people doing it and hiding behind religion? Isn't religion supposed to be for those who love their god and each other? Priests should love their charges not love abusing their charges.

Whether they are aging celebrities or priests or bishops they are all paedophiles and should all be treated as such whether they are religious or not. 'Paedophiles' is what they call them but I find the word puzzling. Isn't this the wrong word altogether? The suffix '-phile' means lover of. A bibliophile is a lover of books. A Francophile is a lover of the French and an Anglophile is a lover of the English so why are the abusers of children called paedophiles? They certainly do not love children do they? Can you love a child and abuse them at the same time? Perhaps you can if the crime is committed within a religion.

I know the next practise has stopped these days but again the Catholic Church comes to mind in the past abuse of youngsters. The Magdalene Sisters or Maggies in Ireland were girls who either did have sex, and possibly children, out of wedlock or were suspected of having sex or were even suspected of encouraging boys to want to do so. For their 'terrible sins' these girls were taken from their families (with their parents' consent) and were locked away with nuns to guard them while they lived miserable lives working in laundries. They were barred from any interaction with the outside world and were treated viciously by nuns and priests. It is estimated that as many as 30,000 such girls and women were locked away in Magdalene asylums throughout the country. Some never left the asylums and all their work (slavery really) made money which went straight to the coffers of the Catholic Church.

Many of their babies were taken from them and 'sold' to the highest bidder without their mothers having any knowledge of who they were with or where they went and that in itself says bundles about the 'mercy' of God and the church. Sex was deemed as being such a sin and yet surely, in the eyes of the Catholics, it must have been their god who made those girls and who gave them the urge to explore the sexual side of life and all the pleasure it can bring. Perhaps if the nuns who imprisoned them had indulged in it a little they may have been less frustrated and less uptight about life themselves.

It seems incredible that this barbaric practise continued unabated right up until the 1990s with the last laundry only closing in 1996.

Girls' lives were ruined through no real fault of their own and those who locked them away may have hidden behind religion but were far bigger sinners than any of the girls ever were and because all this was headed by religion it was seen as being fine by the government of the day. Any non-religious slavery would have been jumped upon and those responsible heavily punished. The Maggies were heavily and systematically punished by the nuns as their superiors counted the cash.

I am sorry if some of the incidences I have recorded above are horrendous but they all happened and were all perpetrated by us human beings. I nearly said the ones with the big brains etc. again but no, not this time.

In this world I have met some wonderful people and of course there are many more wonderful people out there that I have not met. It is not hard to be good, kind, benevolent and caring and I'm sure all who are find it as rewarding as I do. Just to stop on the road and wave another driver through brings be joy. Buying my Mags an occasional bunch of flowers brings me joy. Just looking at a smiling grandchild brings me joy. There is so much joy to be had in just being a decent person so why do people get such a kick out of hurting others? Where does all the hate come from? I am not kind to others because of some religion or any fear of God or for fear of what may happen in any afterlife. I just like being kind. It is what makes me tick.

In no way am I nice to the point where everything anyone says is right no matter how wrong it is. If I was that nice I would not be writing this book. No, if what someone says or does is wrong and does not make sense I will certainly say so and so should you. I do love arguments and debates. That is where I learn.

Arguments and debates are great so long as they do not turn into rows. Rows breed contempt, bad feeling and then wars. How many families are at war with each other just because an argument was allowed to get out of hand?

There have been times in my life when it would have been easy to have had rows with family. If I had entered into any bitter argument I may have lost relations with my relations. Instead, I have talked calmly, put my point forward and then have always agreed to disagree. I have not rowed or backed down. I have kept calm and kept my family.

I am not a great lover of television soaps because when you look at them all they do in their scripts is pit one person against another to the point where they fall out and have a great big fight. This is just television though isn't it? "Oh no it isn't," you say! Do these cheesy programmes actually reflect life these days?

When you look at them you see everyone fighting, everyone having sex with each other and everyone even murdering each other. What gets me is how many viewers revel in the sheer misery of it all.

You could never move to Emmerdale, Coronation Street or Walford for fear of being beaten up, becoming a junky, becoming an alcoholic, being raped, getting pregnant, being murdered, having your house burned down or suddenly becoming a homosexual. They aren't even allowed to get married without more mishaps on the day than most people ever suffer in a decade. No, I certainly would not want to live in any of those places. I think I am better off living where I am in my small village of Midsomer.

I have never been a great lover of sports either although I was once quite good at ten-pin bowling and probably driving. People do, very rightly, follow sports to a great extent but let's look at sports today.

We see competitors cheating at every possible opportunity whether that cheating is in football, cycling, motor racing or even the steady old game of snooker.

I remember F1s supremo Bernie Ecclestone once saying it was getting harder and harder to fix who was going to win races. This was in a season where espionage between teams had been discovered and, to my mind, 'silent consequences' then had to be enforced.

How many times have we heard of so called 'sportsmen' using performance enhancing drugs to boost their chances of winning. How can they call it winning when they have cheated to do so? No one who cheats can ever be a winner but of course sport isn't 'sport' these days is it and cheats do prosper because there is too much money involved.

I was sitting with my brother and a friend once while a football match was being played on the television. An England player took a dive in the penalty area, was awarded a penalty and consequently scored a goal. I was jeered at because I did not cheer and get excited. But why should I have cheered and got excited? That player who was probably being paid hundreds of thousands of pounds each week for his so called skills was in fact just a cheat. What excitement was there in that?

I was walking through Hull one Saturday afternoon when I came across a cricket match. All the participants were having a great time and it did look like real sport. Everyone was in it for the game. Isn't it a shame these sports are ruined when they are not in it for the game but just for the money.

When we were children we used to play cards and my mother was always accusing us of cheating. She would always look at us threateningly and say, "Come on you lot, If you can't cheat fairly don't cheat at all." It was another of her wonderful sayings that made no sense whatsoever.

I have looked up the definition of the word sport and nowhere does it say it is something in which grown men cheat at in order to gain accolades and make money. That isn't 'sporting' at all is it?

The 2012 Olympic Games in London were a terrific and runaway success and even I, a non-lover of sports did enjoy them greatly. I usually hate opening ceremonies and cannot see the connection between them and the sport that follows but this one was great and I was almost entranced. It was all a wonder until you think deeper and have to wonder just how many of the medals were won through cheating. I know just how hard true sportsmen and women have to train to become Olympians and wouldn't it be sad if any of these great people did lose out on a medal to someone who had cheated to get to the top? I suppose it is best not to think about it too much but isn't thought just what real life is all about?

How many times have we seen footballers fighting or getting into silly little tempers only to be awarded a red card and a sending off? They stomp off like some snotty toddler. The same goes for the fans of the teams. They fight and hate each other and some have even been murdered because of who they follow. How pathetic again. Football is a 'sport' and in the end does it matter one jot who follows which team and who scores the most goals? Surely in sport it is all about being 'sportsmen' and having a damned good time. Everyone has their favourites and everyone loves their favourites to win but at the end of the day does it really matter? I went to Egypt on holiday with my brother and in the evenings we sometimes played pool. In a total of about twenty games I only won one because I am useless at it but it didn't make me hate him and want to stab him did it? I just bought him a drink and admitted I was rubbish.

Politicians:

They say that if you do not vote then you have no right to complain. If you think about it quickly you could do nothing but agree. It sounds quite philosophical but if you think about it a little more slowly what are you voting for and who are you voting for? I am not going to knock all politicians as no doubt there are some somewhere who really care. There are also many others who are only in the business to line their own pockets and I feel by voting for them we are only encouraging their actions. In recent years we have seen so many fraudulent and excessive claims for expenses which can only show these people are only helping themselves. Look at a few of the claims:

Fake receipts for expenses.

False claims for cleaning and gardening.

Redecoration of designated second homes.

Taxpayers money used for advertising at football and rugby matches.

Swimming pool cleaning.

Duck house in pond.

Excessive food claims.

Christmas tree decorations.

One MP claimed £10,000 for the redecoration of his London flat when his main house was only eleven miles away. He sold the flat for a good profit and all at our expense.

I could go on and on about this and it has all completely ruined the creditability of all MPs. Even the honest ones are seriously doubted. Who are the honest ones now? They are all under suspicion and I don't know how that suspicion can ever be lifted and forgotten. The trouble is the considerable wages paid to these people are found from the wages of many hardworking and honest people who are living on a shoestring. If they must contribute then they should know their cash is going to a good and worthy cause.

Corruption such as this is not just limited to MPs is it? The whole world is governed by corruption from top to bottom and the more money and influence you have the more money and influence you have to be corrupt with. Then the more corruption you enter into the more money you make. Many people have made a great deal of money for themselves and the best of luck to them I say but how many have actually made that money in a totally honest fashion?

I once visited a school which was situated at the base of Mount Kilimanjaro. The students came from very humble backgrounds and poor living conditions but every one of them wore a huge smile and immaculate clothes. We fell in love with them all and decided that, as we had spare money in our lives we could probably send them a little sometimes to help fund their school. Later, in the local market, we were sought out by someone who put us wise. We were told not to bother because we were assured that not one penny of any money we sent would ever reach the school. It would just go straight into the pockets of officials. We said perhaps we could send parcels instead and were told any parcel would end up in the same place. Any parcel would be opened and sold. Sad isn't it?

Back to politics:

In 1980 I went to see my bank manager because I wanted to borrow money to buy a new car. I only needed £3,000 but the bank manager looked at me as if he was some kind of god and said quite sternly that as I did not have any collateral I was wasting my time. I wanted the car for my newly formed driving school and showed the bank manager my diary which was stacked full of work. He didn't understand what I was trying to say so I explained to him that as my diary was full I had plenty of work and would therefore have no problem whatsoever in making the necessary repayments. Again he looked sternly at me as if I was the king of idiots. "I cannot lend you the money," he said again. "Because you do not have the collateral behind you to guarantee it." I think this was the bank that liked to say no so I raised the money by another means.

Just a couple of years later I took out a home insurance and decided to pay it in monthly instalments of £7. I had only paid three months when I received a letter saying that as I was such a valued customer did I want to borrow up to £7,000? How things had changed in just that short time. Almost overnight credit was readily available and everyone took it. I am not saying my bank manager was totally correct in refusing my loan but he did have his reasons and standards but with this new available credit his type of standards had suddenly disappeared.

From that time on the country's (and world's) economy grew and grew but it grew on credit. It was so obvious then that it could not be sustained but no one cared. Our politicians just revelled in their good fortune and people took out one credit card after another and one loan after another and spent every penny. They lived on credit with no idea or thought whatsoever as to how they were going to pay it all back.

Politicians (most of whom had received a good public school education) either could not see what was happening or they closed their eyes while the hungry lion approached and then

249

what happened? We ended up with a giant, worldwide credit crunch, the coming of which to any thinking person was obvious and had to happen. No one, whether it is a person or country can live on credit without it turning round one day and biting them. Why didn't these so well educated and elected MPs see it and do something about it?

They say we are now, years later, coming out of the credit crunch but how are we doing it? We are getting people to borrow money again and are starting the whole disturbing cycle once more.

The country as a whole spends far more money than it actually makes and like a person the practise cannot be sustained. We may, as a country, be borrowing slightly less each year but the figure still runs into many billions of pounds. We need far more austerity measures and strong leadership to sort the matter out. We as either people or countries can never live well while we are spending more than we are earning.

Another thing that amazes me with the powers that be is why they have allowed house prices to reach such a ridiculous level. In reality no house is worth anywhere near its market value and what happened is this. People in the country struggled to buy a house for their family so someone had a bit of a silly Eureka moment and suggested mortgage companies should not just take one wage into consideration for granting a mortgage but two.

"Great." everyone said. They could now all buy a house. They could get a £200,000 mortgage instead of a £100,000 mortgage. Sounded good but they now had to pay back twice as much and had less money left to purchase other items. They call it 'disposable income'.

And then what happened? The law of supply and demand came into effect and because everyone wanted the few houses that were on the market the price of a house suddenly sky-rocketed so in a short amount of time large mortgages were having to be taken out on houses that could have been bought previously with just the one wage being taken into consideration. The situation changed and everyone was then buying the same houses they could have previously afforded but were paying out a far greater proportion of their money to pay for them. So they were all then living in the same kind of houses but with less disposable income to spend. Everyone ended up worse off as did the country they lived in because that too suffered due to a lack of trade. As with the credit crunch why couldn't politicians see this would happen? Wasn't it obvious?

Another thing that came about was the fact that manufacturers and dealers in house building products had a field day. Suddenly houses were making more money so they could ask and receive more for their products. There was money flashing around everywhere and they were only too willing to snatch it up. They and the mortgage companies made plenty of money but most people lost out.

When I was a youngster, many years ago, I thought the politicians who ran our countries were chosen for their intellect, wisdom and understanding. I was wrong wasn't I? Just look at England's House of Commons and watch them all jeering at each other like silly spoilt children. Why can't they be the adults we are paying good wages for and why can't they just talk to each other like adults should do? Why can't they appreciate what we pay them, sometimes out of very small wages and also why can't they appreciate they have been voted into office by us because we need them to run our country for us? Their job is important and carries much responsibility. I'm sure we would all appreciate them manning, or womanning up (Is that a word) to the task.

And another thing. Why does one side of the House automatically think they have to go against every word that the other side utters? Even if one party said the queen's name was Elizabeth the other ones would have to say, "No, she is called Gladys." How sad. Surely the country would be served so much better if they all took a little maturity, intelligence, honesty, effort, thought and civility into the Commons rather than sheer stupidity. Please show me some maturity and honesty and I shall vote again.

Racism:

'People are somehow different because they are a different colour or race'. Why should this be? Why do so many people think this is so? And why have people been hated or have lost their lives because of it?

In the bible it says nothing about God creating a white person and then a black one and then a yellow one and perhaps a red one. One reason it does not say so is because we were not made by a god and the other reason is because we are not different in any way at all apart from those looks and our upbringing. We came about by evolution and that evolution has caused the changes in the ways we have developed in different parts of the world. It just happens that people of African origins have developed black skins and people from the Far East have a yellowish tinge to their skin and are generally slightly shorter. Even Mediterranean people look different to Britons or Americans and those from North Africa are different to those from Central Africa. Look at the difference between white settlers in Australia and New Zealand and their indigenous peoples the Aborigines and Maoris.

'They say Captain Cook discovered Australia but I do think the Aborigines probably discovered it a long time before he did.'

Surely if they had all been created by a god and evolution was not a factor they would all look the same. Why would a creator make such slight differences from country to country which then result in making quite vast differences from one side of the world to the other? There are vast differences in our looks, traditions and ways of life but why be racist about it? It is just fact. Believe me underneath all these differences we are all the same. No race or no person is worse or better than any other. We are all in it together.

Friction does occur, and perhaps quite rightly, if immigration brings with it those who wish to upset the apple cart of life. People do move into the home country of others and try to impose their own beliefs and traditions upon that country. As they rightly say 'When in Rome do as the Romans do'.

If I was to move to a different country I would only do it after first totally researching that country and making sure I could live my life according to their standards. I would also make sure I understood and could uphold their traditions, ideas and beliefs. If I could not I would stay at home. I have seen people ranting about how terrible the English are. The trouble was these people were immigrants into that country and were glad enough to be receiving our benefits as they were ranting. They were running us down while we were paying for them to do so.

Of course this behaviour only goes to feed racism but those people ranting on the streets were being racists themselves anyway. What else could they have expected?

But why do any of these people think one race of person is different or worse than them? A little saying of mine has always been;

'The only person who is worse than the next person is the person who thinks they are somehow better'.

I think it makes sense.

Yes we do live in a world where people move from country to country and yes we are going to find different races everywhere these days but why should that be a great problem? Years and years ago the white folk of the United States hated the blacks (and some still do today) and segregation was imposed but who were these black people? They were Black African Americans which makes any thinking person question the hatred straight away. If they were Black African Americans why were they in America and not at home in Africa? Some of them may well have come across the Atlantic of their own free will but others were descendants of the poor souls who had been dragged there as slaves. They should have received great apologies not hate.

Slavery then and now, because it still goes on today, is a totally horrendous and hideous thing. How can any person ever 'belong' to another? Above I have slated white people for the enslavement of blacks and it did happen but their captors in places such as the Gambia were actually fellow black people. They were encouraged by the white traders but saw little wrong in selling off their fellow countrymen for a few shekels or whatever money they had. They themselves were racists as they only picked on those of different tribes. Obviously, as today, they thought their 'tribe' was the best.

Different races will always act differently. Even if I did move to a different country and did uphold totally their way of life I would still be me with all that was bred in me. No Muslim family who immigrate into England are going to suddenly eat pie and mash, wear mini-skirts and become Christians are they? This though should never make them targets of racists should it? What is wrong with people from different countries, religions and races providing they all live good honest lives without hurting each other?

They say 'love thy neighbour'. We should rightly do so although that neighbour is very likely these days to be of a different race to us.

I have known many people from many different countries and believe me under each façade lies a normal human being who is just trying to make a decent way in life. I am no better than an African American and no worse than a Muslim. They are who they are and I am me. Be yourselves and treat everyone else with the true love, respect, consideration and dignity they deserve.

Homophobia:

During my earlier life the act of homosexuality was completely frowned upon and deemed illegal. To many it was thought a disgusting thing to do. Two men or two women falling in love? My goodness! The next thing you know is they will be having sex with each other! Where was common sense? Of

254

course, homosexuality had been going on for millennia but people chose not to talk about it. Heterosexuals frowned upon it but homosexuals obviously could see nothing wrong with it and being the way they were they quite enjoyed it.

In the United Kingdom a law was passed in 1967 called the 'Sexual Offences Act 1967'. It decriminalised sexual acts between two men in private providing both men had reached the age of 21. For some reason though this new and quite provocative law did not cover the merchant navy or armed forces. You may question why. Perhaps they thought homosexuals were not butch enough to be in the army and kill people. I don't know but at least the act was a step forward.

This was a United Kingdom law but it was not actually decriminalised in Scotland until 1980 and not in Northern Ireland until 1982. It has all taken time but we have seen Civil Partnerships and now the fight has been won for full homosexual marriages although the church is in the red corner of the fight against it. In their wisdom the Church says it is wrong and will not accommodate such services. I say if they want nothing to do with the practise perhaps they should keep out of the argument altogether. It would be like me arguing against a new bus service through my village. If I didn't have to pay for it and had no intentions of using it or supporting it I really should mind my own business. If the church doesn't wish to play the game then perhaps they shouldn't try to make the rules.

Will the Church eventually give in to popular belief and take the much needed cash for the services? I would not be at all surprised. Not too many years go the Church frowned upon sex before marriage and a child conceived before marriage was a terrible thing. It would not even marry anyone who had been divorced but how things have changed. The Church used to have so much money it could then be picky but their traditions and beliefs have had to be bent rather to accommodate their wallets. One of my daughters (a divorcee) married her husband (a divorcee) in church with their daughter and my granddaughter

Lucy (born out of wedlock) present. They and we were all greeted very warmly as was the fee we paid to the Church. How necessity changes beliefs, dogma and ideas.

Before I go on here I will be honest and make an admission. Being a heterosexual man I can easily tolerate in my mind the thought of two women having sex together but the thought of two men doing the same thing does turn me off rather. Obviously if a heterosexual man thinks of two women having sex together he thinks of two female bodies, bodies he is normally attracted to but if he thinks about two men having sex he has to imagine two bodies like his own and they are certainly not bodies he is attracted to. To me the thought of two men together is quite horrendous but that is just my natural instinct. Where an intelligent person wins through is the fact he or she will always see beyond their natural instincts.

A short while ago I looked at some smoked mackerel being served up for someone's dinner and remarked how wonderful it looked and smelled. Someone else looked at me and said the mackerel was disgusting. I tried but could not explain to her how she was wrong. Her natural instinct was that mackerel were disgusting and that was that. She may well have thought that but if only she had the intelligence to see that mackerel is one of the tastiest and healthiest foods you could ever possibly eat. She was entitled to her feelings but those feelings should have been tempered with thought.

I also know someone who hates mushrooms and therefore cannot see why other people eat them. Could he possibly just think a little and realise the problem is only his?

No, I could not relish the thought of two men having sex together but like the chap with the mushrooms that is my problem. I was born and grew up as a heterosexual and have only ever wanted to have sex with females but if I had been born as a homosexual or a bi-sexual my thoughts and feelings would obviously be totally different.

No one just wakes up in the morning and decides on a whim that they are going to be homosexual that day and no homosexual wakes up in the morning and decides they are going to be heterosexual. We are all what we are and providing it doesn't hurt anyone what is wrong with it? Rape or paedophilia is wrong whether you are heterosexual of homosexual just as consensual sex between either has to be totally okay. What is wrong with anyone leading their lives as they wish providing no one is being harmed in any way?

Someone once told me if his son came to him and admitted he was a homosexual he would have to kill him. I asked why he thought that way when all his son was, was the product of his father's genes. Anything the father saw as an imperfection was ultimately his own fault anyway as those imperfections had to have come either from him or the child's mother.

Half of all heterosexual marriages end in divorce. Let's hope homosexuals can make a better job of it. Good luck to all of them.

The growth of hatred:

When I was a lad at school boys and girls would fall out and sometimes they would fight but all fights were short lived and almost harmless. Someone might have received a quick smack, didn't like the pain and then they backed down. The worst I ever saw was a black eye. The fights were short and generally silly and almost as soon as they were over the two contenders were best of friends again.

We all squabbled, argued and bickered and despite it being a relatively rough school with us ruffians in it there was never any real bitterness. Even after all these years I do still sometimes bump into one or two of my old schoolmates and we talk of the time with great fondness.

What has happened today though? In my day if someone was down on the ground they were just seen as having lost but today there is so much hatred that when someone goes down the boots go in and they get a good kicking or worse.

My headmaster gave me four strokes of the cane once and he hit me so hard he brought out blood blisters across both hands. I had done wrong and it was his job to punish me and many years later we actually laughed together about the situation. He did feel sorry for what he had done and I felt sorry he had to do it. This in those days was what life was all about but just recently we have heard of a schoolboy not liking his teacher so he felt the need to stab her to death. Why oh why? Even the toughest, roughest and most hardened of us at our school would never ever have dreamed of harming a teacher let alone murder them. This type of crime is very rare in the UK today but what of the future? It has always been said that whatever happens in the States will eventually happen in England and as we all know mass shootings in schools in the States are becoming quite commonplace.

In saying what I am saying, believe me, I am not knocking all youngsters as did my father in my younger days. To him if you were young you were an automatic waste of time, space and good oxygen. No, there are many millions of lovely kids throughout the world and I praise them all for it but so many these days have become disaffected, totally hardened and hold no respect for anyone. The problem with those who do not have respect for others is that eventually they have no respect even for themselves.

Many youths, mainly in cities, are members of gangs and these gangs soon learn to hate each other and the hatred goes so deep they often stab each other, sometimes to death. Even worse, there is a gun culture and they are not afraid to use them, even if an innocent child should happen to be in the way as they shoot. I saw a youth being filmed for television and as he was being filmed another youth was seen walking along the opposite side of the road. The first youth said the other youth had to be 'sorted' and when asked why, he was shocked at the question and apparent naivety of the questioner.

"He doesn't belong to our gang," the youth answered. "And he is in our area so he has to pay for it."

How can someone have to be 'sorted' just because they walk down a road? The lad wasn't of a different colour, creed, race or religion and he was doing no harm whatsoever other than being a member of a different gang.

We see the hatred vented towards other people but I wonder what it must be like having to live with all this hatred inside you. I live with a very light feeling towards the world and those in it. My mind and body are always chilled. Even if someone annoys me (and they do) I try hard not to get angry and let it affect my life. I just carry on in the same relaxed manner but what must it feel like to be permanently angry, to live life with a volcano of hate erupting inside? It cannot be good can it? So why not ditch any anger, try to understand the feelings of others and live a relaxed life? You will never stop other people being stupid or angry but at least you will feel better yourself.

I know we have always had crime and a certain amount of hate and always will have but just as with global warming it is all becoming far more prevalent and wanton.

On entry to night clubs these days revellers are searched to stop knives being taken inside so what have these people done? They have disguised knives as other items. I have recently seen one disguised very convincingly as a perfectly normal looking comb. Within seconds this 'comb' could be taken apart to kill someone. Surely these people should just be going into night clubs to meet friends and have a good time. This is not the old Wild West. They do not have to go into a bar with weapons. Even when they come out, many of them have consumed so much alcohol that they start fighting.

In the sixties we did have trouble with mods and rockers but they were just silly boys and girls. What is happening now is completely serious and out of hand.

What is wrong with the world when so much alcohol and or drugs have to be consumed just to have a 'good time'? The trouble is they are not really having a good time are they? All they are doing is masking and getting away from a life that they cannot really handle. If they had respect for themselves at all they would never need to get plastered to that extent anyway. It can be wonderful meeting friends, having a few drinks and maybe a dance with a pretty girl or handsome lad. Surely that is what going out should be for but for more and more going out is just a way to get smashed and divorce themselves from reality. The trouble is once the alcohol kicks in the inhibitions melt and all kinds of bad behaviours ensue. I tell younger people that I used to go out with £1 in my pocket, buy a gallon of petrol for my Ford Cortina, buy two or three pints of beer and a Castella cigar, have fish and chips in town and then still have enough left over for a prostitute on the way home. I do exaggerate a little because even in those days a prostitute would have cost 50p and I was too tight for that. The rest you could have bought for the £1 though. It was a simple but enjoyable life. We did not need to get paralytic or high on drugs to escape from the world. We were satisfied with the world we lived in but perhaps today the world is much more complex.

So we have a huge population, are running short of fuel, our air is heavily polluted and we have all this hatred in the world. Am I right with my thoughts and are we already experiencing the *'Mr and Mrs X syndrome'*?

Bullying:

Someone asked me the other day if I was bullied at school and after thinking about it I realised there was no real bullying in our school. We all had bad days with someone picking on us but those days were few and far between and we couldn't possibly class them as bullying. Very occasionally someone did shed a tear over what had been said by some loud mouthed oaf but that was as far as it went. Today you see children committing suicide because of it. What sort of bullies can actually continue so relentlessly right up to the point that a person takes an overdose of pills or hangs themselves? Can they not see and feel the abject torment, terror and pain of the person concerned or are they so twisted that they actually do not care?

We hear of youngsters being bullied by text or through social network sites. I would say to anyone who is being bullied, and it probably will not help their torment but what I say is always remember that no bully is happy within their own mind. Any bully does it because they are tormented themselves in some way and are venting their anger at you. They are all pathetic little people and should be ignored although that isn't easy is it?

One good piece of advice I would give is if you are being bullied by text then change your number and if you are being bullied on any social network site then do not go to that site. There is life without computers but if you feel you are incapable of surviving without one for even a short while then use it for something else. They can actually be used for things other than social networking or silly games. Why not put your experiences down and write a book as I have done. I know bullying is terrifying and the bullies have no feelings but if you give in to them life can be hell. You and everyone else are better than any bully, all of whom are just silly little souls with nothing better in their lives to think about.

I know I am just being an old codger here but when I was young there was no such thing as a home computer. This is why we saw the proper Wonderment of the world. I know of youngsters who have frightened themselves stupid by spending most of the night playing computer games and then wondering why they cannot function through the next day, the next day and many of the days after as well in fact. I am going on about 'the good old days' again but we were always told of the saying;

'Early to bed and early to rise makes Jack healthy, wealthy and wise.'

Whether your name is Jack, Jill, Agnes or Godfrey I do feel the above words are very true. Some may feel it an old and perhaps outdated phrase but if it was still practised today its theory would work well.

Going back to my dream of living life as an existence farmer or hunter gatherer, a good and very positive thing that would come from it would be the appreciation of the real things in life. We would see (and would need to see) the Wonderment of the weather, the changing seasons and life around us. Our whole lives would be governed by the weather and the seasons and our lives would have to be led in sync with the wildlife around us. We would soon learn to appreciate what is around us and life would become just what it should be today, real. So much of life for so many people today revolves around falseness.

Let's look at the falseness of the world:

(The following are items of falseness but I must say I do mention some of them in a 'tongue-in-cheek' manner)

We have what they call 'reality TV' shows and many do watch the rubbish but 'reality TV' never reflects any of life's reality whatsoever. What do the makers and watchers of these shows actually think life is all about?

How about medical programmes on TV? At the start of them these days they tend to say something like, "This programme does show scenes of a medical nature." What? Of course it does! It's a medical programme isn't it? It's like saying a film of Lady Chatterley's Lover may have a sexual content. Doesn't the title offer a slight clue? I say if we are hurt or offended by such content we just have to turn the thing off or over. Surely there are plenty of other channels to watch or other things to do.

People think they are something special because they buy and wear 'designer' clothes. What are designer clothes? How do we distinguish between designer clothes and non-designer clothes? How can clothes ever be non-designer? Whether it is a £3,000 purse or a £1.50 T-shirt it had to be designed by someone didn't it?

On the same theme people say they are buying an 'architect designed' house. Again what does a non-architect designed house look like? Isn't that what architects do? They design houses. Would you go to the chemists or greengrocers or Specsavers to ask them do design your dream property?

I laugh when I regularly see a restaurant menu or a television chef saying 'Pan fried' this or 'Pan fried' that. They may be advertising 'pan fried' scallops or 'pan fried' squid or 'pan fried' egg and chips but why the emphasis on 'pan fried'? Of course you fry things in a pan. What else would you fry it in? I'd like to see them try to fry things in a cardboard box. They don't say 'oven' cooked roast beef or BBQ fried BBQs do they?

Why is it we see footballers become revered actors and cooks become revered television stars just because they show violence and contempt to those around them? Why do we love a villain and ignore those who do great deeds?

Why is it when some so-called 'celebrity' dies of drugs misuse so many people wail and weep when if it was a highly intelligent person no one would have even heard of them let alone care?

I do not buy celebrity magazines but have glanced at one or two. They are so funny. One thing I have noticed is how they sneak up and take photographs of celebrities wearing swimming costumes and then they comment on how 'life has not been good for those involved over the years as their bodies are not what they used to be'. How false can they get? The bodies of us all sag and degenerate as we get older. It is all natural and does it matter? They are still the same people. When I was twenty-five I had a decent body. You should see it now. Or, no, perhaps you shouldn't.

When you come back home after a holiday the first thing your friends or family say is, "Oh, it can't have been too good a holiday. You haven't got much of a tan have you?" Or, "Look how brown you are. That must have been a good holiday."

Makes you weep doesn't it? Maybe the reason you haven't got much of a tan is because you have been on a wonderful and passionate honeymoon to Iceland and maybe the reason you have got a tan is you had a dreadful holiday in some really hot country and had been thrown out of your hotel and had to live and sleep on the beach. How does a tan determine what sort of holiday you have had? What is a tan anyway? All it is, is

263

damaged skin and can damaged skin possibly make for a better holiday or a better you?

The manufacturing and selling of make-up products is a multi-billion pound industry and it fascinates me. Why do women (and some men) wear it? They only wear it to try to look as good, or better, than the next person when if no one wore it at all they would all look the same, and probably much better, anyway. Heavy make-up can make a person look far worse (to my mind anyway) and how many people dislike themselves so much they actually just wear it to hide behind? Recently I was walking along a small harbour in Norfolk when I saw a young girl of about twenty years of age. She was plastered in make-up and stood in a prominent position so everyone could see her running her fingers through her long bleached blonde hair. She tried her best to give the impression of 'Oh look how lovely I am'. She wasn't though. The whole image was so in your face and cheap that in reality she looked ridiculous although I must say I had just walked eleven miles and was caked in mud so could I really give an opinion? At least my mud was free and real. Obviously there was some gap in this young lady's brain that needed filling and she filled it with complete falseness. Underneath all the filler and gloss you could see she was not a bad looking girl. She had a cute face and a lovely figure and I'm sure if she stood naturally at that harbour with all the make-up removed many a man would have been highly impressed.

I love to look at the advertisements for these products. They are all portrayed in a false way, give false claims and are said to contain miracle chemicals that no one has ever heard of.

"This product," they may say, *"Contains Pro formula feline uronic acid extract."*

People do buy the product, not because it has been proven and is good value but because of what it contains and what the marketers promise it will do. No one knows, though, what Pro formula feline uronic acid extract is but by golly it does sound good and could work wonders on your complexion.

I have made up the term Pro formula feline uronic extract bit but so many would fall for it because it has been mentioned in a classy and glamorous advert but if the additive was real it would have to have something to do with rubbing your face with cat pee.

And why is everything these days called pro this and pro that? Again people fall for it. It may sound good but it is just a word. My dentist recommends a product which begins with the word pro. It is actually a very good product but she does not recommend it because it is a good product, she recommends it because she is sponsored to do so by its manufacturers.

I have seen advertisements on the television for a certain men's deodorant. It shows a man who has used it being chased down the street by several young bikini clad women, all of whom have gorgeous looks and bodies. The first thing I must say is, 'why the hell is he running away?' Why isn't he running towards them? And the other thing I must say is why, when I wear it, does nothing happen? Could the claims in these adverts be just a little exaggerated do you think? However, they do claim this should happen so maybe when it doesn't happen to me I have a good case for misrepresentation and compensation.

And what about products given names like 'World Sabre Superglide II' or 'I Shave Meteor Pro'? I have made up the names because I do not wish to name names but you get the gist. The adverts' claims are always wonderful and glossy but they are all for simple gents razors. They show things like a razor zooming around a bathroom like a fighter jet leaving a trail behind it before being used by a young muscle bound man with looks to match his muscles and stubble. He manly grabs the razor in a manly fashion and gives a cheesy smile for the camera. Why do they never show me first thing in the morning with my five for 20p razors from the supermarket super-savers line? I end up with a smooth face just the same as these younger chaps do with their 'Smooth Slide Super Satin Seductive Sensor VIs'.

I do love adverts for their sheer stupidity. What about the man who sits in a dragster to sell a cleaning product. His spray is supposed to have 'Turbo Power!' How can a household domestic cleaning spray possibly have turbo power? It is such a cheesy advert but what of the man who is selling the stuff? Good luck to him I say. If the advert is appealing to an audience, is selling his product and he is making his fortune then what else can you say but, "Good on you!"

Probably the silliest of adverts are those selling perfumes but when you think about it, in a way, they have to be as you cannot put across the smell of the perfume which is just the thing you are trying to sell. We have invented much but no one has yet come up with smelly vision. The trouble is though that as the smell cannot be put across they then tend to portray the product in as glamorous and false a way as possible. Men and women who try to be so glamorous that they come across as being almost ugly, pose in what are thought to be seductive ways and some husky man in the background says something like, "Possum Pooh, the fragrance by Kevin Kiln." Why can't they just say, "Buy this one because it is only £8.99 and it smells nice."

A product was advertised yesterday with the claim that it was judged as better than every other product in its class. Sounds good but what if their product was just expensive rubbish while all the other products were complete expensive rubbish? And many of them say their product is an 'award winning product'. What they don't say is who awarded the award. Was it to themselves by themselves?

Another advert which is for a foreign shampoo claims you must be quick to get some because it is selling extremely fast. It doesn't take a huge intellect to work out the fact that if it is selling so fast that you have to rush to buy some then why are they bothering to pay good money to advertise it?

And lastly because I am enjoying this but probably boring you, when they show a hunky young man eating a chocolate bar have you ever noticed how he holds it? He always grips it fully and firmly in his large hand. His hand completely envelops the bar and then he looks at it in a macho way as if to say, "I am going to devour you once I have finished looking stupid." The problem is he looks at the bar for so long as it is clutched in his grip that the whole thing must melt before be takes a bite.

Advertisements, whether they are on television, radio or in the press cost money and most of them cost a lot of money so no one would pay for them unless they knew the advert would sell the product concerned. All the above adverts are rather sad but they must work. Obviously many people in many countries are falling for them. The Latin phrase 'Caveat Emptor' is a phrase I remember from my young college days and the phrase means 'Let the buyer beware'. As with the rest of this book, look and listen to the advert, dissect it and think about it before you part with your money. A great deal of money is made from those who do not think.

People have been made rich and others have been murdered because of diamonds. This is another thing that I cannot understand. Why all the fuss? What is a diamond? Is it some mystical item or an object that can bring happiness to millions? No. It is sometimes seen as an object which portrays wealth and the bigger it is the better off you are and therefore the better person you are but what is a diamond in a real world? It is a piece of stone isn't it? It is something dug up from the ground. A 118 carat diamond was once sold for \$30.6 million but what use did it have? None at all really. It might have made a good doorstop but you may as well just have bought the 118 carrots. At least you could eat them.

Early humans treasured flint because it was useful. Flint is a stone exactly the same as is a diamond. Why don't we put a piece of flint in a ring and say "Oh look at me"? Then we could all have a big one?

No stone, whether it is a diamond or a piece of flint will ever make you a better person. It is just the same as make-up. However big the stone you own is or however much make-up you have plastered on your face you are still the same person.

Cosmetic surgery is another multi-billion pound industry today but who needs it? Yes, there are people who do genuinely need cosmetic or plastic surgery and it should be there and free for them but why do so many people pay so much money to go through so much pain and discomfort when, in the end, they are again still the same person afterwards?

Why do we live in a world where women must have big boobs no matter how they get them and no matter what chemicals they have stuffed inside them? What is so great about big boobs getting in the way whatever you are trying to do? And how many of them look real afterwards? If a woman suddenly has big boobs is she suddenly a better person? She may be bigger and less feminine perhaps, but not better.

I sat talking with two young ladies once and the subject turned to looks. One young lady said she hated her body and asked the other if there was anything about her body and features she actually liked. The reply was there was nothing about herself that she liked apart from her nose. I smiled but then realised they were both being completely serious. I couldn't believe it. Both of these girls were truly gorgeous and I tried to tell them so but it was already too late. They had already spent years convincing themselves they were ugly and believed it deeply.

I have seen people who have had cosmetic surgery and have become quite depressed after. They go in for the procedures thinking they will come out of them looking just as they have dreamed and they also come out of them thinking they would be a totally different person but, of course, this does not and can never happen. They may look different and probably sometimes a little better but a nose job or a tummy tuck can never change a person's personality. Post op patients are still the same person inside and no operation can change that. What we have to do is learn to totally accept who we are as we are. We need to dump self-loathing and be ourselves.

Where has all this self-loathing come from? Of course it has come from television and soppy celebrity magazines full of soppy people. Men and women everywhere have been silently brainwashed into believing these kind of people should be revered and looked up to. None of the people in any of these soppy magazines are ever any better looking than normal people but they had been put on such high pedestals that they are almost worshipped as gods and goddesses. I suppose if there was such a thing as a great god who was all-powerful and all-seeing then we could well be tempted to aspire to his looks and ways as well.

These so-called 'celebrities' are just ordinary everyday folk who just happen to have had a lucky break or two in life and most of the photographs shown in the magazines have been touched up to hide warts, blemishes, lumps and bumps anyway.

We see them all strutting around like proud hens on the now obligatory 'red carpets'. Their looks, manners and poise all shout, "Oh look at me. I'm on the red carpet and I am special!" Does standing on a red carpet make you a better person as well? All my carpets are a light brown colour. Where does that put me on the carpet colour scale? Quite a way down I would imagine.

I once knew a woman who had such a drastic face lift she ended up with a goatee beard.

(Think about it.)

Today's so-called 'Celebrity Culture' drives me mad when the soppiest of people are so highly revered when they look stupid, have done nothing and have achieved nothing. Some time ago a 'celebrity couple' were going through a divorce (Bless their little hearts) and I heard one person ask another which of the two people involved they she felt sorry for. I only felt sorry for anyone who was the remotest bit interested. This isn't life and these people are not 'real'.

I do jest to some extent but I genuinely do think we should try and get away from glamour and falseness and focus on the true realities of life. Our planet is heading feet first into uncertainty and possible oblivion and no amount of make-up, cosmetic surgery, designer goods, celebrities or red carpets are ever going to stop it.

Another little thought.

If financial advisers are so good with money why do they have to work for a living?

Before I move on to what is, to my mind, the most important chapter of the book can I please point out that I am not just a grumpy old man. I may be a grumpy old man but I am not 'just' a grumpy old man. I am other things as well. I do feel strongly that we should all try to live in a real world and get the best out of life that we can for ourselves and those around us. I may come across as being a grumpy old man but believe me in reality I am totally happy and content and have a great love and lust for life.

Let's stop talking about me though and talk about the 'Wonder of You' which, I'm afraid does contain some more bits about me. It is my book after all.

We will proceed. P.T.O. (That means Please turn over, not Please turn off.)

1 3
The Wonder of You

This chapter is the last and most important of all as it is all about you.

"You are everything and everything is you"

The Stylistics song 1971.

You are everything and that is fact. We all love others dearly but in the end the most important person in your life has to be you.

But before we begin properly we have to ask the question "Why are you here"?

Religionists say in unison that you are here because a god made you. It is a god's will that you live and it will be his will that dictates when you die. This must be the way of it all because if you are not here at the behest of a god and you are not here to serve that god then there can be no purpose to your life at all and you would simply not be here.

So can we just say?

God made you.

God watches you.

God expects you to sing and pray to him.

God listens to you.

God judges you.

God rebukes and punishes you.

God takes you.

God decides whether you go to heaven or hell.

Is this really all that a child's life is, being the property of a god? If it could be true then this would be the same for every man, woman, child or animal and there the Wonderment would end.

So can you exist without a god? If you have a god you have life. If you have life you have to have a god. That is what religionists would say but again, what a simple answer to a vastly important question. I nearly said a vastly important and complex question but it isn't is it? You are here because you are here. It is as simple as that. I like Cornish holidays and ice cream but there is no complex reason why. I just do.

I am here and so are you but why are we really here and what is the real meaning of life? So many have pondered the true meaning of life, they have thought long and hard. Even the most educated of us all have pondered it and no one has been able to come up with any answer at all and do you know why? There is a good reason why one has not been found and that is simply because there isn't one. Why should there be a meaning to life? Why can't we just accept that we evolved, are here and that is it. I am me and you are you. We are here and we are happy.

They say what is the point of living if life has no 'meaning'? Of course our lives have meaning as we live them but why should life have had a meaning to evolve? The chemicals were there and it just did and we are here to make the best of it.

I like a cold beer on a hot day but does there have to be a reason for it? I don't enjoy it because a god made me enjoy it. I just enjoy it. Why must everything be so complicated?

In the universal scale of things we are just tiny animals living on a tiny planet which orbits a tiny star. In the great scheme of things we are nothing. We could all be wiped out tomorrow and the universe would be none the poorer for it. One day the earth will die as a liveable planet and will then be consumed by the sun but the universe will carry on. Our planet will die but so many more will either carry on existing or will evolve from other dying stars. So are we so totally insignificant? No, of course we are not. While we are here on earth every one of our lives is totally significant. Every one of our lives is totally unique, special and precious in every way. Let's look at why.

You and I are here because life has evolved so that our parents could come together and create us and without going into the ins and outs of sex too much let's discuss what happened to make us.

To create a person or a python, a fish or a fox, a bat or a badger, or a hippopotamus or a horse a sperm from a male has to come together with an egg from a female and fertilise it. This fertilisation can take place within the body of the female or, as in the case of a fish, on the riverbed or seabed but wherever it takes place the process is much the same. We are humans so we will concentrate on us.

For a human couple to reproduce the man's penis has to enter the woman's vagina and as he ejaculates many sperm are released and they then have to race to the woman's egg and fertilise it. During an ejaculation a male will emit anything up to 300 million sperm cells while only one is actually needed for reproduction. This, I suppose, could be seen as all being part of the survival of the fittest regime. The sperm that actually reaches and penetrates the egg first must be the fittest and healthiest and therefore the best candidate for reproduction. Sperm are produced constantly in men while women are born with all their eggs actually inside them already. They are not really actual eggs at this point but are what we call 'follicles'. Inside a baby girl's body there are approximately $1 - 2$ million follicles but only around 400 of these actually survive and mature into fertilisable eggs.

This brings us to a sum. The chance of any one sperm reaching and fertilising the egg first could be somewhere in the region of 300,000,000-1 and the chance of a particular egg being fertilised is somewhere in the region of 400-1 so the chance of a particular sperm fertilising a particular egg and producing you is around 120,000,000,000-1. That is 120 billion to one against you or I being born.

If you won the Lotto jackpot you would think you were quite special but the chances of that are a mere 14 million to one. This means you are up to 8,571 times more likely to win the Lotto than you are actually being born. Now how special does that make you? Very I would say.

So the chances of us existing are very slim but, as with all life on earth, it must have happened because we are here. You are here and so am I and we are all special. Your sperm did reach the egg first and nine months later you emerged as a tiny bundle of joy for your parents. You may have been an odd and wrinkly little thing but all of you had formed and so had many of your characteristics. The split second your father's sperm penetrated your mother's egg your fate was sealed. As with the beginning of the universe there was basically nothing but everything was there to form you and your character. Your traits and your ability to think were also there, soon to be packaged in your tiny brain. We are shaped by the world we grow up in and the different things we encounter but so much of 'you' is already there as the sperm meets the egg. Life is a combination of character and experience and sometimes these can become obscured but together they do make us.

Two children brought up in the same household can become two totally different and distinct characters. I know I have touched upon this before but let's look at another analogy:

Brothers Roger and Richard were born just over a year apart into the same household and to the same parents. They grow up with turbulence around them as their father regularly gets drunk and beats their mother. They witnessed it on several occasions but were only small and were completely powerless to help. Their mother was a good and kind wife and mother and Roger was shattered and heartbroken. Richard, on the other hand, witnessed it all in relative silence.

Roger and Richard grew up and both married. Probably due to his experiences Roger was a quiet man. He didn't speak much to his wife about what had happened in his childhood but he knew very deeply and strongly that his father's behaviour was totally wrong and unforgivable. He therefore very seldom drank and treated his wife with the great kindness and respect she deserved and she became a doting wife and mother because of it.

In Richard's case though things were different, he had witnessed the same as his brother and although quiet at the time it had all worried him greatly and this worry turned him to drink and the drink turned him to violence. He married but his wife's fate was much the same as his mother's.

Was it his father's violence that drove Richard to drink or was the need bred in him in the first place?

Did he become violent himself because he thought as that was how his father had behaved it was somehow the natural thing to do or was the violence bred in him as well? Did the drink breed violence or did the violence breed drink or were they both inherited?

Did Roger rebel against the violence and drink because of his experiences or did he manage to inherit his gentleness and sobriety from his mother?

As you can see, life does mould us but much of what we are is what we are when we are made. Also though you can see how both issues can be clouded together to a certain extent.

Whether we are what we are or we become what we are as we grow or whether we are an intertwined mixture of the two it does make us all very complex individuals and because of all this we are all completely different and that again is a wonder. There are seven billion humans on the earth and every one of us is completely different in character and therefore completely special. I am me and you are you. We are all the same but completely different. If any god had created us we would all be the same and not different at all. Let's say God did manage to make us. How could he ever have come up with seven billion different characters?

Some people 'love' themselves, some people hate themselves and some of us just have a healthy respect for the people we are but no matter what opinion you have of yourself always remember you are special. We are all special and we are all different and also in many ways we are all flawed. We have faults and we have traits, some of which it is hard for others to understand.

I have formed a theory in my mind which states that we think but the exact opposite of what we think is sometimes the case. Funnily enough I have named my theory *'The Theory Of Opposites'*. It goes something like this:

A person is quiet and you therefore think he is miserable when, in reality, he is totally content in his world and just likes to let others talk so as not to be rude. Also by listening to their conversations he is continuously learning. In no way is he miserable. He is just happy, kind and accommodating.

A person such as my young lady example at the Norfolk harbour wants you to look at her in all her make-up so that you think she is something special when underneath all her mask she is actually a very insecure individual who feels a strong need to be accepted.

It probably doesn't usually happen but have you ever sat on a train and looked at someone who is reading the Guardian newspaper? He or she may be taking it all in with great intent and knowledge but the next time you look just give it a slightly different stance. Maybe the person cannot read at all but has picked up a copy of the Guardian just to try to impress you.

A man in a pub is drinking pint after pint of beer and looks like he is having a wonderful time. He thinks he is being manly but far more likely he is only doing it because it is the only way he knows to mask the fact that he cannot cope with life.

A lady buys drink at a bar and as she hands over her money she purposely lifts up her finger to display a huge diamond set in a ring. She is trying to say she is special but in doing so all she is saying in reality is 'look at me. I need this piece of stone to try and prove I am something, anything at all'.

I am not a great lover of Christmas and because of this people say I am miserable. Again, the complete opposite is the fact. I adore life 365 days a year and therefore do not find 25th December particularly different. It is great for religionists as it is supposed to be the birthday of Jesus although there is not an actual register of his birth so no one knows when he was born. Certainly no one can deny it is a wonderful time for children.

I think times have changed and Christmas has lost its magic and sparkle because we are all so much better off these days. In my younger days (Here we go again) my parents had to save hard for just a big chicken or small turkey and because of this it was special. Now most of us could have chicken or turkey every week or even every day of the week if we wanted.

I could go on and I know I do but let's get back to the book.

Going back to the slim chance of us ever being born. The chances were very slim but we made it and we were born but none of us ever asked to be born did we? We were all thrust into the world as living, breathing, seeing and hearing creatures without any choice of what kind of person we would become in the wholly uncertain life that lay before us. We came into the world with nothing and with absolutely no idea what we were going to do with it. All we can possibly do is try our hardest and do the best we can. Some will see their lives as a success and some will see things totally differently. Some will see money as a success. Others will see knowledge as the best thing. Others yet will wonder what the hell life is for at all.

This is the point of this chapter. You may not have asked for life but you have it. You were born and you are stuck with the fact. In reality you have two choices. You can either take life as bad luck and live your life in misery or you can grab life with both hands, give it all you have got and love it. I would strongly suggest the latter as it is fun. There can be no contest between happiness and misery so why choose misery? We may never achieve all our dreams and aspirations but we should all have fun in trying. There is true Wonderment in being born and there is even more Wonderment in living the life you were given to its full.

Talking of dreams and aspirations takes my mind back to the Channel 4 television serious 'Derek' again. The scene went something like this.

A man who has money and continually aspires to be richer is talking to Derek and says,

"What is it like living without a lot of money?"

"It is the same as living with a lot of money", Derek answers. "But with a lot less money."

Derek is portrayed as a man without a huge amount of brains but underneath his almost childish exterior is a man of some wisdom who is admired by everyone.

In his answer Derek is actually saying that life is life and life is special no matter if you are rich or poor and he is absolutely right. As I said in my Wonder Of Wonderment chapter you do not have to be wealthy to enjoy the best things in life as they are truly free.

I will try to put this across in another story:

A young man works hard to better himself financially. He starts a business and from the proceeds of it he buys and renovates a small cottage. Life is quite sweet and because he is young he can tolerate the 75+ hours of work he has to do each week. He could be satisfied with his lot and live a simple but quite comfortable lifestyle in his cottage but he is not like that. Either because of ambition or insecurity he is motivated to do 'better' so he starts another small business and then moves to a larger house which can accommodate that business within its grounds.

In the meantime he had worked hard and felt the need to buy himself a hugely powerful sports car as this was something he

had always wanted even from being a small child and leafing through a 1960s Observers Book of Automobiles.

The new property he bought and moved to had four bedrooms, a swimming pool and a barn at the bottom of the land which would house the new business.

So here was this young man who after just a few short years had moved from a rented bungalow to his own small renovated cottage and from that to a four bed house, swimming pool, two cars and two businesses.

Things were rosy and looking up for a while but then the person started to have quite serious health issues. A childhood back problem flared up badly and caused him much pain and discomfort and he found work difficult. Coupled with this was the fact that the first of his businesses ran into difficulties which meant he had to rely too heavily upon his new fledgling business which saw the demise of that as well.

Money and health issues caused the loss of the house, the swimming pool, his cars and businesses and this man and his family were forced to move out and into council accommodation with ill health and little money.

It would seem they had lost everything but no, they hadn't. They had lost all the trappings of life but they still had life and they still had each other and as the man always said, "It doesn't matter how wealthy you are you still have the same birds singing outside your window each morning".

Some of my analogies are probably untrue and a little far-fetched but this one is absolutely true and I know so because the man in question here was me. Yes, those times were hard. We did still have life and had life around us but I cannot say it was all without physical and mental anguish. The thing is though that we did cling on to life and each other and yes, they were the same birds singing outside our window. I was not a wealthy man or a healthy man but we still managed to go out and see all the Wonderment around us. No wealthy and healthy person could have seen anything different. Like me in my earlier days, they would probably have been too wrapped up in their dreams and aspirations to have noticed anyway.

Whether it is someone drinking heavily to hide their failings or someone wearing too much make-up or someone trying to show he has money when either he has or he hasn't or someone bullying someone else it is all down to a crippling condition called 'insecurity'.

Why do some people verbally run others down for no real reason? It is through the insecurity inside them.

Why do people comfort-eat so much they become morbidly obese? It is through insecurity.

Why do people develop other eating disorders? Again, it is through insecurity.

Why did Adolf Hitler try to rule the world? It all basically came down to the same reason.

So why do so many people feel insecure, so insecure in many cases that it can wreck their lives?

Insecurity, I suppose, can be seen along the same lines as having an inferiority complex, or are they the same thing?

Again I have to talk about me to demonstrate the whole thing. Please bear with me again.

I am not a bad person and I am no better or worse than anyone else. I certainly am not inferior to anyone else in any way and I also am in no way unworthy but without thinking, this is what my parents did their best to instil in me as a youngster and to a large extent it worked.

As children my sister and I were not perfect. No child or adult ever is. We did wrong sometimes, sometimes unknowingly and sometimes knowingly with the hope we would not get caught but in our naughtiness we were never bad. Everything we did do wrong though was pounced upon mainly due to our father's insecurity. Being wholly in charge was his way of satisfying his own insecurities and ego. He could never praise but boy could he find fault. We were put down for the slightest thing, not usually in a physical way but in a psychological way which hurt far more than any beating and had far longer lasting symptoms and consequences.

I laugh about it now but I remember once when I was about eight years old we visited my uncle, aunt and cousin who lived on a farm. My uncle was the farm manager. It was autumn and my cousin and I wanted to go onto the farm to find conkers. We were allowed but were told in no way were we to go to the conker tree on the edge of the field of black beans. Off we went excited at the prospect of filling our bags with choice conkers ready to thrash everyone at school the next day.

A while later we found a huge conker tree on the edge of a field and I asked my cousin what the plants were in the field and he shrugged his shoulders and said they were broad beans or something. We gleefully threw sticks into the tree and started to fill our bags but then my father and uncle appeared. I said hello but quickly saw my father was rather more than angry. He was absolutely one hundred percent bouncing up and down with rage and I feared his head was going to explode. He was waving a large stick around like a whirling dervish.

We were roughly shepherded out of the field under all kinds of threats and abuse but still I did not know why. When I did manage to get a word in edgeways and ask what was wrong my father became even more enraged and said he wanted to hit me with the stick. I was dumbstruck. My father had always been a law unto himself and had never actually been a caring and loving sort of chap but now it seemed he wanted to knock me about with a stick without explanation.

Luckily my uncle managed to stop him hitting me and he said, in a calmer voice, that we were told not to go in the black bean field and we had defied our orders. I tried hard to explain that in no way did I know we were in the black bean field but my father's angst was inconsolable.

I was eight years old for goodness sake. Up to that day I had never even heard of a black bean. I had heard of baked beans but they were orange. My father's rage was not wholly aimed at me though was it? Much of it was aimed at a world in which he could not quite fit, a world which made him angry because he always wanted everything his way and although he mostly did get his way it was not all of the time and he resented the fact. Through his own insecurities he reacted far too strongly to our little misdemeanours and this did make us feel insecure ourselves. I did not know which bean was which but my father never would believe me so in the end I just had to let it drop. The truth was he did not want to believe me. He felt good in being right so why should he ever listen and let himself be proved wrong? He did manage to calm down after a month or two and life did return to something near normal.

Another little incident comes to mind that happened just a few weeks before the scandalous 'case of the black bean'. I had been in bed for a few days after contracting German measles and as I lay there I took to drawing and drew an aircraft. It was no masterpiece but I was proud of its looks, its fuselage and its biplane configuration. My mother saw it and complimented me, which was very unusual in itself but when she showed it to my father he completely and utterly refused to believe I had drawn it and plainly and simply called me a liar. He said it was a drawing done by someone else. Who else was in the bedroom? Was it Father Christmas hiding up the chimney?

As children we were rubbish and we were made to know the fact. I do honestly believe my mother loved us even then but she did not say it until just before she died many years later. No affection was shown to us and no affection was ever shown between my mother and father, well not openly anyway.

On the day my father died it fell to me to visit my mother and tell her what had happened. It was something I was proud to do (And rightfully of wrongfully glad to do). She was in bed when I arrived at her house and I woke her as I opened the door. In her heart she knew the reason for my early visit but I sat beside her on her bed and calmly told her. She sobbed and sobbed but even today I question the reason for the sobbing. Was it because she had just lost the great love of her life or was it because he was such a tyrant and she was glad to see the back of him? In truth

282

the reason had to lie somewhere in between but she is also gone and I shall never find out.

Getting back to my insecurities. I worked from the age of twelve to buy my own clothes and other nice things but my father never did thank me for that. When I was sixteen I bought a battered old scooter from our local Saturday auction for eight pounds and to go with it I bought a parka coat. My father actually said the coat was the best thing I had ever bought. I took that as a compliment as it was the closest thing to one he had ever uttered or would ever utter.

Apart from the parka coat everything I ever did was wrong no matter how right it was and I became painfully insecure.

Long hair was in fashion when I was young and I dreamed of mine one day coming down to and touching my ears but my father would always insist on a 'short back and sides'. I looked like a Second World War soldier who had just been demobbed and luckily I worked to buy my own clothes because otherwise I would have been dressed in hobnail boots, my granddad's trousers and a demob suit for Sundays.

When I reached the age of sixteen I had my scooter and more freedom. I worked hard and bought myself a purple silk shirt, sunglasses, hipster trousers and winkle-picker shoes. I also let my hair grow down to my shoulders. I was becoming a man and had the freedom to do what 'I' wanted at last. I wanted it all. I wanted to look myself, not something my father had moulded and I managed it. I screamed Hurrah!!!! at the top of my voice but looking back I now laugh because I had rebelled so much I did look a bit of a pillock.

I love to love and be loved and always did. When I was at high school, or secondary school as we called it in those days, some girls used to fancy me. One even said at the dinner table that she preferred me to all the other boys and she was extremely pretty too but did I do anything about it? No, of course I didn't. She was pretty and I was me. She was gorgeous and had practically thrown herself at me but I was far too unworthy. I did nothing but later when I saw her walking hand in hand down the street with one of my mates I was stunned. Life can be hard sometimes.

Even when I took home my first real and serious girlfriend the first thing my mother said was "She is far too good for you."

I married that girlfriend and have my lovely daughter and son by the marriage but even after becoming a man, getting married and fathering children, my insecurities still dominated my life. I have banished them all these days and have a very healthy respect for the person I am but it does still pain me just a little that my childhood relationship with my parents was not more loving and rewarding.

The moral of the story is no child is ever asked if they want to be born. They are made out of choice by their parents and it is up to those parents to give them as big and good a chance as they can in their childhood. Most children do go off into the world to find their own way eventually but kind, helpful and loving guidance beforehand can be priceless.

Many children are unloved or if they are loved they are not told so. This leads to all manner of problems which can blight lives. A lack of love can lead to my kind of insecurity which luckily was something that, step by step, I managed to banish from my life but it can also lead to stronger emotions such as self-loathing or self-disgust. These then lead to depression, self-harming, anorexia, bulimia, drug and alcohol abuse or even the contemplation of or the actually act of suicide.

I wonder how many children have sought out sex in the mistaken belief what they were getting was love. They sought affection but in reality only received attention.

I should imagine my insecurities were and still are symptoms suffered by many people and those symptoms were relatively harmless. I have learned much from them but for those symptoms to lead to more drastic and consequential actions is very worrying and sad.

I did have a wonderful upbringing with all the freedom and Wonderment the world had to offer but that great early life could have been enhanced so much more if it was founded upon love, care and compassion. I had a father who had no wish to give love and a mother who desperately wanted to but had no idea how, but I am me and who wants to feel bitter?

I would advise in the strongest way possible that all parents should show love to their children and very much to each other in front of their children. Of course badly behaved children should be rebuked but well behaved children should always be praised and loved. As I have said before, today I have a very healthy respect for myself, if only I had been able to feel some of that self-respect when I was a child. As is always said, 'If only I knew then what I know now'.

It has to be the duty of all parents to teach their children self-respect because it is only through having respect for themselves that they will ever show full respect for others.

I did not loath or hate myself I just never had any respect for or confidence in myself. Back then I would willingly have been anyone rather than me but now if anyone was to ask me if I had the choice to be reincarnated as anyone at all who would it be? I could honestly hold my head up high and give the answer "ME PLEASE!!!" You too should always feel the same.

I have mentioned anger and bitterness before in the book and obviously my father suffered from both but he was certainly not unique as it seems more and more people feel the same as time progresses. We seem to be developing what I would term as a 'Self Society'. This is a society in which the population in the main is only interested in the happiness and fulfilment of themselves and their egos. They do not give a hoot how anyone else is feeling so long as their own personal urges and needs are satisfied.

I look at the amount of time I can sit at a junction waiting to pull out as traffic bundles by. It would be so easy for someone to just ease off the accelerator a little and give a wave but no. Their little lives and getting home ten seconds quicker is all that matters to them.

One evening I sat so long at a local junction waiting to turn right that I felt to get out I needed to edge forward to show someone my intent. I moved forward but cars still drove round the front of me. Even when the traffic stopped they parked in front of me instead of leaving a gap. This led me to experiment. Just how far forward would I need to go before someone let me out?

I moved forward so far that a car coming from my right almost crashed with a car from my left as he squeezed through in front of me.

I am not saying this is dangerous because it nearly caused a minor accident but the whole 'Self Society' thing is dangerous because in a society we all must care for each other otherwise there is no such thing as a society at all.

Why can't people give a little? There are great rewards to be had by giving and working together. My life motto is this:

"If you give me 50p I will give you £1. If you don't want to give me 50p then forget it."

(Actually the 'forget it' part is a very mild way of saying what I actually say normally but for the sake of the book I will have to leave the rest to your imagination.)

I always live by this and it is very rewarding. My Mags loves and looks after me well and I then tend to pay for most of our holidays. My family look after me and I look after them. My grandchildren give love to me and I give twice as much back to them. Some people just want to take from me though and in their case they get nothing.

Also in this 'Self Society' we see people thinking they can disobey every law whether that law is a criminal law or just a law of decency and think they should not be punished.

I have worked with people and have been their immediate superior. They have done wrong and I have calmly told them so but the next thing that happens is I am approached by someone, who is my superior, because I have upset the person concerned. What is the point of being in a position of authority when you cannot use that authority for fear of someone getting upset? To them their own little bubble has just been pricked and I have affronted their selfishness.

I have watched programmes about police chases and arrests and it amazes me the amount of times someone is stopped for an offence only to argue with the police that it is the police's fault all along. The typical case scenario is a man who has been stopped for driving whilst using his mobile phone. Of course the police were totally wrong to stop him. According to him it should seem obvious to the police that they should have been hunting down real criminals and should not be 'victimising' him.

He rants and raves irascibly because he will not see. Using a mobile phone whilst driving is dangerous and against the law and he has just been caught using one, has broken that law and therefore has to be punished. The police are not about to give him fifty lashes and lock him up for life are they? He has done wrong so why can't he just say, "It's a fair cop guv," and take his ticket? It wasn't the police who put the telephone in his hand. He used it, it was his choice and he should take the punishment. We all make choices in life and we must all be bound by them and be made responsible for them.

This brings me to another television programme. One in which a young girl lived her life by shoplifting. She, very rightly in her own mind, justified the activity by stating that everything she stole was insured so it cost no one anything and therefore she was harming no one. Again her 'Self' was the only important thing to her. Who does she think it is who pays for the insurance? It is added to the price us 'honest' people pay. She cannot ever justify being a thief.

We are living in an ever growing 'Self Society' world and it needs to be stopped. Why can't we fulfil our own 'Self' by obeying laws and looking after others?

In the piece above I said I was someone's 'superior'. I only meant that in a work hierarchy way as neither I nor anyone else can ever be superior to another person. We are all here because of the race to fertilise the egg and every sperm and every egg may have been different but none of them were superior. Whether you are a road sweeper or a ranch hand or a restaurateur or a royal you all won the same kind of race and are just a human being because of it.

I have great respect for the Royal Family. They bring in a huge amount of money to the country and are great figureheads for it also and although they live lives of great privilege I certainly could never wish to be one of them. Every single thing they do is under a spotlight and intense scrutiny. How much of their private lives can ever be actually private? I do have great respect for them but I cannot see them as 'special' as is it expected of me. They call them 'Their Royal Highnesses' or 'Her Serene Majesty' and people bow to them constantly but to my realistic mind they are just lovely people who are the same as you or I. Their sperm reached the egg first just the same as yours did. It just happened to be a sperm from another royal.

I always say if a tramp says a London bus is red it is red. It is not green just because the Queen says so. Respect has to be earned, not commanded or expected but I do respect them.

During the cold war several nuclear shelters were built. Many millions of pounds of tax payers money was spent making these shelters but in a nuclear incident just who would have been invited in and who would have been locked out? Everyone had paid their share but only a 'select' few would have been chosen. Who would these 'special' people have been? Who thought they were so special they actually gave themselves the role of compiling the list? Who was willing to fight off all the others who had contributed and after a nuclear attack what did these 'special' people think they would see and what sort of life did they think they would have when they came out again?

It makes me think of the book Animal Farm by George Orwell which gives a statement something like this:

"All animals are equal except some are more equal than others".

Always remember as you go through life that your life is just as equal as anyone else's. We are all here and if we live our lives according to the laws of the country and show decency to others we are all just as important.

A cleaner who works for a company is just as important as the CEO. A chauffeur is just as important as the person he is chauffeuring. Everyone in any company must be important otherwise they would never be employed in the first place. No one pays wages to a person if they are not important and needed. They are all equally important despite their position, badge or intellect.

My mind here goes back to my days as a driving instructor. I taught several members of the same family to drive but one member of the family has stayed in my mind particularly. I am not going to name him for real but for this piece let's called him Peter.

Peter was a man of about forty years of age and had come to driving later than usual. The reason for this soon became apparent. He had not learned to drive earlier because of his fear of learning the Highway Code. He explained to me with some acute embarrassment that he could not read.

I did not see it as a problem though and I just taught him the Highway Code alongside his actual driving. We had to travel twelve miles to the town where he was to eventually take his test so on each lesson we had twenty-four miles for me to drum the Highway Code into him. Learning it this way was no problem to him at all.

Despite not being able to read, Peter became a very gentle and competent driver. He listened to everything I said and if he did not fully understand he would ask until his mind was assured. He never argued with me because he realised he was paying me good money for my knowledge. He just listened and learned and passed his test.

Not only was Peter a gentle driver, he was a true and gentle man. He was not a Royal or an academic. In matters of intellect he was way down the cue when it was being handed out but this didn't stop him being one of the loveliest men I have ever met.

I know George Orwell said 'some are more equal than others' but believe me it is not true. In a real world we are who we are and we are all the same.

Peter did not have the ability to learn anything intellectual but what he could learn he did with gusto. We should all take a leaf from his book and do the same. We should never be too afraid to learn and we should never be too arrogant to listen.

Throughout this book I have made reference to television programmes and it does sometimes make me wonder if I have watched too much of it but, at the same time, it is a medium from which so much can be learned. Some people read books, some watch television and some just sit and think but at least they all are learning. I feel the greatest harm you can do yourself is close your mind off to learning but many do. I feel we have a duty to learn and progress through life. How sad it must be to live the same life with the same knowledge only to lay on your deathbed and think "Oh I wish I had listened".

I see people making a rash statement and then closing off their ears and minds and not hearing any counter argument. They are being rude and missing out on the chance to learn. These same people tend to be the ones who will not take constructive criticism. Criticism is seen as an affront to them and they cannot see how much they would benefit from listening.

Peter always listened, always learned and was never afraid to admit he was wrong. This was what made him the wonderful person he was and hopefully still is today.

I have talked about insecurities wrecking people's lives but another very common condition is a lack of self-discipline. As far as we know we only have one life and that life is precious. It is up to us to make it as pleasant, enjoyable and as easy as possible for ourselves.

Look around you these days and you see more and more obese people. They say now that half the population is overweight and a good percentage of those people are either clinically or morbidly obese. If their condition is brought about by choice then who is to say they are wrong but are people fat purely from choice? I suppose there are those who just think they will eat and enjoy what they want and worry later about the consequences but in a realistic world I would say inside each fat person is a thin person they would really like to find so they scream for help. Help though is already there. It is there in the shape of self-discipline. It was them who pushed in all the food and it has to be them who stop doing it.

Billions of people together have spent billions of pounds on various diets when, again, let's look at it in realistic way. If you consume three thousand calories per day and use up only two thousand you are going to become fat. If you consume two thousand calories and use up three thousand you are going to become thin. How simple can it be and who needs expensive fad diets?

All my younger life I was a skinny as a rake. Even at twenty years of age I only weighed about ten and a half stone. Then suddenly the weight began to go on. I hated being skinny and at first the extra weight was a treat. I went through eleven, twelve and thirteen stone and felt better and better. I was a young man and worked hard physically on building sites and much of the extra weight turned to muscle. I reached thirteen and a half stone and felt lovely. For once I actually looked good too but then I changed my career and became a driving instructor and the weight still came but as I was constantly sitting down the muscle deserted me. I thought little of it but my weight crept up to fifteen and a half stone and one day I walked passed a shop window and was aghast at the reflection. I looked and looking back at me was this almost obese figure who looked much older than his years.

There and then I decided to do something about it. Being that large was not an option so I dieted back to the thirteen and a half stone I was happy with. That was over half my lifetime ago but thanks to good old self-discipline I am still at the same weight today. I have had a few weight peaks during this time but I have it under control.

So many obese people stay obese because of a lack of discipline and the same goes for giving up smoking or drinking. "Oh, it is so hard to stop smoking," they say. Of course it is not easy but the cigarettes don't just jump up into your mouth do they and the whisky doesn't pour itself does it? Every person should be in charge of their own lives and bodies. It you do not overeat you are not fat. If you do not light up a cigarette you are not a smoker and if you do not pour drink down your throat you are not an alcoholic. Complain all you like and seek whatever assistance you like but I am afraid in a realistic world it is perfectly true. In the end it is up to you.

We have talked about debt before and much of this is also down to a lack of self-discipline. Many people borrow money and when needed there is nothing wrong with it but the discipline comes in being in control of just how much you borrow and making sure you have a plan to pay it all back. It is the same as going to war. You cannot commit yourself without first having an exit plan.

Work hard and think hard and life can still be a bitch sometimes. No matter how many times you get up it can still knock you back down. Life can be hard enough on its own without you joining in and making it harder for yourself as well.

Life can be a wonder if it is used correctly but the first thing we have to do is live ours to the full without hurting ourselves or others. Does it matter if we are tall or short, fat or thin, blonde or black? Does it matter if we have big noses or small noses, long legs or short? Or round bottoms or flat ones? In a real world the only thing that matters is we treat ourselves in the best way possible and care for others in the same vein. That is all we can do.

Something has happened over the past few years and a habit has proliferated among mostly young people. It is the infernal use of the 'L' word and I hate it. The word 'like' is just a word and used in context is as good a word as any other but why oh why do people use it these days in the wrong context and in just about every stupid sentence? Let me explain.

I was shopping in a well-known supermarket, the name of which I shall not mention but it begins with the letter T, one day when I overheard a group of young ladies talking. What one young lady actually meant to say was,

"When I go out on a Friday night I put a few extra ones in my handbag".

I don't know what she was talking about but what she actually said was this,

"Like when I like go out like on a like Friday night I like put like a few like extra ones like in my like handbag".

This 'like' business has been going on for some time and it is happening almost trans-globally but what the heck is it all about? I thought the word 'Like' meant to 'enjoy' or 'similar to'. I like (enjoy) knitting or that duck is like (similar to) that other duck. You can either use the word like or enjoy in the first statement or the words like or similar to in the second. Try to use them in the statement heard being made in the supermarket and where does that lead you? It leads into a world where people are not only not thinking about the world around them but they are not even thinking about the grammar they are speaking?

Why is the word like used in such a way? Let's look at the same sentence with a different word inserted.

"Pig when I pig go out pig on a Friday night I pig put a few pig extra ones pig in my pig handbag".

You will immediately say that this sentence in nonsense and makes no sense at all and you would be perfectly correct but what sense does it make with the 'L' word used instead? No more I would say.

This 'L' word does bug me somewhat but there are several other 'L' words which we should love and live our lives by. Let's look at a few of them.

'Love'

Love is only a four letter word but isn't it the greatest word ever invented?

'Lust for Life'

There is much wrong with our world today but there is still plenty of life out there to lust for. Without a lust for life, (or even just a lust for each other) life would be all too boring.

'Listening'

We must never be afraid to listen. Only by listening will we ever expand our knowledge.

'Learning'

If we listen we expand our knowledge and if we expand our knowledge we learn. If we learn we have better and much more fulfilled lives. We must all learn and it doesn't matter what we learn. I have heard people say, "What is the point of learning long division or Pythagoras?" Why not I say? It is all learning and it all broadens the mind. I strongly feel the more we use our minds the better they become and hopefully the longer they will last.

'Labour'

Whether it is the labour of work, the labour of a hobby or just the labour of watching the Wonderment around us we can gain so much by it.

'Leisure'

If we labour we deserve our leisure and even in our leisure we can learn. We go to the beach to paddle but in doing so we can learn so much of what is around us. We fly a kite and look beyond it into the sky. We cycle to keep fit but it also gives us the chance to look into hedgerows at all the flora and fauna that lives there.

'Liability'

We live our lives and enjoy it all but we must also remember there are boundaries and we are always liable if we should cross them.

'Laughter'

Laughter is the best medicine they used to say, and probably still do, and they are completely and utterly one hundred percent correct. What in life can ever be better than a good old laugh and does it matter what it is we are laughing at as long as no one is being harmed by it? As I have said, I grew up with a low esteem and subconsciously I used to try and counteract this by trying to make people laugh. With much practise I seemed to manage it and still do today. The trouble is they all seem to laugh at me rather than with me but I love it.

Maybe it is just me but I think one of the best sights ever in human life is someone who tries to stifle a laugh but just cannot. You may be short or fat, rich or poor. You may be American, African, Asian or Afghanistanian. No matter what you are in life you can always laugh and laugh you should. I would say the 'L' words love and laughter are the best words ever.

There are a couple of 'L' words that come immediately to mind that we should avoid wherever possible. I will group them together as they are virtually one and the same. They are:

'Listlessness' and 'Lethargy'

Life is for living and so much can be gained from living it but life will never just come to us. We have to seek it out. I have seen so much listlessness and lethargy and people being 'bored'.

How can anyone ever be bored when we are surrounded by Wonderment? We all just have to get off our butts and go for it.

Many of these 'lethargic' people seem to rely on another 'L' word. That word is 'Luck'. They 'laze' and 'loaf' around in a 'languid' state of 'lifelessness' needing a 'large laxative' to get them going and their only hope is luck. I'm afraid we all have to make our own luck in the world. Even if a lazy person was to win the lotto jackpot they would still be a lazy person and would still not enjoy life to the full.

We all need to get up and get going!

Life is not always easy and others do drive you up the wall at times but a big thing I have learned is never to worry or argue when I am tired. A small niggle can seem magnified into a vast drama or crisis when you are tired or a small verbal slight from someone can seem like a giant punch in the ribs. If you are tired and feel you should be worried just go to sleep on it and believe me it will seem much lighter in the morning.

In the case of an argument you have to always put your brain in gear before you engage your tongue. I know this is not always easy but it has to be done. When someone says something to you that you do not like or agree with your first instincts have to be:

A. Is the person correct in what they are saying and if so do not argue whether tired or not.

B. Is the person incorrect in what they are saying and if so am I too tired to respond in a measured manner?

It is so easy to just rely on instant gut instincts, have a blazing row and lose a friend or relative.

None of us are perfect and what is 'perfect' anyway? As I have said before, beauty has to be in the eye of the beholder. You have faults and so do I and the best thing we can ever say is,

"In no way am I perfect but bugger do I try hard!"

The problem comes when (I have seen it any many people) someone admits they have far too many faults but still expect everyone else around them to be perfect and if they are not perfect they are severely berated or chastised by the imperfect person concerned. We can never be perfect. We just have to do our best.

The best we can do is totally accept each other for what we are. Yes, we can moan at sheer stupidity in the hope that the person concerned will learn and yes we can argue if we are sure what someone else is saying is wrong but let's do it all in a constructive and measured way and not get bitter because of it. Bitterness ruins lives and our life is the only one we have.

There are all manner of people out there who have a healthy respect for themselves and who treat others in a similar manner but there are many who act precisely in the opposite way. They have no respect for society, no respect for others and, ultimately no respect for themselves.

I know my life motto of 'give me 50p and I will give you £1' is simple but I'm sure if we all adopted the same principle life would be so easy and so rewarding.

So many people lean on religion and other superstitions as they feel they need support. They seek comfort in what is not real and therefore any comfort they receive is not real and yet they somehow feel comforted by it. Many people find a kind of comfort in things that are not real because often they cannot face up to reality. At the very beginning of this book I gave a story of a lady who told me I was the 'kind of person who only believed in things that are real'. In my real world this did not make sense but looking at it from her world she felt far better in a non-real world. She felt so comfortable in it all that she felt her religion and other superstitions were the best place to hide in. In a way she was so immersed in her unreal world that, to her, it had become a reality. Does that make sense?

We can have religion. We can have superstitions. We can have daydreams and fantasies but in the end, in reality, reality is all there is. Searching for anything else, as many do, can only bring tears.

We can rely on religion or we can rely on psychiatrists or we can rely on spirituality or astrology but in the end none of these will do you any real good because there is only one thing, in a real world, that we can truly rely on and that is ourselves. We have been given the wonderful gift of life and it is up to us to live it to the full and we must do it under our own steam and with our own unique brain to guide us. We must do it all for those who love and care for us and we must do it all for those around us but most of all we must do it all for ourselves.

Conclusion

In this book I have jabbered on from nothing and the beginning of the universe and the beginning of our own planet, planet earth, through to evolution, war, love, illness and loss, drugs, superstitions and the future of our world, so what conclusion can we draw from it all?

The earth was formed 4.5 billion years ago and life has been evolving for 3.5 billion of those years. In that time many millions of animal species came and went. Those that could adapt to nature's requirements survived and those that could not became extinct. Some were only on the planet for a relatively short time while others that evolved many million years ago such as jellyfish, crocodiles and dragonflies are still with us today.

People lean upon a religious beginning because in their minds it is a simple way of explaining the 'creation' of the planet as it negates any need for thought but the real origins of life are much simpler than this. How difficult must it have been for a single god to have made the world and everything in it in just six short days compared with it coming to where it is today, step by very tiny step, over a period of 4.5 billion years?

People cannot seem to get their heads around it but where is the complexity of evolution? There is none. It is simple. The world is made of simple chemicals and we are made of those same chemicals. We all know if you were to mix two buckets of hydrogen and a bucket of oxygen together you would get three buckets full of water. So if you did this and if you then progress to add a few more chemicals into the mix you get us. The four main chemicals that make us are hydrogen, oxygen, carbon and nitrogen. It all took time but it happened. It is as simple as that and it is far easier to explain that than trying to work out how a god did it all in six days from dust.

Throughout the world's history there have been mass extinctions but life has come through and adapted again. After each event new niches have formed and different animals that have been able to fill them have thrived. For example, 60 million years ago many of the dinosaurs died out and the mammals took over.

For billions of years everything was fine. There were good and bad times for life as it evolved but generally everything was governed by nature but then came an ape species which would quite quickly spread from the African continent, populate the rest of the globe and then eventually learn to defy nature at every turn. That species of course was us. We learned to take every single thing from the planet that we felt we needed to suit our every need and desire which was fine at first but as the population grew rapidly through the seventeen and eighteen hundreds we began to take too much. The earth began to suffer as did the other animals we shared it with and we started yet another mass extinction.

Man is, in general, a greedy species. We are not content like other animals. They eat, drink, breathe and reproduce. That is all they want and wish for but we are different. Because of our great brain capacity we need more. We demand it and we get it. Other animals walk to where they wish to go but we demand transport. Other animals migrate to where they can find food while we demand it is brought to us. Other animals build simple nests while we demand cities. They exist on the heat from the sun while we demand fossil fuels. Other animals do sometimes fight for existence but we go to war simply on a whim and any whim will do. Other animals just wake up in the morning and get on with their lives with only themselves for support while we seek the help of God and again, any god will do. We want everything and want it now. What we cannot get for ourselves we pray for. We do not care if God is trying to sort out major world issues when we interrupt him because, in our 'Self Society', it is only our own little lives that are important.

We are a race that cannot seem to face reality. We live in dreams and fantasies while everything around us crumbles. We close our eyes to the troubles we face while the *'hungry lion'* approaches.

We live in an unrealistic world which holds an unrealistic amount of human beings. Wars are more and more prevalent and something has to be done. The *Mr and Mrs X* syndrome is biting hard.

Even after thousands of years religion still has a grip upon us and certain religionists or religious groups seem to think theirs is the best and they want to rule the world by it. This is causing wars and strife and the deaths and suffering of many millions of people. We still worry about cutting our nails on a Sunday or putting our shoes on the table or walking under a ladder but we don't seem too fussed about children being bombed and blown to pieces.

Religious people are supposed to be the ones who care and 'heathens' like me are supposed to be the uncaring ones but if you took all religions out of the equation then the world would be a better place for it and we could all live in peace. Again this is an example of my *'Theory of Opposites'*.

We do need to forget about all superstition whether it is religion based or whatever. We have reached the 21st century and we need to do something completely drastic and probably unthinkable if we want the world to survive as we see it today. We need to get real. The only other answer is more war and strife until so many are dead the earth will be able to support us once again but in a far simpler way and lifestyle. We need to get real and if we are to avoid the apocalypse of overpopulation we have to act now. We have to stop dreaming and enter the real world with real thinking and a real purpose by real people.

We need the governments of all countries to be strong. We need them to stop acting like children and do the real job they are paid a good wage to do. They do not need to stand up and jeer at the opposition they just need to stand up and be counted.

We are the ones with the big brains and intellect and I'm sure if we really used them to the best of our abilities we could find solutions. We need to stop killing each other and work together. We need to dump this 'Self Society' and work for the good of us all. We need to dump all hatred and learn to love each other no matter what race, colour or religion we are. We need to elect the best of us to lead us through what is rapidly becoming a hugely difficult and demanding time. We need to learn to think for ourselves and love each other and then perhaps we can survive. We need to watch that 'hungry lion' and keep him at bay.

Above all we need to begin to be satisfied with living simpler lives and enjoy the Wonderment around us because in a real world that is all there is and it is all we need. 'We cause ourselves and others danger and stress every time we start to search for anything else.'

Time is rapidly ticking away but it is not too late. We have to act drastically and quickly but together we can do it. Together we can all work hard and enjoy the fruits of our labours. Life is by no means all bad and with thought, love, selflessness and determination it could become great again.

'Is this the real life?
Is this just fantasy?
Caught in a landslide.
No escape from reality.
Open your eyes.
Look up to the skies and see.

Queen. Bohemian Rhapsody

Epilogue

And so you have read my book. I have thoroughly enjoyed writing it and I truly hope you have enjoyed reading it. I know I have knocked just about everything in life but I have done so to illustrate the kind of life pattern we humans have fallen into. I have knocked and knocked again but I have also tried my hardest to inform and teach everyone to look, listen, think and learn in order to live better and more fulfilled lives.

Whether you have now learned to think of me as an intellectual man or someone who knows a bit of life or just someone who thinks or even if you now think of me as a complete jerk at least you are thinking and your thoughts are yours and you are entitled to them. Whatever you do think of me I do hope you have learned a little something and I do thank you most sincerely for reading my book and listening to my thoughts, principles and beliefs.

In the book I have tried my best to dispel what I think is the complete myth of religion but if, after reading it, you are still convinced that I am totally wrong then all I can say, in all sincerity, is "God Bless You".

Bless you and thank you sincerely.

Barry R Boughen